D1453273

Opening the Field

Opening the Field

Irish Women: Texts and Contexts

Co-edited by
Patricia Boyle Haberstroh and Christine St Peter

CORK UNIVERSITY PRESS

DEDICATION
To Charles Haberstroh and John Tucker

First published in 2007 by
Cork University Press
Youngline Industrial Estate
Pouladuff Road, Togher
Cork
Ireland

British Library Cataloguing in Publication Data

A CIP catalogue record for this book is available from the British Library.

ISBN 978-1-85918-410-3

Typesetting by Red Barn Publishing, Skeagh, Skibbereen, Co. Cork.
Printed by ColourBooks Ltd, Baldoyle, Co. Dublin.

www.corkuniversitypress.com

Contents

Acknowledgements

Patricia Haberstroh acknowledges the support of the Fulbright Foundation and La Salle University in Philadelphia, Pennsylvania. Christine St Peter acknowledges the support of the Social Sciences and Humanities Research Council of Canada and the Faculty of Humanities at the University of Victoria, British Columbia.

Grateful acknowledgment is made to the following sources for permission to quote excerpts and to reproduce images: Carmel Benson, 'Crouching Sheela' from a solo exhibition at Graphic Studio Gallery, Dublin, 1990 and 'Seir-Kieran Sheela-na-gig Travels' from a solo exhibition *Into the Pattern,* at the Hallward Gallery, Dublin, 2003, reproduced by permission of the artist; Ruth Carr, 'Community Relation', from *Word of Mouth*, Blackstaff Press, Belfast, copyright © Ruth Carr, 1996; Susan Connolly, 'Sheela-na-gig', *Brigid's Place* and 'Female Figure', *For the Stranger*, quoted with permission of the poet and Dedalus Press, Dublin; Katie Donovan, from 'Underneath Our Skirts', *Watermelon Man*, quoted with permission of Bloodaxe Books, Tarset, Northumberland; Paula Meehan, from 'Not Your Muse', *Pillow Talk*, quoted with permission of The Gallery Press, Loughcrew, Oldcastle, County Meath; Mary Morrissy, from *The Pretender*, quoted with permission of Greene and Heaton Ltd., London, copyright © Mary Morrissy, 2000; Kate Newmann, 'Sea horses', from *Word of Mouth*, Blackstaff Press, Belfast, copyright © Kate Newmann, 1996; Kate O'Brien, from *As Music and Splendour*, Penguin, from *Farewell Spain*, Heinemann, London and from *Mary Lavelle*, Virago Press, London, quoted with permission of David Higham Associates, Ltd., London; Katherine Arnold Price, 'Curithir and Liadain', from *The Field Day Anthology of Irish Writing*, Volume 5, quoted with permission of Cork University Press, County Cork; Elizabeth Shane, 'Fiddlin' Kate', from *The Field Day Anthology of Irish Writing*, Volume 5, quoted with permission of Cork University Press, County Cork; Ann Zell, 'Nature Programme', from *Word of Mouth*, Blackstaff Press, Belfast, copyright © Ann Zell, 1996.

Introduction

Patricia Boyle Haberstroh
Christine St Peter

One of the defining moments in late-twentieth-century Irish literature occurred with the publication of the *Field Day Anthology of Irish Writing* (ed. Seamus Deane et al.), which appeared in three volumes in 1991 and immediately created a controversy. A huge collection covering more than a thousand years, the anthology was marked by the virtual absence of female writers and a consequent spotlight on the all-male editorial board that had produced the work. The media attention surrounding this controversy led to a proposal for an additional volume (later to become two volumes) which would highlight the accomplishments of women writers. This decision created its own controversy, raising the question of marginalization, but it also led to the valuable two-volume 'addition' to *The Field Day Anthology* (ed. Angela Bourke et al.) in 2002, and to an ongoing analysis of the place of the female writer in Irish literary tradition. From this point on, definitions of the Irish literary tradition would change.

While the publication of the first three volumes of *The Field Day Anthology* may have sparked the fire, the fuel had been long smouldering. Anthologies implicitly establish canons, suggesting that the material in them constitutes the best and most representative work of a people and a culture. The anthology also came under attack for other biases, including nationalist ones, but the outcry at the under-representation of women was one of the loudest, for it followed on the heels of an increasing interest in texts by women. We should note here that the quarrel was not just a case of the anthology neglecting to recognize more recent writing by women; it also highlighted a failure to acknowledge the contribution of women writers in Ireland's past.

Many factors influenced the protests raised at this time. The growth of women's movements internationally had spurred feminist movements in Ireland to focus both on women in Irish history and culture and on Irish stereotyping of women and women writers. In women's studies courses and programmes created in Ireland's national universities, scholars and students began to examine the place of women writers, and were confronted not only with the problem of locating and accessing this work, but also with the criteria for evaluating texts which assumed a male writer and paid little, if any, attention to the possible differences in works by women. The frustration over

1

this resulted in various challenges to mainstream definitions of Irish literature and canons; to a call for the scholarly work of recovering lost texts; and to valuable debates over the ways in which literature by women might demand an expansion of the boundaries of genre and of established criteria for evaluation. Just such work had, in fact, been going on in Ireland for some decades. Arlen House, for example, was created in 1975 to publish women's writing, and as early as 1945 B.G. MacCarthy's two-volume critical work, *The Female Pen,* had argued convincingly the importance of women's contributions to Irish literature. This made the omissions in the first three volumes of *The Field Day Anthology* even more glaring.

Anthologies devoted to writing by Irish women had appeared as the interest in women's writing increased. *Woman's Part: An Anthology of Short Fiction By and About Irish Women 1890–1960* (ed. Janet Madden-Simpson); *The Female Line: Northern Irish Women Writers* (ed. Ruth Hooley); *Pillars of the House: An Anthology of Verse by Irish Women from 1690 to the Present* (ed. A.A. Kelly); *Wildish Things: An Anthology of New Irish Women's Writing* (ed. Ailbhe Smyth); *Stories by Contemporary Irish Women* (ed. Casey and Casey); and *Territories of the Voice: Contemporary Stories by Irish Women* (ed. Louise DeSalvo, Kathleen D'Arcy and Katherine Hogan) were all in print by 1990 to be followed in the 1990s by, among others, *Voices on the Wind: Women Poets of the Celtic Twilight* (ed. Eilís Ní Dhuibhne); *Virgins and Hyacinths: An Attic Press Book of Fiction* (ed. Caroline Walsh); *Wee Girls: Women Writing from an Irish Perspective* (ed. Lizz Murphy); *Alternative Loves: Irish Gay and Lesbian Stories* (ed. David Marcus); *Word of Mouth: Poems* (ed. Ruth Carr et al.); *The White Page: Twentieth Century Irish Women Poets* (ed. Joan McBreen); *Ireland's Women: Writings Past and Present* (ed. Katie Donovan, A. Norman Jeffares and Brendan Kennelly); *The Wake Forest Book of Irish Women Poets 1967–2000* (ed. Peggy O'Brien); and seven volumes of poetry in the *Women's Work* (1990–1996) project commemorating annual National Women's Poetry Competitions. Nevertheless, a survey of the most publicized, frequently reviewed and popular anthologies of Irish literature published during this time still continued to under-represent significantly the achievements of women, just as *The Field Day Anthology* did.

But we need also to note that it has been easy to ignore the work of Irish women writers and feminist scholars, to dismiss it as marginal or of limited interest, to suggest it will be read only by certain groups (read *women*), to define it as the production of some radical separatist conspiracy, or, finally, to consider it as unimportant work on minor writers by scholars involved in esoteric research who refuse to accept established canons. All these dismissive attitudes have been enabled and perpetuated because the work of Irish women writers has not necessarily been readily available or accessible.

An audience for a writer's work depends on many factors beside a dedicated group of readers and scholars: the text has to get into print (or back into print), has to be reviewed, has to be taught in literature classes and has to be written about. A study of major Irish publishing houses still shows a noticeable disproportion of male to female writers, and reviews of the work of women writers still lag significantly behind those of their male counterparts. Few publishing houses actively pursue and promote women writers, especially emerging writers, and those that have in the past, like Arlen House or Attic Press, often go under due to the difficulty of maintaining their energy over a period of many years in the face of so much cultural resistance – although Arlen House was resuscitated in 2000 and Salmon Publishing has been an important outlet for women poets. Cork University Press undertook the publication of the fourth and fifth volumes of *The Field Day Anthology*, a huge contribution to the cause of women's writing in Ireland, and also assimilated Attic Press's list when Attic could no longer publish. The *Irish Journal of Feminist Studies* published nine issues between 1996 and 2003, and was crucial to the growth of feminist scholarship in Ireland, as was the *Women's Studies Review*, started in 1992 and still publishing, albeit under a new name, *Irish Feminist Review*. While cheap editions of romance novels by women were beginning to appear in the bookshops, other work by Irish women writers was often heading outside of Ireland, to publishers like Bloodaxe in Manchester; finding them in Ireland's bookstores is not easy. Irish libraries, even those in the universities, still do not have many of the texts by good women writers.

Volumes IV and V of *The Field Day Anthology*, then, more than ten years in the making, represent a major step in correcting the omissions in the first three volumes but, as mentioned above, these later volumes created their own controversy. While some hailed the recognition brought to women writers, others argued that, rather than mainstreaming women writers, Volumes IV and V represented a 'women in the annex' marginalization. (See Gerardine Meaney's essay in this volume for a discussion of responses to Volumes IV and V.) And as the editors of Volumes IV and V explained, organizing the volumes presented difficult challenges, given that women writers do not necessarily fit into the genres and categories that traditional anthologies, including the earlier *Field Day* volumes, had followed.

For the male editors of the first volumes of *The Field Day Anthology*, defining Irish identity was a major issue; their stated aim was to expand that definition and to make available a more diverse body of literature. The Field Day group in Northern Ireland, which had evolved from the Field Day Theatre of the 1980s, had produced, prior to the anthology, a series of pamphlets that focused on Irish revisionist history and literature. Influenced by postcolonial theory, and the ongoing debate in Ireland over nationalism, the editors of Volumes I to III also sought to redefine 'Irish' literature. Immediately after the anthology's publication, the editors were accused of promoting a nationalist agenda, even though they maintained that they were countering earlier images of Ireland, like those popularized by the Celtic Twilight Movement of the late nineteenth and early twentieth centuries. The criticism of the under-representation of women in their anthology, therefore, was part of a broader challenge to the work.

Long before Volumes I to III appeared, however, women had already begun to challenge definitions of Irish identity which applied primarily to males, illustrated in a historical record that passed over the achievements of women, a literary canon that ignored many important women writers, and a literary culture uninterested in recovering the lost work of women writers. The LIP pamphlets, a series published by Attic Press between 1989 and 1994 under the editorship of Ailbhe Smyth, addressed these issues. One of the most important of these pamphlets, Eavan Boland's *A Kind of Scar: The Woman Poet in a National Tradition*, focused on the absence of women in recorded Irish history and canonical literature; Boland used her own experience as an Irish woman and poet as example. In her poetry and in her important collection of essays, *Object Lessons: The Life of the Woman and the Poet in Our Time*, Boland challenged what she saw as a prevailing image in Irish literature of woman as object not subject, an image which created serious problems for Irish women writers, who could not see themselves as part of a literary tradition. Describing her own struggle to write within that context, Boland challenged the idea of a male-focused nation. Although she shared the Field Day editors' desire to present a more diverse picture of Ireland, she chastised them for the absence of female writers in the early volumes. Boland's emphasis on this, as well as her own encouragement of women poets, contributed much to making the situation of Irish women writers more visible.

But assumptions like Boland's soon became the focus of their own critique, as some critics saw her vision as too limiting and overly personal. In another LIP pamphlet, *From Cathleen to Anorexia: The Breakdown of Irelands*, Edna Longley argued that Boland's Ireland was itself narrowly defined. She claimed that Boland's location in the Republic resulted in her taking little notice of the non-nationalist segment of the island's population: 'Boland holds to unitary assumptions about "a society, a nation, a literary heritage".' Troubled about 'the woman poet', she takes 'the national tradition for granted – and perhaps thereby misses a source of her trouble' (PD 16). Longley had essentially the same objections to what she considered *The Field Day Anthology*'s nationalist ideology, and she joined others in objecting to the absence of women in the early volumes. But Longley blamed that absence on a nationalist culture's failure to recognize the achievements of women, a culture which, Longley charged, Boland implicitly accepted and promoted. This debate largely paralleled an ongoing discussion within international women's studies which stressed the need to acknowledge the diversity of women's lives and experience and to emphasize not 'woman' but 'women.' However, while Longley argued that Boland and others ignored a non-nationalist culture, Longley's own work did little to recognize women writers, especially those long neglected in Northern Ireland.

The issue of the multiplicities of Irish identity was further complicated by other theoretical debates developing in academic circles, as well as the growth of women studies departments in Ireland's universities. How does one define 'women'? How does one describe 'Irish'? Many early feminist discussions had centred on the simplified image of the heterosexual, maternal woman prevalent in Irish culture. But what about lesbian, bi- or trans-sexual women? Lesbian studies and queer theory provided the opportunity to reconsider Irish literature and women writers from another perspective, uncovering dimensions of literary works missed or ignored. Soon questions of the relationship between sex and gender and the importance of class, ethnicity, genre and popular culture became part of the discussions in feminist literary criticism. In *Sex, Nation and Dissent in Irish Writing,* a collection of essays edited by Eibhear Walshe that focused on gay and lesbian writing, Anne Fogarty argued that the work of Kate O'Brien and Mary Dorcey is important not only for their 'sexual dissidence but also because they utilize this potential subversiveness to explore the otherness of Irish society', and that 'they find themselves in a position to critique those aspects of modern Irish identity which they find confining and anti-democratic' (PD, 171).

On this issue of Irish identity, postcolonialism, which had a strong influence on both Field Day and Irish critical writing in general, and postmodernism have become increasingly popular lenses through which to view Irish culture and literature. But postcolonial theory in Ireland has tended to be centered more on narrow political than on cultural or social forces, and women, as before, have generally been left out of the equation. This latter tendency, evident in Irish nationalist history, used the idealized icon of Mother Ireland/Cathleen Ní Houlihan to create a symbolic female victim of the male colonizer, a symbol challenged by feminist theories on body imagery (Gerardine Meaney, *Sex and Nation*; Anne Crilly, *Mother Ireland*). With regard to Irish political feminism, Margaret Ward suggests that there are two strands: 'One emphasizes the centrality of the colonial relationship and links the struggle for women's emancipation to the movement for national liberation. The other emphasizes what it considers the essential qualities of feminism to the exclusion of external political issues. There are great differences of strategy, not only *between these* two strategies, but also within each' ('Nationalism, Pacifism, Internationalism', p. 61). In an attempt to combine those two strands, more recent work has applied postcolonial theory to literature by Irish women, for example, in the work of Angela Bourke ('Language, Stories, Healing') and Sarah E. McKibben on the oral lament ('Angry Laments and grieving Postcoloniality'), or on female Irish language writers. Nevertheless, the old republican–unionist political conflicts have been at the heart of much published Irish postcolonial analysis, forcing out much needed attention to gender issues.

Postmodernism might serve as a useful corrective to such binary thinking, as this theoretical stance works from the position that a coherent subjective identity is illusory; that binary concepts of male and female are limiting; and that to speak of a woman's voice or individual female subjectivity gives a false sense of identity. Margaret Kelleher has argued, however, that 'unlike other European feminisms, the influence of poststructuralist criticism in the Irish field has been relatively limited; one reason, perhaps, is that Irish feminism is by and large unwilling to let go of its female subject' ('A Retrospective View on Irish Women's Studies', p. 166). But Irish feminists are not alone in debating this issue, as the need to identify a female subject or to 'hear' a female voice is undercut when the concept of a coherent female subjectivity is challenged. Yet some feminist critics have suggested that just as women began to discuss the need for a female subject or voice, the 'loss of subject' theorists began to speak. Those challenging a stringent postmodernist approach note the irony of a critic/subject promulgating the insignificance of the individual speaking voice. Moynagh Sullivan writes: 'Whilst the rhetoric of the postmodern differs from the modern, its speaking or writing non-subject remains within the very modern paradigm it claims to want to escape . . . the postmodern refuses to play that game anymore, whilst still retaining the right to name the game. It would appear, then, that the authoritative subject is still very much abroad, and now positionally hidden not only from others, but also from itself' ('Feminism, Postmodernism and the Subjects of Irish and Women's Studies', p. 245).

Sullivan, nevertheless, is unwilling to ignore the value of postmodernist perspectives and maintains that feminists, like postmodernists, are engaging in deconstructing false concepts of identity. She seeks to negotiate between a 'postmodern which disowns its own subjectivity' and traditional 'Irish studies which actively asserts its subjecthood' (p. 248). Acknowledging Eavan Boland's early image of woman as object in Irish literature, Sullivan suggests that Volumes IV and V of *The Field Day Anthology* evidence the beginnings of a dialogue which will recognize the value of different approaches. She writes:

> If, however, questions of the positioning of the subject of Irish studies are placed side by side with historicized expressions of variable womanhood, then woman is no longer available as an object to serve the function of grounding Irishness, but rather serves the purpose of unsettling any articulation of Irishness predicted on the object's silence and ahistoricality. Small wonder, then, that the hospitality extended to all the micro-narratives that constitute Irishness in *The Field Day Anthology of Irish Writing* did not extend to the micro-narratives of Irish women writers and to feminist theoretical concerns. (p. 250).

Such reactions to the first *Field Day* volumes demonstrate that women writers and critics not only had been examining images of women in Irish literature and culture, but also had developed a number of different approaches in a complex feminist debate. One purpose of this collection is to illustrate the variety of those approaches. To demonstrate this, the editors asked contributors to describe an approach to reading Irish women's text, to explain the value of that approach and then to apply it to a text of their choosing. In many cases, they draw from their own experience reading and teaching these texts.

The most valuable asset of this collection is its diversity, neither narrowly ideological nor monolithic; the writers, texts and perspectives chosen offer a clear indication of the many ways in which women writers can be read. These essays reflect most of the contemporary theoretical approaches to literature, as the writers successfully develop the inter-relationships between feminist and other theories. The theoretical approaches of psychoanalysis, lesbian studies, queer theory, materialist feminism, postmodernism, body theory, post-colonialism, gender theory and cultural studies are all illustrated in this volume. The collection adds another layer of analysis in those essays which also incorporate the contributor's personal experience in reading, teaching and writing about certain texts. In some of these essays, the writer describes her own coming to terms with literary analyses and a literary, critical and cultural climate in which women's voices were muted or absent, and chooses to use her personal voice instead of the more genderless one advocated in some contemporary criticism. Equally important, these essays demonstrate the ways in which traditional readings are both challenged and enhanced by considering that the text is written by a woman. Covering fiction, poetry, visual art and drama (text and performance), this collection examines a variety of texts from the nineteenth and twentieth centuries.

The organization of the volume is roughly chronological, moving from the first essays on nineteenth-century writers through those of the early twentieth century up to the present. It begins with Gerardine Meaney's 'Engendering the Postmodern Canon? *The Field Day Anthology of Irish Writing, Volumes IV and V: Women's Writing and Traditions*', because her essay introduces a number of issues other contributors discuss, as well as describing the landscape for Irish women writers and scholars in the twenty years preceding the beginning of her work as an editor on the later volumes of *The Field Day Anthology*. Explaining how the anthology project soon became a much larger task than she and other editors had anticipated, Meaney suggests that the construction of Volumes IV and V needed to follow two different but parallel paths: the first was 'differencing' the inherited canon by rereading the known in the light of new aesthetic, intellectual and political frameworks; and the second was the unearthing of unknown and forgotten work which then had to be re-evaluated in the light of new critical approaches – what Meaney calls making Irish writing 'strange to itself'.

In her essay, Meaney illustrates the workings of the editorial process with a case study of her own work on representations of the 'figure of the woman artist' in the work of vernacular poet Elizabeth Shane and modernist poet Katherine Arnold Price. She invites us into the place of uncertainty she inhabited in her own exploration and argues that the 'unworked nowhere' (Medbh McGuckian, *Captain Lavender*, p. 75) of forgotten poetry is a 'stranger and more interesting place than anyone could have anticipated'.

Illustrating some of the strategies that Meaney describes, the two essays that follow Meaney's examine novels written in the early nineteenth century.

Each might be said to illustrate one of the two guiding principles used in constructing Volumes IV and V of *The Field Day Anthology*. In the first, we find Eiléan Ní Chuilleanáin rereading a novel by the highly regarded Maria Edgeworth (1767–1849) in the light of new aesthetic, intellectual and political frameworks; in the second, Heidi Hansson unearths a work by Harriet Martin (1801–1891), an author rarely mentioned in studies of Irish literature, including the *Field Day* volumes on women writers. Choosing *Ormond* (1817) as text, Ní Chuilleanáin focuses on Edgeworth's exploration of the construction of patriarchal masculinity. Ní Chuilleanáin poses a number of questions as a way into *Ormond:* Can a woman writing through a male protagonist shirk, as it were, the concerns of her own sex? Is the masculinity Edgeworth writes a natural or a social fact? And most important to her discussion: Does Irish history make a difference? Ní Chuilleanáin brings these to bear on the novel's treatment of its male hero whose history and evolution, she argues, self-consciously echo and challenge two famous literary classics, *Tom Jones* (1749) and *Sir Charles Grandison* (1754). In one of her most evocative suggestions, Ní Chuilleanáin claims that *Ormond* creates a character who is a critical reader, passing judgement on the literary classics – and the cultures – in which they are created.

Harriet Martin, the subject of Heidi Hansson's essay, was, like Maria Edgeworth, the daughter of a prominent Anglo-Irish father, well situated within the *literati* of her time and wealthy enough not to need to write for her living. Unlike Edgeworth's work, however, Martin's has been largely ignored in Irish canon-building even though the novel under discussion in Hansson's essay, *Canvassing* (1832?), was popular enough to remain in print throughout the nineteenth century and was reprinted in 1979. Originally publishing under a pseudonym, Martin had the freedom to tackle what Hansson calls a most 'unwomanly theme': the interconnections between the Irish election practices and the marriage market of her time – 'two equally corrupt systems'. Using the theories of Elizabeth Grosz, Judith Butler and Margrit Shildrick, Hansson points out that the body, too, is fluid, 'a surface inscribed by a particular time and ideology' that defies the homogenizing category 'woman' or even 'women'. As postmodern feminist theory makes impossible the question 'what is woman?', a more useful question emerges: '*where* are women?' If no aspect of identity is ever central and fixed within an unchanging hierarchy, then circumstances – or 'place' – determine how the self can be constructed. Hansson demonstrates the valuable results of paying scrupulous attention to the historical elements of time, place and social context in which the work was produced.

The distances between the worlds of these two nineteenth-century novels and that discussed by Patricia Coughlan in the next essay could hardly be greater. Here we find a study of the two-volume autobiography (1936 and 1939) that Great Blasket Islander Peig Sayers dictated to her son Micheál Ó Gaoithín. Neglected by scholars of various disciplines and suffering from ideological distortion in a national debate over ownership of 'Peig studies', these works offer remarkable opportunities for an understanding of both women's writing and of women's history. But this recovery will need to overcome the various constructions made of Peig Sayers' life and work during the twentieth century, from a false version of 'Peig' as female icon of saintly female virtue and passivity created for the De Valera era to the contemporary modelling of her in public discourse as a representative of a 'sentimental, backward-looking and ruralist ideology' with little value for contemporary Ireland. The contestation of her meaning, argues Coughlan, 'crystallized the roles women might and might not be allowed to occupy in Ireland'.

Katherine O'Donnell's essay considers a novel exactly contemporary to Peig Sayers' autobiographies, but imaginatively and materially worlds away from the Great Blasket Island, despite its author's west of Ireland location. O'Donnell provides a reading of Kate O'Brien's *Mary Lavelle* (1936) which is informed by lesbian studies and queer theory. Unlike some advocates of queer theory who eschew feminist analysis, O'Donnell situates her study *within* feminist analysis but uses the insights of lesbian and queer readings to interrogate feminist readings of the novel which she finds trapped in 'heterosexual presumption'. Thus she approaches the foregrounded adulterous love story of the Irish governess, Mary Lavelle, and the wealthy Spaniard, Juan Areavaga y Parajo, with a close reading of an occluded text made possible by her knowledge of the intertextual relation of this novel to O'Brien's other fiction, history and autobiography, as well as to the hidden language of queer discourse in English literature in that period. She argues the importance of this step because O'Brien was a lesbian writer in the days of heavy Irish censorship of any explicit sexuality, much less same-sex love, in literature and she experienced the banning of her work, including *Mary Lavelle,* by the Irish Censorship Board.

O'Donnell's reading against the grain of heterosexist assumptions is set against another equally radical theory in the next essay: that a dramatic text written in the realist tradition with 'its grim patriarchal landscape' mirroring reality outside the theatre may *in performance* not just challenge but actually overthrow the written text. Cathy Leeney, a professor of theatre as well as a professional director, uses her practical knowledge of the theatre to demonstrate her argument in a study of Marina Carr's *Portia Coughlan* (1996), which features a monstrous anti-heroine and was widely produced throughout Europe and North America. Conjuring up the familiar and painful experience of the feminist performer, critic, teacher or audience confronted with powerfully negative representations of the female and the womanly, Leeney demonstrates how Portia, an abject failure as a mother, wife and daughter – angry, promiscuous, foul-mouthed and slovenly – becomes in performance a radical representation of a woman rejecting all the categories traditionally used to define women. Gender, found wanting, becomes the test of the limits of realist drama and the social reality beyond the theatre walls.

The celebration of possibility and change offered by the staging of the monstrous Portia Coughlan finds a parallel in recent feminist recuperations of the shocking medieval figure of the Sheela-na-gig. These naked icons, carved onto the walls of churches and castles throughout Ireland and Europe, display their genitalia in outrageous exhibitions of women's physicality and sexuality. The essay by Luz Mar González Arias explores the ways modern artistic representations, including the poetry of Susan Connolly and the painting of Carmel Benson, flood their texts with women's bodies, drowning the inherited notions of 'Irishness' that 'have depended on, or better, have been constructed at, the expense of the female body'. Revealing that which should be invisible, contained and subdued is a powerful way of resisting inherited 'somatophobia', and helps the 'Irish body claim a space of its own in the creation and transformation of culture'. Their plural meanings, changing over time according to the cultural needs of specific contexts, make the Sheela-na-gigs particularly appropriate as representations of powerful bodies that refuse the damaging constructions of Irish womanhood in various Irish discourses.

Finding voice amid the din of male-dominated discourses is probably nowhere more difficult than in a war zone. In the next essay, whose subject is the contemporary poetry of Northern Irish women, Rebecca Pelan situates this little-studied topic in a useful overview of women's artistic work in the North, comparing its development to women's art in the Republic. Although now a women's studies professor in the Republic, Pelan was born and raised in Northern Ireland and knows intimately the codes, customs and linguistic traps of that region. But years of feminist teaching in Australia have also made her an insider-outsider whose vision is mediated by years 'away', where she learned to see beyond the rigid binaries enforced by the Troubles. She reflects on the consequences of the North being 'astonishingly gender-blind' in terms of roles and politics, a situation in which women's concerns continue to be secondary to the dominant politics, and the artistic production, of the region. Arguing for the value of materialist feminism as a way of allowing Northern women to speak their own radical and oppositional discourse, Pelan demonstrates these insights by reference to the poetry of Medbh McGuckian, Kate Newmann, Gráinne Tobin, Eilish Martin, Mary Twomey, Sally Wheeler, Ann Zell, and particularly to that of Ruth Carr, who has been one of the most consistent animators of Northern women's poetry writing and publication during the last generation.

The final essays, by Ann Owen Weekes and Anne Fogarty, offer studies of two different novels by Mary Morrissy. Morrissy's experimental postmodern texts do not easily reveal their secrets; each is a multi-layered fiction about the lives and subterfuges of shape-shifting heroines whose psychic states reveal the troubled power relations between the familial and the social during the twentieth century. Illustrating the diversity of feminist approaches and the bridges that can be built between feminist and other contemporary literary theories, Fogarty and Weekes offer different perspectives on Morrissy's work: Weekes from a psychoanalytic stance, Fogarty from a postmodernist.

Using Adrienne Rich's analysis of motherhood as a political institution, and Jessica Benjamin's theory of the fantasy of maternal omnipotence with its resulting sense of failure and guilt, Weekes argues the this 'funny, terrible' novel, *Mother of Pearl* (1996), figures the pathology at the centre of Irish family life and politics. Three female characters offer versions of mother–daughter dyads. The first, mother-bereft and obsessed with having a baby, steals an infant from the hospital; the second mother finally reacquires the missing girl at a terrible cost; and the third is the divided child who grows up in the course of the novel, but is torn apart between them, drawn back and forth across a contested border. The novel addresses, Weekes maintains, the hidden but deeply enshrined narrative reverberating across the society: Irish Catholic *and* Protestant misreadings of *Genesis*, 'emphasizing female culpability and inherited sin'.

The final essay by Anne Fogarty uses recent discussions and theories of female subjectivity in order to explore Mary Morrissy's *The Pretender* (2000). This novel offers a multi-layered fictionalization of the life of Franziska Schanzkowska, a Polish factory worker and the Pretender of the title who claimed to be Grand Duchess Anastasia, daughter of the Russian Imperial family who, according to legend, escaped the Bolshevist execution of her family in 1917. Situating this novel as a feminist postmodern text, Fogarty suggests that Morrissy has created a heroine that neither historians nor biographers could imagine. Morrissy takes advantage of the multiple selves the Anastasia legend provides, and Fogarty shows how Schanzkowska's dramatic afterlife in Morrissy's fiction can disclose and also question the ways in which women's lives are shaped and commemorated. Through the exploration of narrative structure, patterns of imagery and the narrative technique of *style indirect libre*, Fogarty illustrates how Morrissy creates a postmodern view not only of a female subjectivity which can embody conflicting subject positions, but also of 'the global dimensions of modern identity'. Placing these issues in the context of recent debates within feminist criticism, Fogarty demonstrates that in *The Pretender* Morrissy has created a form that 'represents the problematic dimensions of female subjectivity' while it also 'shows the necessity of discriminating between stories while taking cognizance of how women's lives might be interconnected'.

One of the noteworthy achievements of these essays is the degree of care and insight each contributor displays for the artistic text examined under her respective lens, and we hope that this collection will provide useful tools for readers, critics and teachers of Irish literature and women's writing and art. We are reminded of the value of this kind of exercise by an observation Katherine O'Donnell makes at the end of her essay, an idea that underlies not just this book but the whole enterprise of literary and cultural criticism: that the enjoyment of engaging with stories, poetry and plays, and the conversations we have about our readings of the texts, can provide 'some of life's best educational experiences'.

These essays offer much material for such a conversation – numerous perspectives on the work of Irish women that cover multiple genres and different approaches to the texts under consideration. The contributors offer as well, at the end of each essay, information about the biographical and critical contexts of each author. Some of the essays recover 'lost' texts; others bring us new ways to read more popular texts; still others introduce us to writers who ought to be better known to a reading public. But, as the beginning of this introduction suggests, and as the debate over *The Field Day Anthology* shows, a conversation that excludes the voices of women, a 'canon' that under-represents their achievements and a critical practice that does not include women's scholarship can offer only a limited and exclusive educational experience. The critical work that follows demonstrates how rich and varied the conversation can be now. And just as clearly we see that while the ideas and issues in the literature discussed here need to be read in the context of Ireland, they belong as well to the larger contexts of international movements of women's writing and multi-faceted feminist scholarship.

Works cited

Boland, Eavan, *A Kind of Scar: The Woman Poet in the National Tradition*, LIP pamphlet (Dublin: Attic Press, 1989).

——, *Object Lessons: The Life of the Woman and the Poet in Our Time* (Manchester: Carcanet Press, 1995).

Boland, Eavan et al., *A Dozen LIPs* (Dublin: Attic Press, 1994).

Bourke, Angela, 'Language, Stories, Healing', in Anthony Bradley and Maryann Gialanella Valiulis (eds.), *Gender and Sexuality in Modern Ireland* (Amherst: University of Massachusetts Press, 1997), pp. 299–314.

Bourke, Angela et al. (eds.), *The Field Day Anthology of Irish Writing: Irish Women's Writing and Traditions, Volumes IV & V* (Cork University Press in association with Field Day, 2002).

Carr, Ruth et al. (eds.), *Word of Mouth: Poems* (Belfast: The Blackstaff Press, 1996).

Casey, Daniel J. and Linda M. Casey (eds.), *Stories by Contemporary Irish Women* (New York: Syracuse University Press, 1990).

Crilly, Anne (dir.), *Mother Ireland* (Derry, Northern Ireland: Derry Film and Video, 1989).

Deane, Seamus et al. (eds.), *The Field Day Anthology of Irish Writing, Volumes I–III* (Derry, Northern Ireland: Field Day Publications, 1991).

DeSalvo, Louise, Kathleen D'Arcy and Katherine Hogan (eds.), *Territories of the Voice: Contemporary Stories by Irish Women* (London: Virago, 1990).

Donovan, Katie, A. Norman Jeffares and Brendan Kennelly (ed.), *Ireland's Women: Writings Past and Present* (Dublin: Gill & Macmillan, 1994).

Irish Feminist Review, vol. I (Galway: Women's Studies Centre, National University of Ireland, 2005).

Fogarty, Anne, 'The Ear of the Other, Dissident Voices in Kate O'Brien's *As Music and Splendour* and Mary Dorcey's *A Noise from the Woodshed*', in Eibhear Walshe (ed.), *Sex, Nation and Dissent in Irish Writing* (Cork University Press, 1997).

Hooley, Ruth (ed.), *The Female Line: Northern Irish Women Writers* (Belfast: Northern Ireland Women's Rights Movement, 1985).

Irish Journal of Feminist Studies, vols. I–IX (Cork University Press, 1996–2003).

Kelleher, Margaret, 'A Retrospective View on Irish Women's Literary Studies', in Munira H. Mutrun and Laura P.Z. Izarra (eds.), *Kaleidoscopic Views of Ireland* (Universidade De Sao Paulo, 2003), pp. 161–78. (Reprinted in 'The Field Day Anthology and Irish Women's Literary Studies', *The Irish Review* (30) 2003, special issue on contemporary literature, pp. 82–94.)

Kelly, A.A. (ed.), *Pillars of the House: An Anthology of Verse by Irish Women, from 1690 to the Present* (Dublin: Wolfhound, 1987).

Longley, Edna, *From Cathleen to Anorexia: The Breakdown of Irelands* (Dublin: Attic Press, 1990). (Reprinted in *The Living Stream, Literature and Revisionism in Ireland* (Newcastle-upon-Tyne: Bloodaxe, 1994)).

MacCarthy, B.G., *The Female Pen*, 2 vols. (Cork University Press, 1945–7).

Madden-Simpson, Janet (ed.), *Woman's Part: An Anthology of Short Fiction By and About Irish Women 1890–1960* (Dublin: Arlen House, 1984).

Marcus, David (ed.), *Alternative Loves: Irish Gay and Lesbian Stories* (Dublin: Martello Books, 1994).

McKibben, Sarah E., 'Angry Laments and Grieving Postcoloniality', in P.J. Mathews (ed.), *New Voices in Irish Criticism* (Dublin: Four Courts Press, 2000), pp. 215–23.

McBreen, Joan (ed.), *The White Page – An Bhileog Bhán: Twentieth-Century Irish Women Poets* (Cliffs of Moher, Co. Clare: Salmon Publishing, 1999).

McGuckian, Medbh, 'Timed Chess', in *Captain Lavender* (Loughcrew, Co. Meath: The Gallery Press, 1994).

Meaney, Gerardine, *Sex and Nation: Women in Irish Culture and Politics* (Dublin: Attic Press, 1991).

Murphy, Lizz (ed.), *Wee Girls: Women Writing from an Irish Perspective* (Melbourne, Australia: Spinifex Press, 1996).

Ní Dhuibhne, Eilís (ed.), *Voices on the Wind: Women Poets of the Celtic Twilight* (Dublin: New Island Books, 1995).

O'Brien, Peggy (ed.), *The Wake Forest Book of Contemporary Irish Women Poets 1967–2000* (Winston-Salem, NC: Wake Forest University Press, 1999).

Smyth, Ailbhe (ed.), *Wildish Things: An Anthology of New Irish Women's Writing* (Dublin: Attic Press, 1989).

Sullivan, Moynagh. 'Feminism, Postmodernism and the Subjects of Irish and Women's Studies', in P.J. Mathews (ed.), *New Voices in Irish Criticism* (Dublin: Four Courts Press, 2000), pp. 243–51.

Walsh, Caroline (ed.), *Virgins and Hyacinths: An Attic Press Book of Fiction* (Dublin: Attic Press, 1993).

Walshe, Eibhear (ed.), *Sex, Nation and Dissent in Irish writing* (Cork University Press, 1997).

Ward, Margaret, 'Nationalism, Pacifism, Internationalism, Louie Bennett, Hanna Sheehy-Skeffington and the Problems of "Defining Feminism"', in Anthony Bradley and Maryann Gialanella Valiulis (eds.), *Gender and Sexuality in Modern Ireland* (Amherst: University of Massachusetts Press, 1997), pp. 60–81.

Women's Studies Review, vols. I–IX (Galway: Women's Studies Centre, National University of Ireland, 1992–2004).

Women's Work: An Anthology of Poems by Women, 7 vols. I–VII (Wexford: The Works, 1990–1996).

Chapter 1

Engendering the Postmodern Canon?

The Field Day Anthology of Irish Writing,
Volumes IV & V: Women's Writing and Traditions

Gerardine Meaney

'Is tradition like history? Do we have to invent it?'
Eilís Ní Dhuibhne, 'The Flowering'

'Tradition is . . . not merely what the past leaves us. It must always be understood as selective tradition . . . Tradition cultivates its own inevitability by erasing the fact of its selectivity in regard to practices, meanings, gender, "races" and classes'.
Griselda Pollock, *Differencing the Canon* (p. 10)

The context of the anthology

The final two volumes of *The Field Day Anthology of Irish Writing* have their origins in the controversy surrounding the first three volumes, sharply criticized for their under-representation of women's writing. That controversy focused very much on contemporary writing and the virtual invisibility of the women's movement. The two new volumes are, however, much broader than this in their historical, disciplinary and thematic range. The editorial structure and the methodologies employed were also very different from those of the previous volumes. Three literary critics, three historians and two Irish language editors formed a multidisciplinary and collaborative panel which identified areas for inclusion and commissioned a total of forty-seven other contributing editors, from a wide variety of academic disciplines, journalism, the arts and political groups, to research, identify and edit material for inclusion. The result was the identification of a more complex and diverse range of sources than even that editorial panel had ever envisaged. The enormous number of texts from which the selections had to be made led to the eventual conclusion that the one volume originally planned simply could not do justice to the material. The editorial staff of Cork University Press, who took over as publishers of the project in 1999, arrived at the pragmatic solution of a two-volume set.

Each of the panel editors assumed responsibility for an individual section, early in the commissioning process. My own section was 'Women and Writing, 1700–1960', and it is on the editing of that section, and the issues of selection, research methodology and critical practice which I had to resolve in the process, that I wish to focus here. The eight-member editorial panel was crucial, however, in creating a context where critical and historical certainties were challenged and reshaped. The sections are discrete, but the editorial process was one of creative fusion. One aspect of the volumes which gives me as an editor particular satisfaction at this stage is the juxtaposition within them of poetry, fiction and drama with women's stories from workhouses, convents and prisons and the intermingling of both with the legacy of storytellers, singers and keeners. The very diverse and complex picture of women's history and creative output which results is the outcome of the collaborative and multidisciplinary nature of the project.

My own editorial activity was concentrated in the traditional literary genres, however, and as such my section bears a closer relationship to the first three volumes than do those dealing with oral or historical material. Consequently, the issue of literary canons, their formation and change, was an important one for me from the start. I have kept a shortlist of items which I was originally dismayed to discover were not in the first three volumes as a reminder of how far we have travelled: it was only two pages long. Editing this anthology was a voyage of discovery for me as editor, primarily into the extraordinary wealth of material written by women between 1890 and 1960, which I edited in detail, but also vicariously through the work of contributing editors and my colleagues on the editorial panel.

It became clear after the first year or two of reading and research that the material we were dealing with did not fit easily into any of the existing paradigms for Irish literary history. It also became clear to me, working in the areas closest to those in which the then-prevailing ways of constructing the history of women's writing in the English language had been established, that those paradigms too were challenged by the material. There is no strong tradition of realist domestic fiction, for example, and only limited examples of the female Bildungsroman. In contrast, there are numerous examples of women writing political poetry, drama and fiction, particularly historical fiction, which constituted an important, if often overlooked, intervention into the 'mainstream' discourses of nationalist and unionist politics. In the twentieth century, popular dialect poetry is as strong a current as strenuous modernist experiment with form. Consequently, part of the project for me was to generate new critical paradigms as well as recover lost texts.

Feminist theory, literary history and editorial practice: critical and academic contexts

Typically for an Irish feminist critic, my involvement in feminist criticism was initially an entirely separate development to my education in Irish literature. The origins of both lie in teenage reading. I read a copy of Germaine Greer's *The Female Eunuch* (1970) discovered in a house where I was babysitting: the impact on a fifteen-year-old attending a convent secondary school in 1970s Kilkenny is difficult even for me to imagine a quarter century later. At university, Greer seemed to lead inexorably to Sylvia Plath, Stevie Smith, Doris Lessing and Angela Carter, and, more convolutedly, to Spark, Kristeva, Irigaray and Cixous. Then a friend who was studying French hurried up to me in the library with a copy of Roland Barthes's *Mythologies* (1972), and the possibility of a completely new way of reading opened up. Inevitably my interests led from Barthes to Elaine Marks and Isabel de Courtivrons's ground-breaking *New French Feminisms* (1981). Translations of the key texts of French feminist theory circulated in University College Dublin in the early 1980s in a kind of samizdat form, blurred photocopies of photocopies of photocopies, all originating from Ailbhe Smyth's seminars on women's writing in the French department. By contrast with deconstructing the entire western tradition in philosophy and literature, the content of most of my Irish literature courses seemed unexciting. Jennifer Johnston was the only Irish woman writer I can recall appearing on the university English curriculum, and the impact of *Shadows on Our Skin* (1977) was a profound one at the time. The consensus was nonetheless that there was no tradition of women's writing in Ireland. Instead there were Joyce and Yeats, lots of them. Courses called 'Poetry after Yeats' re-enforced the idea that Irish writing was basically a great plain with those two monumental peaks (and a cliff face called Beckett). Despite the encomiums of Kristeva and Cixous for Joyce, that landscape felt both alien and hostile. In retrospect, it was, of course, the way in which they were read and taught in the early 1980s that produced this effect, which does not entirely invalidate the perception I shared with many of the female students at the time that Irish literature was the exclusive property of the intense young men in our tutorials who so obviously and painfully identified with Stephen Dedalus. It was that conjunction of French feminism and contemporary English literature that inspired my postgraduate work. Consequently, when I decided to attempt an academic career it was to pursue feminist theory and women's writing, not Irish literature.[1] Again like many of my contemporaries, it was reading feminist criticism which forced me eventually to ask myself where the Irish women writers were buried.

The extraordinary facilitating force of literary theory in the 1980s is often overlooked in criticism of its alleged elitism. At the time, the vast majority of undergraduate English literature students were women. The ratio was dramatically reversed at postgraduate level and the presence of women decreased even further among lecturing staff. (This gender bias has, of course, changed its structure but emphatically not gone away.) In 1983, I was one of three women in an M.A. class of sixteen, in a department where only two of the twenty lecturers were women. In that context, theories which challenged the cultural authority of the entire edifice were a practical necessity. They cleared a space for different voices to speak and provided a vocabulary which women could use to speak differently and to challenge the certainties which defined literature. Postmodern suspicion of the grand narratives is a natural position for those whose cultural existence the grand narratives deny. Theory gave a powerful language to those previously outside the parameters of cultural power. In effect, feminist literary theory made it possible to function within and against the academic structure. The development of new ways of reading Irish literature within the context of postcolonial theory evolved in the same period: the *Crane Bag* journal (1977–85) and the Field Day pamphlet series transfigured the critical reading of Irish literature in the 1980s. Sustained rereading of the literary revival's construction of Irish literature in English, from Seamus Deane's *Celtic Revivals* in 1985 to Declan Kiberd's *Inventing Ireland* in 1995, reconfigured the canonical terrain. These developments eventually facilitated an exploration of gender, though postcolonial and feminist criticism remained parallel with little integration until the end of the twentieth century.

Feminist theory, literary history and editorial practice: political and historical contexts

The 1980s were also a time of extraordinary social and political turmoil in Ireland, with the successive abortion referenda putting the issue of changing sexual and gender roles at the centre of political life in the South. Anyone politically opposed to the resurgence of the Catholic right at the time was forced to think about the reserves of cultural hysteria centering on women's bodies in general and motherhood in particular which it was able to mobilize. Kristeva's work on the cult of motherhood in Catholic ideology seemed extraordinarily resonant to me and it gave me a way of analysing underlying cultural and symbolic structures which could account for the origins of the ferocity of the social and cultural conflict of the period.[2] It was an attempt to use feminist theory to understand the sexual politics of contemporary Ireland which initially led me to work on Irish women's writing. I started working on Kate O'Brien, whom Arlen House and Virago brought back to print and critical notice at the time.[3] Working on O'Brien's novels forced me to adapt Kristeva's theory, paying more attention to the particularities of Irish history. In turn that led to a more historicized approach to theory. In effect, O'Brien conditioned the methodology which would inform my selections in the anthology, certainly for the first half of the twentieth century, not least because initial research into women's fiction in the period indicated a very different context in which her writing could be regarded as part of a continuum rather than a controversial exception to the development of the Irish novel.

Women's writing and the canon of Irish literature

The twenty years preceding the inception of Volumes IV and V of *The Field Day Anthology of Irish Writing* had been extraordinarily productive for Irish women, with social change and the women's movement generating vibrant and challenging work in all cultural forms and academic disciplines. Anthologies and journal special issues focusing on contemporary Irish women's writing appeared. Major work by Eavan Boland, Eiléan Ní Chuilleanáin, Medbh McGuckian, Nuala Ní Dhohmnaill and later Paula Meehan challenged the masculine construction of the Irish poetic tradition.[4] The new cultural confidence was haunted by a significant absence, however. This is evident particularly in the work of artists and writers. Eavan Boland has spoken repeatedly of the isolation of the woman poet, with no sense of a tradition of writing by women. Medbh McGuckian's 'The Aisling Hat' in *Captain Lavender* (1994) expressed a similar longing: 'I search for a lost, unknown song / in a street as long as a night, / stamped with my own surname' (p. 44). This sense of absence was not entirely due to an absence of awareness of Irish women's past or their cultural contribution. Most of the groundwork for Volumes IV and V, for example, was laid prior to the 1990s. It was for precisely this reason that the 1991 version of the anthology could be challenged. The re-evaluation and recovery of women's work and history was not, however, regarded as part of the serious and central work of defining and redefining Ireland in the 1970s and 1980s. The contested nature of national and political identity in the period often produced self-enclosed binary oppositions, closed to the questioning of national identities, literary canons and historical priorities which an analysis of the role of gender in their construction would have necessitated.

Given that the focus of the section I edited was on traditionally literary forms, the question of how the formation of the literary canon was gendered in Ireland was a crucial one from the start. Even more important was the question of how to postulate an other, differencing literary history which would disrupt existing discourses. Before I became involved in the anthology I had developed an interest in Sandra Harding's feminist epistemology. In the somewhat polarized debate about the relationship between feminism and postmodernism, Harding's work seemed to offer a third way. As I worked on the project, I watched the evolution of her work, moving from a refusal of the 'either/or' polarities of the feminism versus postmodernism debate to a new understanding that combined suspicion of the 'grand narratives' with an acknowledgement of the need to produce new narratives, particularly for those whose narratives have been foreclosed or occluded by the dominant discourse. This seemed to me to be very close to the dilemma facing an editor and anthologist of women's writing. The very existence of Volumes IV and V challenges the idea that anthologies can ever be more than provisional versions, selections on the basis of criteria that produce and are produced by the values, debates and politics of the culture in and for which they are composed. Their existence also, however, challenges the idea that the absence of claims to totality justifies exclusions of particular groups or points of view. The volumes insist on differences, but it is predicated on sexual difference. The editors had a common desire to undermine the generalization of all Irish women into one type, one history, one 'figure', to recover their differences. To undertake such work is, nonetheless, to propose a provisional narrative of women's relation to writing, to culture and to Ireland. However much it insists on its provisionality, it too will be seen as producing a canon which in turn will be challenged by the work of the next decades in this area.

Here I found Harding's work on standpoint theory particularly useful. Just as the editing of *Field Day* appeared to be ending in 1998 (a false dawn, but it felt like an ending at the time), Harding's *Is Science Multicultural? Post-colonialisms, Feminisms and Epistemologies* appeared. In it she proposed a way of formulating and proposing knowledge that mediated between the claims of truth and relativism in a radical way. The basis of knowledge in this formulation is not a claim to totality or truth but the opening up of new conceptual spaces and dialogue, using a series of strategic maps which make visible the perspective and standpoint from which they are constructed. It is precisely such a strategic map which is provided in the women's writing section of the anthology.

The other important influence on the way I approached the issue of canon formation was Griselda Pollock's work on canons in art history, *Differencing the Canon* (1999). Pollock helped me to bridge the initial gap between my own training in feminist theory and the apparently empiricist requirements of research in bibliography and biography required by the project of retrieving little-known texts. Pollock's aim of 'differencing the canon' particularly appealed to me as it addressed directly the reservation I shared with many critics of the project, that women's writing would be segregated into an 'annex', while the main structure of the Irish literary canon remained untouched. In this context, I held throughout to the decision not to include again women writers already well represented in the first three volumes unless there were very specific and pertinent reasons for doing so. Including again all women writers previously represented would have consolidated a separate canon of women's writing, neatly divided from a male canon which would then assume an originary status as *the* (national) canon. Hence writers from Morgan and Edgeworth to Boland and O'Brien were included again in Volumes IV and V, but thematically, not as the canonical monuments around which the less familiar work could be organized and recuperated into a recognizable version of Irish literary history. To difference the canon, one must combine rereading the known with rendering visible the unknown. Feminist rereading of canonical texts has been an ongoing critical project for several decades. Recovery of the lesser-known work by women was urgently overdue when we began work at the beginning of the 1990s. There were important predecessors, including Janet Madden-Simpson's *Women's Part* (1984) and A.A. Kelly's *Pillars of the House* (1987). In the intervening years, studies of nineteenth- and eighteenth-century literature, increased interdisciplinarity and focus on previously less-regarded genres, such as Gothic and melodrama, have rapidly expanded the definitions of what constitutes Irish literature. Indeed, some of the contributing editors to the anthology had been pioneers of that expansion. The authors included in the anthology for the period prior to 1960 remain little read beyond academic circles, however. The anthology offered an opportunity to make a much wider public aware of their work and, consequently, of a very different Irish writing beyond the canonical horizon. The Irish media response to the volumes has been disappointing in this regard, proving largely unwilling to look beyond writers and issues with which reviewers are familiar. The question of how successful we have been in the objective of making Irish writing strange to itself awaits a much longer-term response.

As an editor, I took responsibility for representing women's contribution to fairly traditional genres; poetry, fiction, drama, criticism and the writing of history, in the period 1700–1960. In doing so, I chose to work within the traditional parameters of the literary, though the volumes' larger structure meant that the literary was not the dominant variety of writing included but one among many forms of expression. Unlike previously non-canonical written forms, such as diaries and letters, these traditional genres demanded a high degree of self-consciousness about the form and content of their expression by the women who worked within them. For the period 1890 to 1960, on which I worked as a contributing editor as well as general editor, this usually also involved a high degree of self-consciousness about issues of national identity and often included questioning the ways in which national identity was gendered in Ireland. I would like to focus on this period and on this section of the anthology in order to look at the issues of aesthetics and politics, nation and gender, feminism and nationalism from a different angle, one provided by the texts themselves. I also want to deal with the issue of literary merit and its relationship with canon construction, with an emphasis on the way in which the critical concerns I have just outlined informed the choice of texts selected. The best way to address this seems to me to focus on the figure of the woman artist in two little-known poems from the period. The figure of the modern woman artist is an important one in fiction of the period, featuring centrally in Katherine Cecil Thurston's *Max* (1910), for example, and Rosamond Jacob's *The Troubled House* (1938). The woman as storyteller and keeper of the records of oral culture figures in Lady Gregory's *The Gaol Gate* (original performance 1906), where, as I have argued elsewhere, the lamenting or keening woman is a surrogate of the dramatist herself. The woman with the frustrated capabilities of an artist features also in Teresa Deevy's play, *The King of Spain's Daughter* (original performance 1939), a devastating retelling of John

Synge's *The Playboy of the Western World* (original performance 1907). It is on poetry rather than fiction or drama that I wish to concentrate, however, on one comic and one tragic figure of the woman artist.

The woman artist: 'Fiddlin' Kate' and modernist Liadain

The section on 'Identity and Opposition, 1890–1960' included poetry, fiction and drama. The section is organized around the thematic and political concerns which these genres shared in the period. Predictably these include matters of gender and national identity, but, more unexpectedly, exploration of the figure of the woman artist is almost equally pervasive. This may have its origins in the suffrage period and the literature of the 'New Woman', but is also attributable to the influence of modernism, particularly its tendency towards self-reflexivity in art. The self-reflexive woman artist in the Irish literature of this period, however, is not exclusive to literature which is stylistically modernist. A very populist and vernacular example is Elizabeth Shane (pseudonym of Gertrude Hine), 'Fiddlin' Kate'. 'Fiddlin' Kate' was originally included in A.A Kelly's *Pillars of the House* and its inclusion in Volume V of the anthology (p. 1024) registers the debt of anyone working on Irish women's poetry to pioneers like Kelly and Anne Ulry Colman. It is also one of a number of poems representing the tendency towards vernacular and dialect verse by twentieth-century women writers, which appears to have been a predominantly Northern Irish phenomenon. Kate, the poem tells us, 'was a quare wee restless thing, / Her laugh was as gay as a bird in spring, / Her eyes were black wi' a dancin' light, / An' she played the fiddle from morn till night'. Both Kate's personality and her art are clearly at odds with her society's definition of appropriate feminine behaviour. Her lover, Mike, 'wanted a wife could bake an' spin / An' he'd no great notion o' fiddling', concluding '"I will not marry a fiddlin' wife. So 'tis the way when ye marry me / Ye'll have the fiddle behind," said he'. Kate successfully defies this disapproval:

> She laughed, an' wi' never a word at all
> She turned where the fiddle was on the wall,
> An' tuckin' it under her tilted chin
> Tunes by the dozen did she begin;
> Till Mike, wi' his heart in a black despair,
> Went out o' the door an' left her there.

Kate later encounters him in an argument with his wife, a fine, domesticated, bad-tempered woman. Kate:

> . . . looked at him wi' her impish grin –
> 'I hope,' said she, 'she can bake an' spin.'
> 'Och, och!' said he, 'If I'd known at first,
> Sure a fiddle itself is not the worst.'

Shane's popular comic verse reflects a highly self-confident self-reflexive strain: she herself was a classical violinist. In the poem, the woman artist is exuberantly free not just to reject the constraints of domesticity, but to fully enjoy her 'tunes by the dozen'. This laughing figure is in contrast to the tortured modernist Liadain, who features in Katherine Arnold Price's 'Curithir and Liadain – II' (*Field Day*, vol. V, p. 1026). Price's poem was a major discovery for me, not just because it crystallized many of the central concerns of the section, but also because it raised the issues of literary merit, aesthetic judgement and canonicity in an acute form.

With regard to poetry, the editorial panel had long discussions about the inclusion of poets who had never had a volume of poetry published in book form. Initially we made a general editorial decision that only poets with at least one volume published could be considered or the project would expand in scale to completely unmanageable proportions: none of the editors had teams of researchers at their disposal, which such an undertaking would have required. However, working through journals such as *The Dubliner, The Bell* and *Poetry Ireland,* the issue of who had access to publication seemed to me highly significant. In general, women working in popular verse, like Shane/Hine had a much better chance of publication, at least in the first half of the twentieth century. There were poets, such as Blanaid Salkeld and Temple Lane, who were no longer even footnotes to Irish literary history, despite the publication of several volumes of poetry. Salkeld, for example, had a high degree of access to publication and a generally positive critical reception but underwent that peculiar fading from the literary record which feminist criticism in the 1970s and 1980s had chronicled so well in other contexts. Then there were the women who wrote, sometimes all their lives, sometimes in a brief flowering, for the many literary journals and periodicals of Ireland, but who never published a volume. Despite the pragmatic principle of excluding this ocean of material from consideration, I was loath to leave Price out. She had, of course, published two books towards the end of her life when she turned predominantly to fiction (in 1980 and 1985), but that simply confirmed the hypothesis that women had greater access to publication and critical regard in fiction than poetry. Including her fiction rather than her poetry would have been to reproduce that bias. Finally, there was the issue of literary value. It is very difficult to estimate what the influence or otherwise may have been of a poet whose poems appeared in a medium as ephemeral as journals and magazines and whose major work, the poems based on the story of Liadain, seem never to have been published in their entirety. It is impossible to postulate even a coherent corpus of her own work, let alone position her within a coherent narrative of Irish poetry or women's poetry. Price's work, however, can work for a contemporary reader if it is situated at the intersection of the discourses of feminism, modernism and nationality. In other words, I thought it would work in the context of this section of the anthology. I wanted it to work, of course, because it seemed to me to have a force and a quality which not only entitled it to set aside pragmatic editorial decisions but which also called into question in a fundamental way the judgements of posterity. Was I then to have recourse to the notion of the neglected genius and set about seeking canonical status for work which had been too advanced for the literary establishment of the time? Price's poem invites this construction, almost demands it:

> . . . breath, the poet's instrument, must utter
> Sounds of authority answering the spirit's will,
> Not testament, nor apologia, nor lament,
> But the articulation of this consciousness,
> This way of being that is mine and me.

Liadain's dilemma is whether to integrate life and art, as Cuirithir exhorts her, or to pursue an art which is pure and fatal: 'I wanted to move always further into pure being / Death, or perhaps several deaths becoming winnowings.' Implicit in Price's poem is a critique of the abstract nature of Liadain's art. The question of whether her experiment is worth the price of life and love is not answered. The poem is informed by an Irish context of sexual repression: it was Liadain's religious vocation in the traditional rendering of the tale that demanded the rejection of sexuality by the lovers.

Another context also informs it, however, one which recurs in all of these images of the woman artist, that of the relationship between sexuality and creativity. Interestingly, the vastly different Shane and Price concur in their poetry that fidelity to art precludes love. In *Max*, Katherine Cecil Thurston's 1910 novel about a woman living as a man in order to train as an artist, Max/Maxine paints a portrait of her female self in order to control and dismiss it. The picture succeeds, but the manoeuvre doesn't. *Max* ends uneasily with Maxine seeking to do what Max has pronounced impossible, combining a life of art with a heterosexual relationship. Rosamond Jacob's *The Troubled House* insists, by contrast, on a positive connection between sexual and aesthetic freedom. The centrality and seriousness with which all of these texts treat this issue in itself renders them marginal to traditions defined by the cooption of the feminine to the materiality from which art is made, in other words, the aesthetics of both mainstream revivalism and avant-garde modernism.[5] It is unsurprising, then, that they are beyond the canon of Irish literature. The question to which Price's work returns us is whether the texts have the retrospective power to interrupt the legacy of that dominant aesthetic structure. Making aesthetic judgements outside the frameworks of canon and consensus is a risky business. The danger with Price was that of reversion to a Romantic ideology of the poet by way of the cult of the exceptional, unknown woman. Such a construction would simply bury her under her own monument, however. Her shorter poems indicate an engagement with the specifics of her society in its time which forces the reader of 'Cuirithir and Liadain – II' back to the relationship between its aesthetics and politics. In poems from a 'Scrapbook for County Down', published in *Poetry Ireland* (9 April 1950),[6] Price includes 'The Special Constables'. The role and significance of this force is not commented on directly in the poem, which instead builds up a sense of menace: 'The three walk heavily together, fear on their shoulders, / Bruising the midnight with authority's boots; / Snouts of their rifles root among the roofs.' The relationship between Irish history and Price's work is usually more oblique, but it is nonetheless powerful. Given the context of sexual repression in Ireland and the role of the church in the original story, the poem is surprisingly absent of any declarations of religiosity on Liadain's part. Renunciation of sexuality is an experiment in renouncing life and the poem is highly ambivalent about the value of the choice. Again, attention to the context of publication is worth bearing in mind. Price's complete poem was never published and, presumably, the choice of this extract was an editorial one for *Poetry Ireland*. The 'Perpetual Dialogue of Cuirithir and Liadain' (from work in progress), which Price later described as the bulk of her long poem on the subject, was published in *The Dublin Magazine* in 1957. The implication is that the complete poem is a balanced and open-ended dialogue, though the extract in *Poetry Ireland* is exclusively from Liadain's perspective. It is consequently easily read as a woman's lament for lost love, if that is what you are looking for in a modern rendering of an Irish myth. From a contemporary perspective it is equally misleadingly easy to read it as a poet's subjective view of the exactions of her art or a woman's lament that she cannot combine independence and love. Yet the poem does not leave Liadain's point of view unchallenged. Even within the extract, there are references to Cuirithir's counterview of life and art. What '[if] I have created a negation . . . as he said; / A kingdom where there is nothing . . . as he said', ponders Liadain:

> Curithir said I was an enemy of living,
> Drawing mesmeric circles to diminish
> Man's dimension; he found the silence minatory,
> Stillness an atrophy; he craves the temporal life,
> Seasonal, repetitive; he needs the diversion of folly,
> The sight of a fool or a cripple to increase him.
> He greets the world as a lover, inhaling its breath
> Inexhaustibly, seeking not mastery, but excess.
> For him the heart was an impediment to adventure.

*   *   *   *   *

The different roles of the poet embraced by Curithir and Liadain as Price formulates them do not easily fit into conventional gender roles. He seeks excess, she mastery:

>   . . . for me
> It was never a question of happiness; not at all;
> It was a question, it is always a question of living,

Of finding a way, a changing equilibrium
Maintained above the mustering of ancient impulses
Intricate before word was; perception running ahead,
Away from darkness, away from the primordial dream
That winds a wild horn for an outrageous hosting;
The will subduing the animal incitements
And the masked irregulars of the mind's mutiny;
No inertia, no cramp of a mesmeric circle
But the balance of outstretched wings, force meeting force,
All the skills of the indivisible self
Creating in counterpoint a calculated entity,
Vision and understanding driving spirit
To generate a form imbued with the art of living.
Using my life, I have made an experiment in living.
Perhaps it has failed; for I am repudiated;
Or is proved; and the corollary is solitude.

Liadain's uncertainty about the success of her experiment is indicative of an ambiguity running through the poem. That ambiguity makes it impossible to construct ultimately any one poetic voice. Curithir and Liadain represent two positions in relation to life and art and Price's poem does not propose any identification between the poet and either one or the other of them. Moreover the poem cannot be assimilated to any preconceived notion about the gendering of poetic power. Liadain is an artist more than confident of her powers. In contrast to the artist in Dorothy Macardle's 'The Portrait of Roisin Dhu', who is fatally oblivious to the power of his art to affect its living object, for example, Liadain has a belief in representation's ability to mould reality which speaks to the concerns of feminist criticism in an unexpected way:

We go round and round, he said, but I shall go backward,
Listening along the blurring trail of sound,
Word by remembered word, phrase by slurred phrase,
Halted by lacunae and half-willed obliterations,
One more dishonest historian with a special plea,
Composing and redisposing the unacceptable,
Subtly changing him to what I would have him be,
Re-creating him, drowning him in legend . . .
No, no, not that . . . I must not even name him;
If I uttered his name it would put a leash upon him.
Naming has power; half-way across the world
He would be halted by my invocation,
My thought would reach him and re-make his mood.
That is a tyranny I must not practise.

Price's poem critiques the tyranny poetry and legend exert over the reality of the past, in a way that foreshadows Eavan Boland, for example, in *A Kind* of *Scar* (1989) and *Object Lessons* (1995). It also imagines that power to be at the disposal of the woman poet. 'The unworked nowhere' (McGuckian, 'Timed Chess', *Captain Lavender*, p. 75) of forgotten poetry is a stranger and more interesting place than anyone could have anticipated .

Conclusion

Differences can coexist, cross-fertilize and challenge, be acknowledged, confronted, celebrated and not remain destructive of the other in an expanded but shared cultural space. Instead of the present exclusivity of the cultural canon contested by fragmented special studies all premised on the binary oppositions of identity politics, insiders/outsiders, margins/centres, high/low, and so forth, the cultural field may be reimagined as a space for multiple occupancy where differencing creates a productive covenant opposing the phallic logic that offers us only the prospect of safety in sameness or danger in difference, of assimilation to or exclusion from the canonized norm (Pollock, *Differencing the Canon*, p. 11).

Pollock's notion of an expanded, shared, differenced cultural space can seem utopian at times. Yet it is difficult to imagine any other kind of cultural space that would create a context in which poets like Shane and Price could be reread in a way which does full justice to their difference and their complexity. The project of recovery of lesser-known and unknown women's writing has the potential to remap the canonical territory of Irish writing, rereading from the margins to reconfigure the cultural space usually designated 'Irish'.

Field Day Anthology of Irish Writing, Vols. IV & V: critical contexts

Given the time span of the contents of *The Field Day Anthology of Irish Writing,* it seems a little premature to assess its impact only five years after the publication of the concluding volumes. The immediate hostile reaction in the Irish newspapers mirrored the earlier hostile reaction to the first three volumes, with the interesting side effect of retrospectively canonizing – in all senses – the earlier set. This was particularly noticeable in the extensive *Irish Times* review. This reaction was predictable, particularly in its emphasis on what was not in the anthology as opposed to what was in it. This might be described as the *Harry Potter* effect in newspaper reviewing: where the text is too long to read or assimilate in the appropriate time frame for newspaper coverage, the reviewer must perforce find an angle from which to generate a thousand words or so without having to engage too closely with the actual book or books under review. In the case of Volumes I to III, this meant that newspapers normally hostile to feminist criticism initially ran the story of the exclusion of women writers. In the case of Volumes IV and V, the familiar construction of a feminist enterprise as necessarily blinkered or exclusive required the rehabilitation of Volumes I to III as exemplars of scholarly impartiality. Changes in the political climate, particularly in relation to Northern Ireland, also meant that the political imperative of hostility to *Field Day* had been removed.

The politics of Volumes IV and V were a somewhat different matter. Even newspaper reviewers with no understanding of their relation to the underlying concepts of feminist scholarship or radical challenges to the notion of literary canons understood that their integration of historical documents and oral and written literature was a challenge to mainstream notions of the status and function of literature. The initial newspaper reaction to that challenge was not positive, but engagement with it has been a feature of the complexity and range of journal reviews. Beginning with Lucy McDiarmid's *Times Literary Supplement* review, reviews in the *Irish University Review, Irish Literary Supplement, Eighteenth-Century Studies* and the *Dublin Review* have begun to unravel what the significance of such a project might be for understandings of Irish culture and history and to propose how it might be used by scholars, students and readers. Margaret Kelleher's discussion of *Field Day* in her 2003 account of the long history of feminist criticism in Ireland and Roisín Higgins's review of Volume V in the *Irish University Review* (2004) have also sought to understand the volumes' relation to their own historical moment.

As an editor, I found both startling and illuminating Higgins's argument that the death of Anne Lovett, commemorated at the time of her review, haunted our endeavours. Perhaps the scale and extent of the undertaking is only explicable as a response to the scale and extent of feminists' alienation from the Ireland they grew up in as a place of secrets and constraints and half-known things, and the Ireland where as adults they lost political battles to forces which seemed to draw on inherited fears and anxieties, originating in that apparently un-narrated place, women's past. Repeatedly we talked of a springboard for future research. Claire Bracken's analysis of the 'rhizomatic' structure of the volumes and their consequent affinity with the internet projects in which a number of the volumes' editors are involved would seem to indicate the springboard worked. The way in which a younger generation of scholars are using the volumes, theorizing and historicizing, criticizing their limitations and exceeding them, is exhilarating.

If the past and present of Irish women was the object of our research, it was assumed that that object could only be provisionally represented, for now, until more is known. In retrospect, amid all the diversity of epistemologies, methodologies, disciplines and training, that was the one constant. The multiplicity of sources and voices and texts and editors can be understood in this context as the mark of a narrative in process, the refusal to construct one story which will make sense – finally – of woman's relation to Irishness and the alternative proposal of a point of dialogue with the past for future use.

Works cited

Barthes, Roland, *Mythologies,* trans. Annette Lavers (London: Jonathan Cape, 1972).

Boland, Eavan, *A Kind of Scar: The Woman Poet in a National Tradition,* LIP pamphlet (Dublin: Attic Press, 1989).

——, *Object Lessons: The Life of the Woman and the Poet in Our Time* (Manchester: Carcanet Press, 1995).

Bourke, Angela et al. (eds.), *The Field Day Anthology of Irish Writing, Volumes IV & V: Women's Writing and Traditions* (Cork University Press, 2002).

Colman, Anne Ulry, *A Dictionary of Nineteenth-Century Irish Women Poets* (Galway: Kenny's Bookshop, 1996).

Coughlan, Patricia, '"Bog Queens": The Representation of Women in the Poetry of John Montague and Seamus Heaney', in Toni O'Brien-Johnson and David Cairns (eds.), *Gender in Irish Writing* (Milton Keynes: Open University Press, 1991).

Cullingford, Elizabeth, *Gender and History in Yeats's Love Poetry* (Cambridge: Cambridge University Press, 1993).

Deane, Seamus, *Celtic Revivals: Essays in Modern Irish Literature, 1880–198* (London: Faber & Faber, 1985).

Deevy, Teresa, *The King of Spain's Daughter,* originally performed in 1939. Published in *The King of Spain's Daughter and Other One-Act Plays* (Dublin: New Frontiers, 1947); *Field Day,* vol. V, pp. 1001–7.

Greer, Germaine, *The Female Eunuch* (London: MacGibbon & Kee, 1970).

Gregory, Lady Augusta, *The Gaol Gate,* originally performed in 1906. Published in *Selected Writings,* ed. Lucy McDiarmid and Maureen Waters (Harmondsworth: Penguin, 1995), pp. 356–62; *Field Day,* vol. V, pp. 906–9.

Harding, Sandra, *Is Science Multicultural? Postcolonialisms, Feminisms and Epistemologies* (Bloomington/Indianapolis: Indiana University Press, 1998).

Higgins, Roisín, 'Review Essay: "A Drift of Chosen Females?": *The Field Day Anthology of Irish Writing,* Volumes IV and V', *Irish University Review* 33:2 (Autumn/Winter 2004), pp. 400–6.

Jacob, Rosamond, *The Troubled House* (Dublin: Browne & Nolan, 1938); extract in *Field Day,* vol. V, pp. 1007–11.

Johnston, Jennifer, *Shadows on Our Skin* (London: Hamish Hamilton, 1977).

Kelleher, Margaret, 'The *Field Day Anthology* and Irish Women's Literary Studies', *The Irish Review* (30) 2003, special issue on contemporary literature, pp. 82–94.

Kelly, A.A., *Pillars of the House: An Anthology of Verse by Irish Women from 1690 to the Present* (Dublin: Wolfhound, 1987).

Kiberd, Declan, *Inventing Ireland: The Literature of the Modern Nation* (London: Vintage, 1995).

Kristeva, Julia, *The Kristeva Reader,* ed. Toril Moi (Oxford: Blackwell, 1986).

Longley, Edna, *From Cathleen to Anorexia: The Breakdown of Irelands*, LIP pamphlet (Dublin: Attic Press, 1990).

Macardle, Dorothy, 'The Portrait of Roisin Dhu', in *Earthbound* (Worcester, Massachusetts: Harrigan, 1924); *Field Day*, vol. V, pp. 997–1000.

Madden-Simpson, Janet, *Woman's Part: An Anthology of Short Fiction By and About Irish Women 1890–1960* (Dublin: Arlen House, 1984).

Marks, Elaine and Isabel de Courtivron (eds.), *New French Feminisms: An Anthology* (London, New York: Routledge, 1981).

McGuckian, Medbh, *On Ballycastle Beach* (Oxford University Press; Winston-Salem: Wake Forest University Press, 1988).

——, *Captain Lavender* (Loughcrew, Co. Meath: The Gallery Press, 1994).

Meaney, Gerardine, *(Un)Like Subjects: Women, Theory, Fiction* (London/New York: Routledge, 1993).

Meehan, Paula. *The Man Who Was Marked by Winter* (Oldcastle, Co. Meath: Gallery Books, 1991).

Ní Chuilleanáin, Eiléan, *The Magdalene Sermon* (Oldcastle, Co. Meath: Gallery Books, 1989).

Ní Dhomhnaill, Nuala, *Selected Poems/Rogha Danta,* trans. Michael Hartnett, introduction by Maire Mac an tSaoi (Dublin: Raven Arts Press, 1986).

Ní Dhuibhne, Eílis, 'The Flowering', in *Eating Women Is Not Recommended* (Dublin: Attic Press, 1991); *Field Day*, vol. V, pp. 1193–1200.

O'Brien, Kate, *The Ante-Room* [1934] (Dublin: Arlen House, 1980).

——, *Mary Lavelle* [1936] (London: Virago, 1984).

——, *Farewell Spain* [1937] (London: Virago, 1985).

——, *The Land of Spices* [1941] (London: Virago, 1988).

Pollock, Griselda, *Differencing the Canon: Feminist Desire and the Writing of Art's Histories* (London/New York: Routledge, 1999).

Price, Katherine Arnold, *The New Perspective* (Swords, Co. Dublin: Poolbeg Press, 1980).

——, *The Captain's Paramours* (London: Hamish Hamilton, 1985).

Shane, Elizabeth (Gertrude Hine), *Collected Poems: Volumes 1 and 2* (Dundalk: W. Tempest, Dundalgan Press, 1945).

Sullivan, Moynagh, *The Woman Poet and the Matter of Representation in Modern and Postmodern Poetics,* Ph.D. dissertation, University College Dublin, 2001.

Synge, John Millington, *The Playboy of the Western World*, originally performed in 1907. Published in *Plays*, ed. Ann Saddlemeyer (Oxford University Press, 1968).

Thurston, Katherine Cecil, *Max* (London: Hutchinson, 1910); extract in *Field Day*, vol. V, pp. 986–96.

Chapter 2

Becoming the Patriarch?

Masculinity in Maria Edgeworth's *Ormond*

Eiléan Ní Chuilleanáin

Maria Edgeworth's novels do not confine themselves to 'feminine' subject matter. While many contain vestiges of a conventional romance plot and end with a marriage, an emphasis on the fate of a heroine is not at the centre of the author's concerns in such fine works as *Ennui* or *The Absentee*. The reader's attention is as often directed to a man as central figure as to a woman, and indeed the aspects of Edgeworth's work most often discussed nowadays reflect her preoccupation with national character, politics, history and class relations rather than the rights or wrongs of women in her age. She seems equally remote from her famous contemporaries Jane Austen and Mary Wollstonecraft, and is more often bracketed with her admirer Walter Scott or, as in a recent accusation of 'patriarchal complicity' (Kowaleski-Wallace, *Their Fathers' Daughters*), with her predecessor as social moralist, Hannah More.

There is plenty of room to argue that in such works as *Belinda* (and *Helen*, as well as such shorter narratives as *Almeria* and *Emilie de Coulanges*), Edgeworth constructs convincing representations of women's lives and discovers perspectives which illuminate issues specific to the historical predicament of women in her day, while admitting that the reader often gathers that heterosexual erotic love is not her main interest (Kowaleski-Wallace, 'Home Economics'; McCann, 'Conjugal Love and the Enlightenment Subject'). In this essay, I would like, however, to consider her interest in men's lives, and to look at themes of masculinity and patriarchy in a novel which addresses these themes very directly, *Ormond*. The questions that arise in my inquiry – can a woman writing through a male protagonist shirk, as it were, the concerns of her own sex? Is the masculinity Edgeworth writes a natural or a social fact? Does Irish history make a difference? – are given an edge by the fact that *Ormond* itself contains a direct critique of a brace of English classics of the eighteenth century whose titles are synonymous with two diametrically

31

opposed images of masculinity: Henry Fielding's *Tom Jones* (1749) and Samuel Richardson's *Sir Charles Grandison* (1753–4).

Ormond was written as a present for the author's own patriarch, Richard Lovell Edgeworth, who actually, though on his deathbed, contributed some passages to the novel. Father of twenty-two children by four wives, philosophical and scientific intellectual, possibly reformed rake, landlord, Member of Parliament, Edgeworth's influence on his daughter has sometimes been deplored. He has been blamed for the 'moralizing' strain which leads her to make ethical problems and principles central to all of her novels except *Castle Rackrent,* even though, in fact, his contribution to *Ormond* is adventurous and romantic. Certainly he is the major presence in his daughter's writing life, collaborating and criticizing, but his experiences also supply her with a periscope which allows her to look obliquely at the world of men and to exploit their experience. Her first formal novel, *Belinda,* drew on a number of the experiences of her father's early life (*Belinda*, pp. xxii–xxiii, 457–62) and the lives of his friends, and in *Ormond* she chooses to send her hero to Paris to meet courtiers and philosophers at a historical moment which falls over forty years before the book's publication, but which corresponds roughly to the date of Richard Edgeworth's travels to France in 1771.

Ormond illustrates a moral theorem: is it possible for a young person who has had a disorderly upbringing to develop, if he later comes under better influences, into a fully moral being and responsible member of society? Harry Ormond is an orphan who is taken in by Sir Ulick O'Shane but then, while his patron's own son is sent to school and college, is 'let to run wild at home: the gamekeeper, the huntsman, and a cousin of Sir Ulick's, who called himself the King of the Black Islands, [have]. had the principal share in his education' (*Ormond*, p. 10). After an incident when he shoots a peasant in drunken anger, he has to leave Sir Ulick's house and goes to live at the Black Islands. At this point in the story, he might be seen as an example of the evils of idleness and intemperance, justly punished by his position as outcast and probably destined for a series of further disasters.

However, if the reader forms such expectations, they are frustrated. The victim of the shooting, Moriarty Carroll, recovers, and becomes Ormond's friend. The benevolent Lady Annaly is impressed by Ormond's penitence and takes an interest in his future. The King of the Black Islands, Corny O'Shane, drinks too much but is hospitable to the young man and respects his resolution to be temperate for the future; he is clearly intended by the author as a portrait of an honest, generous and even admirable representative of the Gaelic and Catholic Irish tradition (Moriarty too is a Catholic; Ormond is a Protestant, and Sir Ulick has converted to Protestantism for political reasons). Ormond educates himself with the help of books and a helpful clergyman, unexpectedly inherits a fortune, travels to Paris, returns to Ireland to bury Sir Ulick, marries Lady Annaly's daughter and takes over the estate of King Corny from his unworthy son-in-law.

My summary has been intended to suggest two possible readings of *Ormond*. The first would find in the hero's story what might look at first like a general moral proposition: repentance and resolution, leading to self-control and application to study, enable one young man to overcome the unpromising circumstances of his early life and emerge as a mature man, a husband and a landlord. The maturing process, the reader may conclude, transforms the erstwhile wild boy so that he can ultimately become the patriarch, taking over from the father figures who presided over his own youth. The efficacy of repentance and gradual maturation and study, however, is specific to masculine subjects. We are early warned that for a girl merely to be 'lively' brings her to the edge of that 'destruction' from which there is no return (p. 74), when Ormond is tempted to make love to the gardener's daughter, Peggy Sheridan, but recoils at the point when to do so would break his friendship with Moriarty Carroll. Later, we encounter in Paris a society in which a married woman having a lover is not regarded as scandalous, but such a state of affairs horrifies the hero and his return to Ireland is in part motivated by his rejection of the aristocratic mores of pre-revolutionary France.

Maria Edgeworth, then, can see the limits of the general moral lesson. The evolution of the young man cannot in this novel be seen as the universal story of Everyman. Class, religion, race, language play a part in her image of the individual's growth, as well as gender. Ormond, in spite of his initial poverty, belongs by birth to the dominant religion and class of eighteenth-century Ireland, so that neither the disenfranchisement of the marginal Catholic world of the Black Islands, nor the exile of the officers of the Irish Brigade he meets in Paris is in any case going to be his fate. The alternative reading of the novel, to which I will return, would see Ormond's history as illustrating the condition of Ireland, in which political and class division rather than individual character is the focus of attention. But while Edgeworth is an Irish novelist, she is also a commentator on, and a contributor to, the tradition of the English novel. I would like at this point to clarify the theories of the masculine individual which affect Edgeworth's treatment of Ormond, and which she identifies explicitly in the first quarter of the story, in the context of the two English novels mentioned above. Both have an impact on Ormond's development, and in Edgeworth's novel are deliberately contrasted with each other.

The very introduction of *Tom Jones* to Ormond's consciousness is comic. A servant is rummaging in a work-basket and throws out the first volume. Ormond picks it up out of curiosity, and though 'in the greatest possible hurry, for the hounds were out', begins to read and is captivated. He 'read on standing for a quarter of an hour, while [Betty, the servant] held forth unheard . . . he carried it off to his own room that he might finish it in peace', but remains unsatisfied as the next volume is missing. The servant does not know where the rest of the book is, but 'having seized on her, he refused to let her go, and protested that he would continue to be the torment of her life till she should find the odd volume. Betty, when her memory was thus racked, put her hand to her forehead, and recollected that in *the apple-room* there was a heap of old books' (pp. 71–2; author's italics). Sexual passion, including the preying on working-class women by the young men of the families who employ them, is a main motivating force of *Tom Jones*. It is parodied and substituted for here by the passion for reading. But sexual passion is licensed by the book, and its hero, Tom Jones, is, in Edgeworth's disapproving words, 'when going wrong, very wrong, forgiven easily by the reader and by his mistress, and rewarded at the last with all that love and fortune can bestow, in consideration of his being – a very fine fellow' (p. 73). The book, in her account, seduces the reader both by its images of licentious behaviour as easily forgiven, and also by the intoxication of its narrative skill and humour: 'he . . . was delighted by the wit – what Irishman is not? And his curiosity was so much raised by the story; his interest and sympathy so much excited for the hero, that he read on' (p. 71).

Like a proper courtship, the introduction of the second eighteenth-century novel is much more orderly, and is effected by the woman whose daughter Ormond is eventually to court and marry. Lady Annaly sends him a box of books, including a 'very few' novels (p. 84), one of which is *Sir Charles Grandison*. This counteracts the influence of *Tom Jones* by presenting a hero who is already good when the reader first meets him. He appears like a knight of romance, the defender of the innocent and protector of the weak, especially women. Ormond's response to this paragon is not immediate; it is gradual and judicious but still enthusiastic, like the love based on esteem he later begins to feel for Florence (who is 'not one of those beauties who strike at first sight', but whose 'countenance instantly kindled into light and life' (p. 219) when she is interested). He finds the book less attractive than *Tom Jones* at first, but it 'won upon him by degrees, drew him on against his will and against his taste'. In reading *Grandison* he responds not only to the excitement of narrative, but also to the depiction of the social role, to the picture of 'a gentleman, who, fulfilling every duty of his station in society, eminently *useful*, respected and beloved, as brother, friend, master of a family, guardian, and head of a large estate, was admired by his own sex, and, what struck Ormond far more forcibly, loved, passionately loved by women – not by the low and profligate, but by the highest and most accomplished of the sex' (p. 82; author's italics). The quality of Richardson's novel that attracts him is less easily definable than the attractions of *Tom Jones*; the process of reading is described by analogy with visual art, 'just as in old portraits we are at first struck with the costume, but soon, if the picture be really by a master hand, our attention is fixed on the expression of the features and the life of the figure' (pp. 81–2), and the reader at last is lost in admiration of the hero.

Edgeworth makes her plot comment on the action of both novels, but more closely on that of *Tom Jones*. Fielding's novel tells the history of a foundling, discovered as a baby by the good Mr Allworthy and raised by him. Tom is generous, loyal, easily deceived, oversexed, over-fond of amusement – virtues and vices which are presented as natural especially to the male human being, and which lead to his getting into a series of more and more ludicrously disastrous adventures. At the book's climax, he is discovered by a twist of the ingenious and elegant plot to be related to Mr Allworthy, to be innocent of crimes of which he has been accused, in particular in relation to the near-fatal wounding of a man in a duel, and thus to be a worthy husband for the novel's heroine, who is passionately in love with him. As Allworthy's heir and Sophia's husband, he has at the moment of his marriage *almost* arrived at the qualifications for being a patriarchal figure as father, landlord and master – but that state is in the future.

A series of incidents in Edgeworth's and Fielding's novels appear so closely related as to suggest a deliberate parallel. At twenty, Tom Jones procures for a gamekeeper, Black George Seagrim (dismissed through Tom's fault by his patron, Mr Allworthy), a position in the gift of a neighbouring squire (who has a handsome daughter, absent being educated under the care of an aunt, with whom the hero later falls in love). His patron's legitimate and hypocritical nephew, Blifil, 'was greatly enraged at it. He had long hated *Black George* in the same proportion as *Jones* delighted in him; not from any Offence which he had ever received, but from his great love to Religion and Virtue; For *Black George* had the Reputation of a loose Kind of a Fellow' (*Tom Jones*, p. 112). Jones, soon after helping him, succeeds in sleeping with Black George's daughter Molly, an episode which is treated in entirely comic terms. The girl gets pregnant but is shown to have had sexual relations with other men, Tom's tutor Square, and a poacher named Will Barnes (pp. 151–3), besides Tom, so that he is absolved of all responsibility. Claims to love virtue and religion are ironically viewed, and women's innocence is shown to be questionable, but when Tom is discovered having sex again with Molly by his enemy Blifil, he is cast out of Allworthy's house. After various vicissitudes and escapades (including an affair with the predatory Lady Bellaston and the duel in which his adversary is badly wounded and almost dies, like Edgeworth's Moriarty Carroll), he is discovered to be the nephew of Mr Allworthy and marries the beautiful and virginal Sophia Western.

Ormond both follows and deviates from this narrative line. At 'not yet twenty', Harry Ormond (who has been expelled from the house of his patron, Sir Ulick O'Shane, because of the enmity of Sir Ulick's wife) promotes the welfare of Moriarty Carroll, whom he has wronged, acquires him a gamekeeper's job from King Corny O'Shane, cousin of Sir Ulick, while Sir Ulick's equally guilty son, Marcus, indulges vengeful feelings. (King Corny has a beautiful daughter, who is absent being educated under the care of an aunt, and with whom the hero later falls in love.) Ormond now is struck by the beauty of Peggy Sheridan, Moriarty's beloved, and almost sets out to seduce her. The strength of his friendship for Moriarty, however, enables him to overcome his selfish passion and he arranges a marriage between Moriarty and Peggy. When Moriarty is wrongly convicted of a crime, imprisoned and condemned to transportation, faithful Peggy prepares to follow him, but justice is finally vindicated after adventurous vicissitudes and the pair are last seen reunited in a rapturous embrace. Virtue triumphs. Ormond grows out of his passion for Dora O'Shane, King Corny's daughter, is confirmed in his conviction that he should not be her lover when he meets her again as the wife of an officer in the Irish Brigade in Paris, and, after inheriting from his father the large estate of the father's second wife, marries Florence Annaly. Ormond's parentage and his legitimacy are established from the first, the guilty episode of his shooting Moriarty happens right at the beginning of the story, and the dangers he runs at its climax are moral (the possible revival of his passion for Dora) and financial (Sir Ulick O'Shane had planned to 'borrow' his money to shore up the fortunes of his failing bank).

Edgeworth evidently wishes to show a central figure whose development towards maturity is a gradual progress. In this she is avoiding the too-great perfection which many readers had found in *Grandison*, whose hero is never seen as a helpless infant but, when he enters the story to rescue the heroine from a kidnapper who intends to force her into marriage, is already in possession of a splendid estate. But she also avoids repeating the casual postponement of Tom Jones's reformation. After Ormond's first act of drunken folly, he cannot forgive himself until Moriarty recovers, and thereafter he is never shown to be in need of a too-easy forgiveness merely because he is an attractive young man. By contrast, Tom Jones is forgiven, in Edgeworth's words, because he is 'a very fine fellow' – one whose masculinity is proved by sexual promiscuity.

Sex between man and woman, in all these novels, has a social significance principally as it affects relationships between men. Edgeworth twice shows Ormond restraining himself when faced with a sexual temptation because of loyalty to another man, combined with, but having priority over, concern for the woman. Thus, his discovery that Moriarty wishes to marry Peggy ends his pursuit of her (*Ormond*, pp. 76–7). Later, in an emotional scene with Dora, he sees a ring she wears containing some of her father's hair, and the thought of King Corny recalls him, and enables him to recall her, 'to [their] senses' and the 'honourable line of conduct he had traced out for himself' (p. 313). The unworthy Marcus O'Shane is in part responsible for his father's ruin because he is sued for damages by a man whose wife he has seduced, the infamous action for 'Criminal Conversation' which was abolished in England in the mid-nineteenth century but remained possible in Ireland until 1981(p. 225). In *Grandison*, the decorous entanglement with a beautiful and virtuous Italian lady, which at times seems bound to prevent Sir Charles Grandison's union with his beloved Harriet Byron, is largely told in terms of correspondence and conversation with her three brothers.

Fielding avoids bringing Tom Jones's sexual adventures into close proximity with any socially serious impact on his position vis-à-vis other men. He succumbs to the charms – he is seen as passive victim – of Molly Seagrim and Lady Bellaston, and the women's fate is seen as no concern of his; perhaps more to the point, they have no male relatives who have any moral right to complain; no valuable social relationship is transgressed. The women are blamed: '[Molly] soon triumphed over all the virtuous Resolutions of Jones: For though she behaved at last with all decent Reluctance, yet I rather chuse to attribute the Triumph to her; since, in Fact, it was her Design which succeeded' (*Tom Jones*, pp. 114–15). Lady Bellaston gives Tom Jones money when he is destitute in return for sexual favours; the author communicates this disgraceful fact, ironically: 'to do Justice to the Liberality of the Lady . . . who, though she did not give much into the Hackney Charities of the Age, such as building Hospitals, &c. was not, however, entirely void of that Christian Virtue; and conceived (very rightly I think) that a young Fellow of Merit, without a Shilling in the World, was no improper Object of this Virtue' (p. 464). Fielding apologizes for showing an upper-class woman in such an evil light as the first mover in a love affair: 'Lady Bellaston was of this intrepid Character; but let not my Country Readers conclude from her, that this is the general Conduct of Women of Fashion, or that we mean to represent them as such' (p. 480). Her 'violent Fondness' (p. 468) and the 'ignominious Circumstance' (p. 473) of taking her money degrade Jones. When he has a chance to speak in his own defence at the end of the novel, he can only declare to Sophia that '[t]he Delicacy of your Sex cannot conceive the Grossness of ours, nor how little one Sort of Amour has to do with the Heart'. She responds, 'I will never marry a Man who shall not learn Refinement enough to be as incapable as I am myself of making such a Distinction' (p. 635).

But when Sophia's marriage with Tom Jones is decided in the penultimate chapter (from which these quotations come), it is settled comically between two male elders, Western and Allworthy. The autonomy she has claimed is over-ruled in part by her own desire and in part by Squire Western's determination. The characters of the father-figures are so different from each other that any degree of understanding between them is impossible; Western is coarse, illiterate and intemperate, singing songs to celebrate his daughter's deflowering (p. 639) and insisting on an immediate marriage, offering 'five Pound to a Crown we have a Boy to-morrow nine months' (p. 637) whereas Allworthy is refined and judicious. Tom is indeed perhaps capable of learning greater refinement and thus becoming more like Sophia, more like Allworthy; what is already proved is that he has the sexual potency to achieve the patriarch Western's wish of begetting boys with Sophia, as indeed the author assures us he has succeeded in doing in the last sentences of the book. If in this novel Sophia is allowed to have the delicacy which will improve Jones's private character, her personality has nothing to do with the establishment of his public position which is done by the father-figures.

Tom Jones thus progresses from nameless foundling to country gentleman, emerging into a realm of public activity and responsibility. While sexual function may be taken as one test of masculinity, for a man to claim the public privileges of a gentleman in England, and more especially in Ireland, in the eighteenth century, he had to deploy another characteristically male characteristic, the ability to fight. The ritual of duelling, while illegal and condemned as contrary to Christian morality, retained great social prestige in both countries. When Jones is attacked in the street by Lieutenant Fitzpatrick, who is suspicious of Jones's motive for visiting Fitzpatrick's estranged wife – a typical 'matter of honour', though for once Jones is innocent – he defends himself and gives his opponent a dangerous wound (p. 567). He is arrested, but 'The Constable, seeing Mr. Jones very well drest, and hearing that the Accident had happened in a Duel, treated his Prisoner with great Civility' (p. 568). When it is said that the wound is likely to be fatal, Jones is committed to prison but is released when the patient recovers. Society takes no further interest in the brawl, and we gather that, on the whole, duelling is condoned.

By contrast, Sir Charles Grandison (who, though the author asserts that he is universally beloved and admired, meets with a surprising number of people who want to fight and kill him) repeatedly refuses to engage in duels. A superb swordsman, he skilfully disarms his opponents, on occasion more than one at a time, and/or overcomes them with his eloquence, courtesy and generosity (*Grandison*, vol. I, p. 253; vol. II, pp. 120–1; vol. III, pp. 69–72). Interestingly, Richardson's readers were not entirely happy with such an example. The argument in favour of permitting duels relates to the expectation that all upper-class males (unless they were in Holy Orders) should be potential soldiers; a sword was an integral part of formal dress (vol. I, p. 248). In an appendix to *Grandison*, Richardson argues that duelling is wrong even for a soldier, and quotes military regulations in support of his case (vol. III, pp. 464–6). Readers had pointed out that a man less skilled in fencing than Grandison would not be able to disarm an opponent in Sir Charles's style, but the author – as a printer, not, of course, a member of the upper classes but a mere tradesman – still anxiously insists that the custom is wrong.

The issue of military honour is relevant to all three novels. A soldier must prove himself not to be a coward, and willingness to resent an insult, to put one's own life in danger if necessary, may be a valuable quality if it equates with courage in war. *Tom Jones* and *Sir Charles Grandison* are both set at the time of the 1745 Jacobite rebellion, and there are important military figures in both. *Ormond*, too, has a strong military theme: the hero at first plans to go into the army as the only profession open to him because of his poverty and defective education, and is urged by Sir Ulick not to do so only on the grounds that 'peace is likely to continue' (*Ormond*, p. 182). Given a date in the early 1770s, when the complex foreign policy of Great Britain in relation to both India and the North American colonies meant that war was often threatened, we can be left without precise information as to where he has expected to fight. His childhood sweetheart, Dora, marries an officer in the Irish Brigade in France; his rival for Florence's affection is Colonel Albemarle; his relationship to Sir Ulick is based on the fact that he is 'the son of an officer who had served in the same regiment with him in his first campaign' (p. 10).

Edgeworth's admiration for *Grandison* does not lead her to show Ormond setting his face against the duel. She herself as a woman, and her moral authorities in the novel, the clergyman Dr Cambray and Lady Annaly, are outside the scope of the military standard and can see the folly of duelling, like Jane Austen's Elinor Dashwood (who 'sighed over the fancied necessity' of the duel between Colonel Brandon and Mr Willoughby; 'but to a man and a soldier, she presumed not to censure it' [*Sense and Sensibility*, p. 184]), but all accept its inevitability in the world they inhabit. Edgeworth had even in *Belinda* satirized the custom by introducing a duel between two women, where the only person who emerges with credit is an Irish girl, acting as second to one of the duellists, who manages to prevent bloodshed (*Belinda*, pp. 48–51). She presents Ormond as necessarily involved in a duel because of the foolish conventions of honour. In defence of the unworthy Sir Ulick O'Shane, he quarrels with an unnamed gentleman and like Lady Delacour in *Belinda* goes through all the rituals, inviting an acquaintance to be his second at the 'meeting' – no mere street brawl here.

Ormond felt that he had restrained his anger sufficiently – he was now as firm as he had been temperate. The parties met and fought: the man who deserved to have suffered, by the chance of this rational method of deciding right and wrong, escaped unhurt; Ormond received a wound in his arm . . . the inconvenience and pain were easily borne. In the opinion of all, in that part of the world, who knew the facts, he had conducted himself as well as the circumstances would permit; and as it was essential, not only to the character of a hero, but of a gentleman at that time in Ireland, to fight a duel, we may consider Ormond as fortunate in not being in the wrong. He rose in favour with the ladies and in credit with the gentlemen (*Ormond*, pp. 213–14).

Characteristically, Edgeworth situates the fashion for duelling safely in the past. However, as she and her Irish readers knew, the political duel in Ireland survived the turn of the century and the Act of Union. Such episodes as the meeting between Daniel O'Connell and John D'Esterre in 1815, when D'Esterre, the challenger, was shot dead, were surely fresh in their memories.[1] O'Connell's public penitence, wearing a glove on the hand that fired the fatal shot for the rest of his life, was at once a show of his disapproval of the duelling culture – he refused all challenges thereafter – an acceptance of its existence as a recognized way of settling disputes outside the law, and a warning, as with Ormond, that he was not a man to be trifled with. He had fought duels earlier in his career but the encounter with D'Esterre, a member of Dublin Corporation who had killed a number of previous opponents, was the first in which he had injured anybody; by contrast, Harry Ormond is for the second time in the novel fortunate in escaping the moral guilt of murder.

Our reading of *Ormond* has brought us to a point at which we can see the author registering the human condition as developed in a particular place and time. The very situating of Ormond's experience in the past, almost two generations distant from the Ireland of 1817, and before such crucial events as the 1798 Rebellion, the Act of Union and, indeed, the American and French Revolutions, emphasizes the changes in structures and cultures that have taken place in the interval, while the highlighting of issues that remained current at the time of writing, such as sectarian and political prejudice, or duelling, raise the question of how little the social problems of a nation are susceptible to change in anything but the longest term.

Edgeworth's relationships with her predecessors in the tradition of the English novel show her altering the lines of the standard plot to signal the difference made to masculine identity by time and place. Thus the misdeed which precipitates her hero's casting out from elite society is not sexual in its motivation but political, in a country where divisions of race and creed lie at the root of so much social evil. The older woman who intrigues against Ormond and those he befriends later in the story, Mrs McCrule, is not a sexual predator like Lady Bellaston but a Protestant fanatic. The author may be rewriting a story about the excesses of masculine sexuality in a style more acceptable to women readers, or alternatively she may be seen as entering into the conventionally male domain of politics.

By 1817 Maria Edgeworth was a celebrated writer who had received much critical praise. We may read *Ormond*, if we wish, as her declaration of her confidence in her own ability to write extensively about masculine as well as feminine concerns. In doing so, she is answering a question, 'how does a woman writer know how men think?', in part by pointing to the tradition of the novel, where male and female readers had over a century encountered male and female writers of fictions in which male and female protagonists had figured, often, indeed, crossing gender boundaries to critical acclaim. By showing Harry Ormond as critical reader, passing judgement on the classics of the tradition, she had told her own readers how a novel might be read. By underlining both Harry Ormond's taste as an Irish reader and his ability to be enthused by a work which is at first antipathetic to that taste, she calls our attention to the reading of fiction as something which takes us beyond the merely natural. By incorporating allusions to her father's life and episodes of his own fictional narration, she reminds us of the way family relationships give insight into concerns which may seem to belong on the other side of a gender barrier. But she also reminds us that our perceptions may be wrong. When Sir Ulick thinks that Florence Annaly must be in love with Ormond because she faints when she sees him covered with Moriarty Carroll's blood, he is mistaken; her affection for him arises only much later and after his transformation is complete. Edgeworth comments that 'Sir Ulick's acquaintance with unprincipled women misled him completely in this instance' (p. 26); is she thinking of Fielding's Sophia who, on discovering that Tom Jones has broken his arm, grows pale and is 'seized with a Trembling' (*Tom Jones*, p. 131), which the author immediately diagnoses as symptomatic of love? *Ormond* situates itself in a dialogue between the men and women novelists about the subject matter and the purpose of novel writing and novel reading. Published in the year of Jane Austen's death, and of the publication of *Northanger Abbey* with its memorable tribute to Edgeworth's *Belinda*, Edgeworth's mature novel serendipitously illustrates Austen's posthumous manifesto.

*   *   *   *   *

Maria Edgeworth: biographical and critical contexts

Maria Edgeworth was born in Oxfordshire in 1767 to Richard Lovell Edgeworth, Anglo-Irish landowner, and his first wife (of four marriages, producing in all twenty-two children), Anna Maria Elers. The family moved back to Ireland when Maria was fifteen and Edgeworthstown, Co. Longford, remained her home until her death in 1849, though she travelled to London and Paris in the early 1800s, and acquired European celebrity. Her father was a popular landlord, a believer in advanced education and in improving the condition of the tenantry, and a Member of the Irish Parliament which was abolished in 1800. She ran the estate with him, and later for her brother who had inherited Edgeworthstown, and many of her works depict the relationship between landlords and Irish tenants. Her first work was *Letters for Literary Ladies* (1795), which examined women's and girls' education, and she continued to write on education and for children all her life. *Castle Rackrent: An Hibernian Tale* (1800) has been her most popular work, for its comic energy and the character of its unreliable narrator, but *Belinda* (1801) was much admired by contemporaries for its picture of fashionable women's lives, while her later Irish novels, *The Absentee* (1812), *Ennui* (1809) and *Ormond* (1817), seriously consider the responsibilities of the Irish landlord class.

She and her father published a spirited analysis of Irish humour, *An Essay on Irish Bulls* (1802). She is credited with establishing the 'national' novel; international political themes include slavery and anti-Semitism (of which she had herself been guilty). Until recently, critics praised her comic talent and deplored her moralizing, for which her father's influence was blamed. Although Marilyn Butler's biography had argued convincingly that Richard Lovell Edgeworth probably had a liberating rather than a restrictive influence on his daughter, the relationship was seen as oppressive by feminist critics in the 1990s. More recently, psychological probing has focused on a possible lesbian subplot in *Belinda*. Meanwhile, another strain of criticism considered her principally as an Irish writer and related her to the tradition of the 'Big House' novel and her links with the radicalism of the 1790s have been stressed.

Works cited

Austen, Jane, *Sense and Sensibility* [1811], ed. Claire Lamont (London, Oxford University Press, 1970).

Bilger, Audrey, *Laughing Feminism: Subversive Comedy in Frances Burney, Maria Edgeworth, and Jane Austen* (Detroit: Wayne State University Press, 1998).

Butler, Harriet Jessie and Harold Edgeworth Butler (eds.), *The Black Book of Edgeworthstown and Other Edgeworth Memories, 1585–1817* (London: Faber & Gwyer, 1927).

Butler, Marilyn, *Maria Edgeworth: A Literary Biography* (Oxford: Clarendon Press, 1972).

Edgeworth, Maria, *Belinda* [1801], ed. Eiléan Ní Chuilleanáin (London: J.M. Dent, 1993).

——, *Ormond* [1817] (Dublin: Gill & Macmillan, 1990).

Edgeworth, Richard Lovell, *Memoirs of Richard Lovell Edgeworth; Begun by Himself and Concluded by His Daughter Maria Edgeworth* [1820] (Shannon: Irish University Press, 1969).

Fielding, Henry, *Tom Jones* [1749] ed. Sheridan Baker (New York/London: W.W. Norton & Co., 1995).

Kelly, James, *'That Damn'd Thing Called Honour': Duelling in Ireland, 1570–1860* (Cork University Press, 1995).

Kowaleski-Wallace, Elizabeth, 'Home Economics: Domestic Ideology in Maria Edgeworth's *Belinda*', *Eighteenth Century: Theory and Interpretation* 29: 3 (1988), pp. 242–62.

——, *'Their Fathers' Daughters': Hannah More, Maria Edgeworth, and Patriarchal Complicity* (Oxford/New York: Oxford University Press, 1991).

Kreilkamp, Vera, *The Anglo-Irish Novel and the Big House* (New York: Syracuse University Press, 1998).

Lefanu, W.R., *Seventy Years of Irish Life* (21 Oct. 2003) *http://indigo.ie/~kfinlay/ lefanu70/lefanuX.htm.*

Maurer, Sara L., 'Disowning to Own: Maria Edgeworth and the Illegitimacy of National Ownership', *Criticism: A Quarterly for Literature and the Arts* 44:4 (Fall 2002), pp. 363–88.

McCann, Andrew, 'Conjugal Love and the Enlightenment Subject: The Colonial Context of Non-identity in Maria Edgeworth's *Belinda*', *Novel: A Forum on Fiction* 30:1 (Fall 1996), pp. 56–77.

McCormack, W.J., 'Setting and Ideology: With Reference to the Fiction of Maria Edgeworth', Otto Rauchbauer (ed.), *Ancestral Voices: The Big House in Anglo-Irish Literature* (Hildesheim: Georg Olms, 1992).

Myers, Mitzi. 'My Art Belongs to Daddy? Thomas Day, Maria Edgeworth, and the Pre-Texts of *Belinda*: Women Writers and Patriarchal Authority', in Paula Backscheider (ed.), *Revising Women: Eighteenth-Century 'Women's Fiction' and Social Engagement* (Baltimore/London: Johns Hopkins University Press, 2000), pp. 104–46.

Richardson, Samuel, *Sir Charles Grandison* [1753–4], ed. Jocelyn Harris, 3 vols. (New York/Oxford: Oxford University Press, 1986).

Tracy, Robert, 'Maria Edgeworth and Lady Morgan: Legality versus Legitimacy', *Nineteenth-Century Fiction* 40:1 (1985), pp. 1–22.

Chapter 3

Stuck on the Canvas

Harriet Martin's *Canvassing* and Locational Feminism

Heidi Hansson

Where you speak from makes a difference. I come from the north of Sweden, a country that has prided itself on its equal opportunity policies for several decades, and when I first started to work with feminist theory, it was with the feeling that it somehow did not quite concern me personally. I was wrong, of course. Even though Sweden has a number of laws to guarantee against the discrimination of women, attitudes have not changed at the same pace. Women still have lower salaries, we still have to be afraid of men physically, we are still subjected to sexual slurs and our words still count for less in public. But the laws and the debates about women's situation have certainly made it easier to expose prejudice, and even though many people continue to support a traditional distribution of gender roles and believe that an opinion pronounced by a man carries more weight, they find it increasingly difficult to say so openly. It is politically correct to be at least superficially a feminist.

When I speak about feminist issues in the academy, I consequently speak from a location where these ideas are generally accepted, even if it is only on the surface. I do not fight on the barricades for a new order, and the reactions I meet with are not outright attacks but more often queries about the value of dealing with feminist matters today when so much has been achieved. Feminism is considered old hat. I cannot accept this as valid – in fact, I believe that designating feminism as out of date is a backlash phenomenon that needs to be contested in every way – but I can accept that the male–female dichotomy that governed the early stages of feminist thought does not quite work as an analytical tool in my society. Perhaps it never did. This has made me view *location* and *negotiation* as key concepts in feminist research, and I suggest that they are especially important when dealing with material from cultures where feminism has had to share space with other struggles for freedom and recognition. Nineteenth-century Ireland is obviously such a place.

When I speak about Irish matters, however, I speak as an outsider. No matter how often I visit Ireland, Irish culture and customs can never really become lived experience for me. The advantage of this is that it makes it easier for me to extricate myself from other political considerations and focus on feminist concerns, and an added bonus is that I automatically pay more attention to the importance of physical and mental place. The obvious disadvantage is that, at some level, Ireland will remain a foreign country. This creates the distance necessary in research, but also the risk of misunderstanding. To minimize this risk I have long worked together with an insider, Dr Anne McCartney at the University of Ulster. Beside the obvious value of working together with someone who belongs to the culture I am studying, this has meant a constant negotiation of cultural preconceptions for both of us. Even when I am the sole author of a piece, another voice is therefore always present in my writing.

Nevertheless, I believe that a valuable side effect of speaking as an outsider where feminist research is concerned is that it helps to keep alive the insight that women do not constitute a homogeneous group. Irish women, now and in the past, are located in a different place from me, which means that their experiences of oppression are also different – from mine, and from each other's. Feminism is a real political alternative only if it does not become another universalizing grand narrative, and attention to location in feminist literary research can help to foreground the many differences between women without denying the similarities. Such an approach is necessarily grounded in the historical reality of the time, place and social context in which the work was produced and recognizes how material circumstances influence aesthetic choices.

A problem for feminist activity in the twenty-first century and a main reason why feminism has begun to be seen as old-fashioned, is that feminist and poststructuralist theories have dissolved a simplistic connection between body and gender. As a result, it has become increasingly difficult to undertake research based on a pre-existing category of 'women', and the idea of 'the death of the author' further complicates any inquiry which sees the sex of the writer as part of the text's meaning. Studies like Judith Butler's *Gender Trouble* (1990) and Elizabeth Grosz's *Volatile Bodies* (1994), among others, have problematized the binary division between woman and man as well as the division between biological sex and social gender, by showing that the body, too, is fluid, a surface inscribed by a particular time and ideology, gendered male or female not through original anatomical features but through a '*stylized repetition of acts*' (*Gender Trouble*, p. 140, author's italics). The subject is neither completely bound by nor completely free from gender regulations, and the relations between the individual and the regulatory codes will vary. Selecting women writers for study becomes awkward against this background, and when the oneness of the body itself is questioned, even such apparently open definitions as the following become suspect: 'what is being (re)claimed is not a homogeneous category of women, but rather a multiplicity of fluid positions linked by the in-common experience of a specific body form' (Margrit Shildrick, *Leaky Bodies and Boundaries*, p. 9). Nevertheless, Butler's performative view of gender does not deny the existence of sexed bodies or gendered identities, only the myth of their original status and of 'true' femininity or masculinity. These myths were under pressure also during the nineteenth century, and when women writers depict the connection between body form and gender characteristics as inherently unstable, they both respond and contribute to the gender anxieties of their time.

But even though it is crucial to recognize that categories overlap, it is also prudent to ask when and in what context it is important to emphasize that women and men do not really exist and explore questions of the body as a social construction. While the body is clearly insufficient when it comes to answering the question 'what is woman?', it still supplies part of the answer to the question '*where* are women?'. No matter how clearly they oppose gender stereotyping and move between different identities, both women writers and the women characters they create are still located in female bodies, and bodies, as Elizabeth Grosz points out 'are never simply *human* bodies or *social* bodies', they are sexed bodies (p. 84). The sex of the body makes a great deal of difference to the kind of social roles an individual can play, and early-nineteenth-century Ireland has to be described as an officially heterosexual, two-sex society, where women were seen as confined to their bodies in ways that men were not. It is therefore necessary to acknowledge that in their culture, nineteenth-century Irish women writers were identified as women. Seeing gender as performance certainly returns some agency to the subject, but at some point – usually at a person's birth – the body is assigned a sex, however unsuitable this might later turn out to be. This sex does not automatically produce a gendered behaviour, but it frequently causes expectations that can be resisted, accepted, rejected, performed, parodied or negotiated.

It is beginning to be a commonplace that gender cannot be analysed on its own. It is not enough to show how women are located in a patriarchal world: women's subjugation cannot be taken as an ahistorical given, since power structures shift and women use patriarchal constructions of gender to gain influence in specific areas. Stressing location therefore guards against a reading where all women writers are somehow the same, subjected to the same kind of oppression and resisting in the same ways. Any analysis of women's writing needs to take account of the fact that women's experiences of patriarchy are as vastly different as their strategies of resistance. Education, caste, age, financial situation and sexual orientation also come into play, and the intersection of gender with class and ethnicity in forming women's identities becomes particularly obvious in the context of nineteenth-century Irish life. All these facets of selfhood can be expressed in spatial terms, as describing women's 'place' in various environments, but as only one of several aspects of locational identity, this place is fundamentally unstable. Both the walls of confinement and the breaches in these walls are uncovered when we explore women's attempts to negotiate their situation.

'Locational feminism' is a means to move away from essential definitions of gender while still acknowledging the specificity of women's bodies. As Susan Stanford Friedman makes clear, 'identities shift with a changing context, dependent always upon the point of reference. Not essences or absolutes, identities are fluid sites that can be understood differently depending on the vantage point of their formation and function' (*Mappings*, p. 47). This means that no aspect of identity is ever central and always uppermost in the hierarchy, but that circumstances – or 'place' – determine how the self can be constructed. While an essentialist view of identity and gender inevitably leads to polarization, a locational view includes the possibility of fluctuation. A concomitant of locational feminism, therefore, is that the subject is to some extent mobile, if not always in physical terms so at least in intellectual terms. The act of writing, for instance, is one expression of this mobility among nineteenth-century women writers who were physically restricted but could express their views in novels, poetry, letters and journals. Mobility is a concept that covers a range of choices from complete adjustment to current norms to total freedom. Place and space, in both real and metaphorical terms, thus become key areas of examination.

A focus on location also inevitably leads to such questions as what position Irish women speak from and where their cultural activities take place. The most basic answer to both these questions is, of course, Ireland, but nineteenth-century Ireland was not an isolated entity, it was a country under global influence, not least because of the transnational experiences of emigrants and workers who spent part of the year in England, Scotland or other parts of Europe. Intellectual and popular discourses were circulated and exchanged between Ireland and England, the continent and the growing Irish communities in North America and Australia. London journals were read alongside Dublin papers, and although Irish publishing revived in the 1820s, after the temporary lull caused by the introduction of English copyright laws following the Union, Irish writers often published in London or Edinburgh. Hence, Irish women writers were part of a British and sometimes international literary establishment as well as an Irish one, and they could frequently expect their audience to be unfamiliar with at least some aspects of Irish life. As a consequence, their works regularly negotiate the expectations of different types of audiences, not only in national, but also in gender terms because while their readers may have been mostly female, their critics were still mainly male.

Irish nineteenth-century women's writing, then, is generally politically ambiguous. This makes women writers unsuitable as nationalist icons but it also undermines any attempt to reclaim them as feminists or proto-feminists, because they cannot be said to speak for some unified community of women.

Feminist issues are certainly addressed, but a final answer is seldom provided – especially not an answer that relates to women as a group. In many ways this corresponds to the rather recent feminist insight that 'none of us can speak for "woman" because no such person exists except within a specific set of (already gendered) relations – to "man" and to many concrete and different women' (Flax, 'Postmodernism and Gender Relations in Feminist Theory', p. 56). Fiction offers the possibility of returning the reductions of group and national politics to the complexities of individual life, and nineteenth-century Irish women writers frequently portray women as individuals, not as representatives of their sex. To pay attention to what they actually say in their texts means to 'attend to the perplexity of women's fractured, divided, multiplied, and contradictory modes of identification' (Gubar, *Critical Condition*, p. 8). What Harriet Martin says in the novel *Canvassing*, among other things, is that social and geographical place makes a difference as to how gender is construed.

Harriet Letitia Martin (1801–91) was the second daughter of 'Humanity' Dick (Richard) Martin of Ballinahinch, Connemara, MP and founder of the Royal Society for the Prevention of Cruelty to Animals (RSPCA). She was named after her mother, who was also a writer, author of such publications as *Historic Tales,* the four-volume novel *Helen of Glenross* (1802) and a booklet of theatre criticism. Her niece Mary Letitia Martin became a writer as well, her main work the novel *Julia Howard* (1850), which, like Harriet Martin's stories, shows intimate knowledge of life in Connemara in the nineteenth century. A distant relative was Violet Martin, who collaborated with Edith Somerville as 'Martin Ross', and, through her father's cousins, the Galway Kirwans, Harriet Martin was also remotely connected to the late-nineteenth-century writer Emily Lawless. The family obviously had cultural interests, apart from the political struggle for Catholic emancipation and animal rights that occupied Dick Martin, and Harriet Martin received a good education at Mrs Clarke's Free College in Bromley, Kent. Letters from her mother while she was at school indicate that she was expected to understand both the social world and human eccentricity from an early age (*Humanity Dick Martin*, Lynam, p. 167), and her writing reveals that she developed an ironic attitude to social climbing and people's foibles reminiscent of that of Jane Austen. Her parents led an active social life in London during the Parliament season, with the express purpose of smoothing the marital way for their daughters, but none of the three daughters of Richard Martin's second marriage ever married. Some of the reasons for this are possibly outlined in Harriet Martin's first novel, *Canvassing* (1832?), where campaigning for votes or for a husband are shown to contain the same mixture of manipulation, flattery and threats, but no dedication or love.

Canvassing was published as one of the 'Tales of the O'Hara Family', together with the novel *The Mayor of Wind-Gap*, written by Michael Banim, and Harriet Martin's second novel, *The Changeling* (1848), is often attributed to the Banims. According to D.W. Gilligan, Martin was invited to contribute to the second collection of 'The O'Hara Tales' after Gerald Griffin had declined, on the grounds that he was unequal to the task (*The Banim Brothers*, p. 245), and apparently she met Michel Banim in Paris some time during the period 1827–34, when the Martins resided in Boulogne (Wolff, vol. lii, n. 32). Another resident of the English-Irish colony in Boulogne was Lady Morgan, whose father had been involved in Dick Martin's theatre projects at the end of the eighteenth century, and perhaps Morgan's success as a writer was an inspiration (Lynam, *Humanity Dick Martin*, pp. 272–4). The fact that the novel was initially published under a pseudonym may explain why Harriet Martin dared both to deal with the very unwomanly theme of a political campaign and to be so outspoken about the unfair distribution of opportunities for men and women, though plain speaking and strong opinions were certainly also characteristics of her father that she might have inherited. It may also be significant that Martin was not financially dependent on her writing and therefore could risk criticizing the establishment. From 1857 when Patrick Joseph Murray's biography of John Banim was published, Harriet Martin was officially known to be the author of *Canvassing* (Wolff, vol. xlix, n. 1), however, which makes it difficult to avoid the suspicion that this amazing novel was lost because it was produced by a woman.

Although there has been some critical interest in the Banim brothers, Harriet Martin is rarely mentioned in studies of Irish literature, and she is not even included in the recent *Field Day Anthology of Irish Writing Volumes IV & V: Irish Women's Writing and Traditions* (2002), which must be considered an oversight. Today, *The Mayor of Wind-Gap* comes across as a laborious and clearly dated story, written in 'overstrained and theatrical prose' (Gilligan, *The Banim Brothers*, p. 540), while *Canvassing* is witty and lively and reveals a sure ear for dialogue. The novel was still in print when Stephen J. Brown's bibliography, *Ireland in Fiction*, was published in 1916, so it was apparently popular throughout the nineteenth century. Brown characterizes it as an 'elaborate tale of matchmaking and marriage among the upper classes, written with a moral purpose' and an incidental 'good picture of an election contest in the first quarter of the nineteenth century' (p. 203), but the picture of the political campaign is by no means incidental to the marriage plot – on the contrary, the juxtaposition of Irish election practice and the marriage market emphasizes the similarities of two equally corrupt systems. Robert Lee Wolff rightly calls the novel 'unjustly neglected' in his introduction to the Garland reprint in 1979 (vol. xliii), though he finds the final section somewhat awkward, perhaps because Harriet Martin, in contrast to most nineteenth-century novelists, does not end with a blissful marriage scene but includes a description of the disastrous outcome of the marriages.

Though most of the novel is set in an unspecified Irish region that has a lot in common with Connemara, it opens in London with an exposure of the unethical political and marital aspirations of one of the main male characters, Lord Warringdon. At breakfast with his father, Warringdon receives a letter from the Irish Mr Wilmot, who is willing to let him have the votes at his disposal and so secure a seat in parliament – as a landlord, Wilmot could expect to control the voters living on his estate. Very cynically, Warringdon's father reminds his son that he 'must admire the daughters' charms' or he 'will lose the father's votes' (*Canvassing*, vol. 2, p. 235) and it is also made clear that it is only an interest in money and power, not a passion for politics, that makes Warringdon wish to become a Member of Parliament. It is later revealed that he in fact thoroughly dislikes politics (vol. 3, p. 119). He is the heir to a sizeable fortune, but finds his allowance too small for the necessary 'presents to opera people, and *douceurs* to ladies' maids' and the only other way he might hope to repair his strained finances is by marrying an heiress, though he is 'in no hurry to run [his] neck into the noose' (vol. 2, p. 226). In Warringdon's world, marriage is primarily a financial arrangement, and love is a pastime that does not include any sort of commitment. Apart from Wilmot's letter, he also receives two letters from 'the prettiest woman in London' (vol. 2, p. 228) and 'the next prettiest woman in London' (vol. 2, p. 229), and states that 'I hate clever women, you know, and make it a rule never to fall in love with any beauties but married ones' (vol. 2, p. 235). In her introduction of Warringdon, Harriet Martin draws attention to his contempt for intelligent women and shows him as completely insincere, when it comes to both love and politics. Further, she shows that he is supported in this attitude by his father, who also views politics only as a potential source of income and does not think 'that a love affair with a married woman was an event requiring his paternal interference' (vol. 2, p. 233), thus locating these attitudes in an English, upper-class environment. They are then matched by the equally cynical views of Lady Anne, Mr Wilmot's English-born wife.

According to Robert Lee Wolff, the careless and extravagant Mr Wilmot is a portrait of Harriet Martin's father (vol. xliv), and he is one of the most sympathetic characters in the novel. Lady Anne, on the other hand, is portrayed in a much less positive light, and like Warringdon, she sees marriage as a purely financial affair:

> Lady Anne, unable to stop her husband's wild profusion, at last contented herself with turning it to some purpose, and as he would have his house filled with company, she took care there should be a fair proportion of marrying men, at a certain ratio of fortune. By this means, she had already got three daughters off her hands; and she blessed her stars, and so did all who knew her, that she had but two remaining; for Lady Anne's reputation as a match-maker had rendered her the terror of mothers who had sons, and the envy of those who had daughters. (*Canvassing*, vol. 2, pp. 238–9)

To make her daughters Maria and Isabel more eligible for marriage, she ensures that they study languages and music and tries to impress on them the importance of not expecting love or consideration from their future husbands. Marriage in *Canvassing* is paradoxically seen both as a necessity, to ensure women's autonomy, and as a prison, because although a married woman is subjected to her husband in many ways, an unmarried woman has no power or opportunities at all. In the Wilmots' social circle, women's value is measured by how popular they are with men, which also renders any female solidarity impossible: 'it is allowed to a woman, by women, to be either pretty or clever; but, to be both together is unpardonable; and they, therefore, liked Maria better than Isabel, because the men did not' (vol. 2, p. 248–9). The novel includes a direct indictment of the view that women's looks determine their worth, when the 'clever' character, Maria Wilmot, unsentimentally ascribes her lack of success on the marriage market to a combination of intelligence and plainness: 'I was not fastidious, you will acknowledge; yet, was I successful? I had sense, and I had not beauty – so alas! no one came a wooing to me' (vol. 3, pp. 13–14).

It is a telling comment on how women are viewed as cattle when Mr. Barham, the utterly foolish but rich English minor whom Maria decides she will trap into marriage, reflects that Warringdon's judgement of female beauty must be correct, 'for I know he is reckoned a better judge of a horse than any man in Melton' (vol. 3, p. 140). Men may be both ugly and disagreeable, but nothing can make up for a woman's lack of beauty since looks are a precondition for marriage and 'a woman who is not married is nobody' (vol. 3, p. 12). The mechanisms of the marriage market are ubiquitous plot elements in eighteenth- and nineteenth-century fiction by women (Lyn Pykett, 'Women Writing Women', p. 91), but Martin makes clearer than most writers that the rules of the market are not universal, but products of a specific social location.

Lady Anne is the product of the same English, aristocratic environment as Lord Warringdon, and to a great extent, Harriet Martin brands their attitudes to marriage as particularly English. England is depicted as a stiff, rule-bound country where such expressions of freedom as laughter are out of bounds. Another reason for Maria Wilmot's failure to find a husband is therefore that she is 'sadly Irish,' because she had 'more than once, not only laughed at herself, but had caused others to perpetrate a similar enormity' (*Canvassing*, vol. 2, p. 241). Maria and her father are the characters most integrated with Irish culture, and part of Maria's frustration at having to live up to the English ideal of femininity is that this also requires her to deny her Irish side. There are intimations in the novel that a longer exposure to the Irish way of life could have made a difference in the outlook of at least Lord Warringdon, who begins to relax a little after a while, finding that 'unfortunately, there is something in the very air of Ireland which acts on the most pertinaciously rigid muscles, and makes those laugh who never laughed before, and never may again' (vol. 2, p. 316).

Like so many Irish writers, Harriet Martin accentuates Ireland's difference from England, primarily stressing its greater freedom. She also constructs

England as a particular kind of 'gendered place' (Linda McDowell, *Gender, Identity and Place*, pp. 144–5), that is, a place which requires specific, gendered conduct of the subject. This is a significant departure from the usual focus on Ireland as the gendered place, an ideological construction in which Ireland is seen as essentially feminine either to justify English domination or to underscore the country's victim status. Martin, in contrast, emphasizes that gender codes are not inherent but reside in particular places and environments. As she presents it, a gendered place is not a location that exhibits feminine or masculine characteristics in itself but a place that demands conventional, gendered behavior. Thus, even though Warringdon represents an Irish constituency, he remains English, and he expects his future wife to adhere to an English, upper-class construction of femininity that privileges beauty before intellect and a shallow display of style and good manners before true feelings.

Canvassing consequently depicts the gender conflict more in spatial than in polarized terms, and Harriet Martin does not view all women as oppressed in the same way. Rather, she shows that women who are located in a specific national and social context become merchandise because in *this location* they are denied other opportunities in life. This means that they have no power over their future, as at least Maria realizes:

> You know she made poor Louisa marry a man old enough to be her grand-father; and that all Louisa's protestations of disgust were nothing in the balance against fifty thousand per annum, and a peerage . . . . We may break our heart (such of us as have one) afterwards, if we like, – that will not be [mamma's] fault, but ours; she does her duty, she gets us good matches, and leaves all the rest, like a good Christian, to Providence. (vol. 3, pp. 3–4)

'*Good matches*' are the keywords. It is their – and their mother's – ambitions for an English, polite lifestyle that force Maria and Isabel to live up to a set of gender rules required by their class, and they are willing accomplices in their own subjugation. Instead of challenging the patriarchal system outright, Martin shows how women negotiate their situation by outwardly accepting the definitions that bind them in order to achieve the power and influence the married state involves. None of the characters in the novel really hopes that marriage will lead to true happiness, and even Isabel, who still retains some belief in romance compares marriage to an execution (vol. 2, p. 254).

To achieve their goal, the Wilmot girls have to hide their abilities and harness their feelings, and the main moral of the novel is that when women are forced to go against their nature and marry because they have no other options in life, everyone suffers.

Women are consequently depicted as powerless only in that they depend on marriage to secure a platform for themselves. The Wilmot women are household managers with complete power and control over domestic matters, and Maria especially, closer to the servants than her mother and sister are, shows a clear head in a crisis and excellent organizational skills when she manages to get everything in order for Warringdon's visit, despite the empty pantry and cellar and the sorry state of the guest room (vol. 2, pp. 269–80). When dealing with nineteenth-century works, it is important to remember that household management among the upper classes could involve supervising a large staff and running an establishment that today would certainly be described in business terms. Though women were barred from most public arenas, the house was not necessarily a 'gendered place' where women were required to be passive. In most other areas, the managerial skills needed would have been designated as male, and women in charge of large houses are the precursors of today's businesswomen.

But Martin also shows that women are intellectually accomplished and that their exclusion from public fields has nothing to do with their abilities. Thus, Isabel helps Warringdon to compose a political address, but 'with so much tact, that she appeared rather to have skillfully embodied his ideas, than to have suggested any of her own; so that he himself seemed even to deserve the whole credit of the performance' (vol. 3, p. 32). The really astute politicians in Canvassing are women, but to succeed on the marriage market a woman needs to hide her intellect and compromise her integrity. Maria comments on how unlikely it is that a man would marry a woman with intellect: 'He may forgive it in a pretty woman, – he certainly will in a rich one, – but she who is neither wealthy nor handsome, and yet possesses it, how does she fare?' (vol. 3, pp. 7–8).

Both Isabel and Maria perform femininity in the way their society and class expect, and that Martin really views women's adherence to a conventional construction of femininity as a matter of performance is borne out by her comment on women's behaviour when horse-riding – where it is imperative for a woman to pretend alarm even when she does not feel it, being 'aware of how interesting a woman appears to a man when claiming, evidently against her own will, or design, his protection' (vol. 2, pp. 329–30).

Martin poses a clear difference between biological sex and socially constructed gender when she shows how Maria, at least, is painfully aware that this kind of performance is alien to her nature. For her, there is no natural connection between her woman's body and weakness, and she fully realizes that it is the way gender is constructed in her society that prevents her from attaining her full potential. Sadly she laments that talent is 'infinitely in a woman's way' and wishes she had been born a man so that she could have 'made Europe ring with my name; now, all my energies can get me nothing but a husband, and that husband a fool' (vol. 3, p. 9).

There is a strong sense of anger and bitterness in Harriet Martin's descriptions of how women are forced to downplay their intelligence and pretend to be weak and dependent, yet she does not offer any alternatives for women of the upper class. Passivity and an outward lack of confidence are vital aspects of their society's construction of femininity, and to show assurance and knowledge means to fail miserably in the marriage game. Therefore, the visitor Eliza Fitzgerald is no threat to Maria's and Isabel's marriage plans because she has not learnt to suppress her abilities, making the supreme mistake of not only knowing Greek, but having the temerity to talk about it about it in front of a possible suitor (vol. 3, p. 76).

The similarities between Maria Wilmot and Harriet Martin herself are obvious, and it is reasonable to surmise that Martin gives vent to her own frustration in her descriptions of how the Wilmot girls are compelled to pretend to ignorance in order to be acceptable for marriage. In her home, Harriet Martin was expected to take part in conversations about politics, she was a good Latin and Greek scholar at a time when women were not encouraged to study the classics, and she believed in the ideals of the French Revolution (Lynam, *Humanity Dick Martin*, p. 187), but she could make little use of these intellectual accomplishments. Lynam further states that Harriet Martin and her sisters were known 'for their general benevolence and their love of animals' and 'busied themselves among other things with good works' (p. 278). The gender roles restricting women of her class meant that there was little else she could do, but in *Canvassing* she produces a scathing comment on this misuse of women's talents.

The irony is, of course, that it is because of the class privileges that provide her with a good education that Maria Wilmot, like Harriet Martin, is bound by gender restrictions that prevent her from using her knowledge. There is no sense in the novel that young women necessarily have to be victims of a patriarchal order. The prevailing impression, instead, is that the rules limiting women's possibilities are a class matter, intimately connected to national ideals. Attending a servant dance, Mr. Barham realizes that things can be very different in Ireland:

> 'So, in Ireland, the women ask the men to dance – what funny girls you must be! but when you want to be married, do ye ask the men to marry ye?'
>
> 'Ax the min to marry us, is it? Musha, faith an' we don't, – why would we? Thank God there's no occasion, indeed, we'd be giving oursel's that throuble any how, they've good warrants to say that much for themsel's.' (*Canvassing*, vol. 3, p. 56)

Among the servants, women can act, and a further example of this is when a number of peasant women drive off a band of supporters for one of Warringdon's competitors in the election (vol. 3, pp. 207–9). Again, Harriet Martin emphasizes that the restrictions placed on women are not exclusively a gender matter, but a question of social and national location as well.

The recent demand in feminist studies for inquiries that combine gender with race and class analyses usually proceeds from the understanding that women belonging to dispossessed groups in society are especially exposed to gender prejudice and oppression. It is certainly true that gender demarcations in nineteenth-century Ireland were confused by colonialism, since the colonial power needed to construct masculinity as superiority to underwrite its right and duty to rule. This meant that the colonized man in Ireland, India or Africa was feminized, which served to both collapse and re-establish the boundaries between the sexes. Like women, the Gaelic-Irish man was commonly identified as 'body' rather than 'mind' in relation to English officials and Protestant landlords, and a common reaction for men in this situation was to transfer the oppression they were subjected to onto women of their own class. Similar patterns can be found in working-class communities, especially in areas where unemployment is rife. This projection of feminine qualities onto colonized and powerless people devalued womanhood in general, but actual women belonging to the ruling class acquired a power not normally associated with femininity. Harriet Martin reverses this view, however. In contrast to the theories that maintain that women are even more oppressed in a colonized situation, she shows that lower-class Irish women's lack of privileges could lead to greater freedom and a stronger sense of self. It may be a little naive, as it erases too easily the negative effects of colonization and poverty, but it is a logical consequence of her criticism of English, upper-class constructions of femininity.

The liberating aspect of locational feminism is that it does not see identity as essence, but as a product of various locations, which opens the possibility of both mobility and temporary alliances. Maria and Isabel Wilmot deny themselves this mobility, because they are entrenched in a world view that regards social success as a matter of access to the aristocratic, English world. As Martin presents it, mobility is situated in the mind, and in the end, both Maria and Isabel marry their English suitors after a series of manipulations mimicking the methods of the election campaign. The result is disastrous on both counts: the Irish voters gain a representative who is totally uninterested in their situation and in politics as a whole, and as the wife of Warringdon, now Lord Glenville, Isabel is expected to put up with her husband's *amours*, and finally leaves him. Maria becomes a successful Paris hostess, but has to admit that she is 'married to a man [she] is ashamed to acknowledge' (vol. 3, p. 303) and when Barham becomes mad from drink and unhappiness, she gives up her Paris life to care for him from guilt that she is somehow responsible, since she trapped him into the marriage that has made them both miserable. The outcome of the marriages is foretold in the servant-girl Peggy's dream, where Warringdon appears as a big, black, red-eyed dog fighting with a small, mewing cat, interpreted as Isabel, and Maria appears as a great, ugly cat fighting with a little, small, white dog, representing Barham (vol. 3, pp. 62–7). The episode indicates that Martin to some extent sees men and women as incompatible, but this is balanced by descriptions of how both Maria and Isabel later meet other men that they respect and love and are forced to realize that happiness would have been possible for them, had they not allowed themselves to accept their mother's definition of success and be blinded by money. The attack is on the patriarchal system that objectifies women, and this is a system upheld not only by men.

The novel ends with Isabel and Maria setting up house together, jointly raising Maria's daughter and occupying themselves with charity. It is a separatist solution, but love is acknowledged, though it is impossible for either woman to pursue it for moral and ethical reasons. Separatism is thus both advocated as a refuge from a bad marriage and deplored as a necessary solution when love is made impossible by social conventions. The final words are given to Mr Wilmot, who criticizes his wife's marital manipulations, suggesting that doing 'nothing at all' would have been a better policy, to which she finally has to agree (vol. 3, p. 316).

Harriet Martin's novel is itself an instance of canvassing. It does not show women as a unified group, nor does it show them as passive victims, but it reveals very clearly how a specific location in time and place leads to a certain type of oppression. Much of the criticism is directed against England, not for the usual reasons of colonial exploitation and repression, but because it has been the source of Ireland being infected with a set of ideals alien to the country. More clearly than many other writers, Martin attacks the marriage market as a corrupt system that ruins both men and women, and none of the characters is absolved from complicity. Rather than a novel about gender struggle, *Canvassing* is a novel about patriarchy as an English, upper-class structure. There is an underlying sense that if Ireland had been allowed to develop on its own, this would have entailed the possibility for women to define their own identities instead of being defined by male, cultural norms. Unfortunately history shows that trusting in an innately more liberated Irish culture would have been futile too.

*   *   *   *   *

Harriet Martin: biographical and critical contexts

Harriet Martin is one of many forgotten women writers, and very little information about her can be found. She is mentioned in Stephen J. Brown's bibliography *Ireland in Fiction* (1916), but her name does not appear in more recent works, such as the *Field Day Anthology of Irish Writing Volumes IV & V: Irish Women's Writing and Traditions* (2002). Some information about her can be gleaned from Shevawn Lynam's biography of her father, *Humanity Dick Martin: 'King of Connemara' 1754–1834* (1989), MP and founder of the Royal Society for the Prevention of Cruelty to Animals (RSPCA). She was named after her mother, the author of *Helen of Glenross* (1802) and other works, and was related to Mary Letitia Martin, author of *Julia Howard* (1850), Violet Martin, the 'Martin Ross' of Somerville and Ross, and the writer Emily Lawless. In the 1820s or 1830s, Harriet Martin met Michael Banim in Paris, and a result of that meeting was that the novel *Canvassing*

(1832?) was published together with Banim's *The Mayor of Wind-Gap* in the series 'Tales of the O'Hara Family'. Thus, Martin is mentioned in D.W. Gilligan's Ph.D. thesis, 'The Banim Brothers: 1796–1874' (1990), and in Robert Lee Wolff's introduction to the fiction of the Banim brothers in the Garland reprint of *The Mayor of Wind-Gap* (1979), which includes *Canvassing*. As far as can be ascertained, Harriet Martin wrote only one other novel, *The Changeling*, published in 1848 and often attributed to the Banims. No individual studies of Harriet Martin exist at this time, although one can glean information about nineteenth-century women's writing in more general sources, such as the *Dictionary of Munster Women Writers, 1800 to 2000* (ed. Tina O'Toole, 2005).

Works cited

Brown, Stephen J., *Ireland in Fiction: A guide to Irish Novels, Tales, Romances and Folk-lore* (Dublin, London: Maunsel & Co. Ltd., 1916).

Butler, Judith, *Gender Trouble. Feminism and the Subversion of Identity* (New York: Routledge, 1990).

Flax, Jane, 'Postmodernism and Gender Relations in Feminist Theory', in Linda J. Nicholson (ed.), *Feminism/Postmodernism* (New York: Routledge, 1990), pp. 39–62.

Friedman, Susan Stanford, *Mappings: Feminism and the Cultural Geographies of Encounter* (Princeton University Press, 1998).

Gilligan, D.W., 'The Banim Brothers: 1796–1874', unpublished Ph.D. thesis, University of Ulster, 1990.

Grosz, Elizabeth, *Volatile Bodies? Toward a Corporeal Feminism* (Indiana University Press, 1994).

——, *Space, Time, and Perversion: Essays on the Politics of Bodies* (New York: Routledge, 1995).

Gubar, Susan, *Critical Condition: Feminism at the Turn of the Century* (New York: Columbia University Press, 2000).

Lynam, Shevawn, *Humanity Dick Martin: 'King of Connemara' 1754–1834* (1975; Dublin: Lilliput, 1989).

Martin, Harriet, *Helen of Glenross: A Novel* (London: G. & J. Robinson, 1802).

——, *Canvassing*, in Michael Banim and Harriet Martin, *The Mayor of Wind-Gap and Canvassing* [1832?], 3 vols. (New York: Garland, 1979), vols. 2–3.

Martin, Mary Letitia, *Julia Howard: A Romance. By Mrs. Martin Bell* (New York: Harper, 1850).

McDowell, Linda, *Gender, Identity and Place: Understanding Feminist Geographies* (Minneapolis: University of Minnesota Press, 1999).

Murray, Patrick Joseph, *The Life of John Banim* [1857] (New York: Garland Publishing, 1978).

O'Toole, Tina (ed.), *Dictionary of Munster Women Writers, 1800 to 2000* (Cork University Press, 2005).

Pykett, Lyn, 'Women Writing Woman: Nineteenth-Century Representations of Gender and Sexuality', in Joanne Shattock (ed.), *Women and Literature in Britain 1800–1900* (Cambridge University Press, 2001), pp. 78–98.

Shildrick, Margrit, *Leaky Bodies and Boundaries: Feminism, Postmodernism and (Bio)ethics* (London: Routledge, 1997).

Wolff, Robert Lee, 'The Fiction of "The O'Hara Family"', Michael Banim and Harriet Martin. *The Mayor of Wind-Gap and Canvassing.* 3 vols. (New York: Garland, 1979).

Chapter 4

Rereading Peig Sayers

Women's Autobiography, Social History
and Narrative Art

Patricia Coughlan

Peig Sayers (1873–1958) was born to a family of subsistence farmers in the remote village of Dunquin, in West Kerry.[1] She reluctantly left school at thirteen, a common fate for much of the population at the time, and worked as a domestic and farm servant in the nearest town, Dingle, and in the surrounding country. She hoped to be sent the passage money to emigrate to America by her beloved childhood friend Cáit Jim Ní Bheoláin, but this never happened. Cáit Jim left but never wrote, and disappeared from view. She may have had an industrial accident in one of the Massachusetts mills where many West Kerry migrants were employed, or suffered some other illness; perhaps she forgot Peig once she herself had arrived, perhaps she simply failed to make good in the United States (Brendan Feirtéar, *Slán an Scéalaí*). Engaged in hard physical labour on a farm, Peig suffered a breakdown in health and was invalided home. After some bitter time spent penniless in her parents' house, a match was made for her with Pádraig Ó Gaoithín from the Great Blasket Island and she went to live there.

The Great Blasket, the last inhabited island of a small chain lying three miles off the coast opposite Dunquin, was an isolated place where a small community lived a life of physical hardship. They often barely wrested a living, mainly by fishing, from the exposed and treeless land; in winter the seas would send spray over the entire span of the island. Islandmen found it hard to get wives, the island community was growing increasingly in-turned genetically, and they were probably willing as a result to forgo the customary dowry, which the Sayers family could not afford to give with Peig. The couple had ten children, four of whom died of ordinary childhood diseases such as chickenpox and measles; five emigrated once old enough. One son was lost in his late teens when he fell from the island cliffs while gathering furze branches for firewood. Eventually moving to the mainland after this life full

58

of hardship and personal loss, Peig became blind and died in 1958 after spending many years of her old age in Dingle hospital.

Peig was best known in her lifetime as an exceptionally gifted performer of oral tales in the Irish tradition. She knew examples of all the European folk tales, and also had in her repertoire the long Irish hero tales which were more usually the property of male storytellers. She became celebrated among scholars of the Irish language and tradition as the finest storyteller of the age. A tall imposing woman with a fine voice, she had an unparalleled command of the language and exceptionally clear and beautiful diction. Though she could not read or write Irish, skills not considered useful acquisitions in Irish National (primary) schools in the period, she was functionally literate in English. As is well known, Peig's autobiographical texts are part of an extraordinary proliferation of literary production associated with the island: Blasket life generated several other works of autobiography, as well as some minor classics in English by visitors deeply impressed by the islanders' sheer endurance, dignity and imaginative wealth.[2]

The folklore records contain a large body of oral stories collected from Peig, but I shall focus on the two volumes of autobiography (1936 and 1939) which Peig dictated to her son Micheál Ó Gaoithín, and on account of which her name is most familiar.[3] The received wisdom among Irish folklorists until recently was that the autobiographical works are greatly inferior in interest and aesthetic quality to the tales. Indeed, some felt that the former are scarcely worthy of notice, being allegedly mere dilutions of a perceived immemorial purity which is preserved in the inherited tales. This question of mediation and of notional interference with a pure source is an important and ideologically-laden one, in a culture so obsessed with seeking origins and with their moral primacy. Among historians, too, with few exceptions, there has been a startling lack of attention to these writings, a circumstance arising from the masculinist and mandarin assumptions of Irish historiography, where both social history in general and women's history in particular have been marginal or occluded intellectual concerns. In scholarly writing, then, more or less technical analyses by folklorists of Peig's oral tales dominate the field. Margaret MacCurtain and Angela Bourke ('Performing – not Writing'; 'More in Anger Than in Sorrow'; 'Languages, Stories, Healing') have both referred feelingly though relatively briefly to the Peig autobiographies from perspectives similar to my own, and the recent scholarly edition of the first volume (1998) has an informative, though brief, foreword by Máire Ní Mhainnín and Liam P. Ó Murchú. Feirtéar's drama-documentary for television, *Slán an Scéalaí*, with English subtitles, retraces Peig's life events with vivacity and feeling. Kerby Miller's distinguished study *Emigrants and Exiles* also draws briefly on Peig's life story in discussing the sociology of emigration in the late nineteenth century.[4]

My argument in this essay is that a rereading of the Peig Sayers texts is long overdue. They have suffered from unwarranted neglect among scholars of various disciplines and also from ideological distortion, and their importance to our understanding both of women's writing and of women's history has not been sufficiently acknowledged. My discussion has three main sections. In the first, I consider what we know about the important question of Peig's authorship of her own story. Central to feminist approaches to women's writing in general, this issue is of especial interest in this case because of the unusual circumstances of composition, not least among them the author's inability to write Irish, the language of the texts. As we shall see, it has been the object of some contention in Peig studies. I believe this contention arises from unacknowledged but fundamentally patriarchal assumptions about the very possibility of women's authorship. I also explore the image of Peig Sayers in Irish national consciousness, its deployment as a prominent gender-role model from the 1940s to the early 1990s and the later reaction against that deployment. Then I briefly consider the ideological context of the period in which the autobiographies were published.

Secondly, I discuss the representation in these texts of women's lives and mental worlds within traditional culture; an important part of this is the representation of the feelings and thoughts of the central character, Peig herself, as subject of the autobiography. The third and final part of the essay focuses on the narrative art and aesthetic effectiveness of the texts, discussing specific motifs and scenes.

On the question of authorship, the production of the first two of the volumes was instigated by Blasket visitors, in the same way as the other most famous Blasket autobiography, by a man (Tomás Ó Criomhthain). Interested Irish-language scholars, some Irish, some from abroad – in Peig's case two women from Dublin, Máire Ní Chinnéide and Léan Ní Chonalláin – encouraged the islanders to write about their lives. Both were teachers and enthusiastic advocates of the revival of Irish outside the Gaeltacht. They saw the people of Corca Dhuibhne (the Dingle Peninsula, including the Blaskets) as vital exemplars in this project. Cultural tourists since 1910 had included distinguished scholars from Scandinavia, France and Britain, notably Robin Flower from Oxford and George Thomson, the English classicist and Marxist, who in a deromanticized way greatly admired the courage, simplicity and solidarity which characterized the islanders' lives.[5]

Ó Criomhthain was literate, but, as we have seen, Peig dictated her story, some opening chapters to Ní Chinnéide, and then all the rest to her son Micheál. Micheál had emigrated to the United States but returned in 1930, and was also a writer, later known as 'Mike the Poet'. Perhaps, then, these works represent an act of joint composition. Hence the first crux of Peig studies: was she the author of her own text? There is a tendency among scholars to assign the autobiographies to Maidhc. I emphatically disagree and I think this is an example of the principle outlined by Joanna Russ – a principle familiar from Maria Edgeworth and Mary Shelley criticism – namely 'she didn't write it: her father/husband/brother wrote it'; or, in this case, her son. Padraig Ó Fiannachta, in 'Mícheál Ó Gaoithín', after first confidently asserting Maidhc's authorship, concludes after studying texts by both mother and son that Peig was very much the prime mover. On the other hand Mac Conghail has reiterated a negative view of Peig's authorship ('she was not the author of her own text' on the *Pat Kenny Show* (1998). Yet a feminist folklore scholar had already shown sharp disparities between Peig and Maidhc both in literary quality and in attitudes to gender (Joan Newlon Radner, "'The Woman Who Went to Hell'"). Her comparative analysis of their two versions of the tale 'The Woman Who Went to Hell' shows that Peig's narrative gifts outclassed her son's; it also demonstrates that Peig had a developed and positive position about women and the value of their contribution to the traditional society in which she lived. By contrast, Maidhc uses the shared inheritance of the tale to represent the female characters censoriously, underline their moral inferiority and stage their punishment. The autobiography's markedly favorable representation of women, itself very much under-remarked, is therefore far closer to Peig's viewpoint than to her son's.

Other compelling evidence – by default – of Peig's primary authorship is to be found in the falling off in interest and quality of a third volume, published long after Peig's death and the unequivocal product of Maidhc's own imagination (Ó Gaoithín, *Beatha Pheig Sayers*). The information conveyed is still interesting, but its effect is diminished by greater religiosity (a characteristic of Maidhc's writings) and less able narrative organization. 'I used to be fishing from her without her knowledge,' remarked Maidhc about his culling of the material for this volume: this implication of surreptitiously exploiting an unknowing Peig is unsavoury, recalling Synge's notorious eavesdropping on the conversations in Aran through the floorboards of his loft bedroom. An intriguing aspect of Maidhc's volume is the variant and floridly romanticized version it offers of the alleged courtship of Peig by her prospective husband, while the earlier account written from her own dictation is the much drier and more pragmatic story of an arranged marriage with a stranger. Finally, regarding Maidhc's literary competence, the view of scholars currently working on an unpublished diary which he kept for a year in 1923 is that it is overblown, meandering and lacking in linguistic and scholarly integrity.[6] The much finer journal kept from May to November of the same year by the 23-year-old Eibhlís Ní Shúilleabháin – a work of great freshness and charm, only recently published (2000) – affords a further opportunity to explore women's perspectives on Blasket life, besides those of Peig herself. Like Peig's friend Cáit Jim, Eibhlín emigrated, but she died in her forties in Springfield, Massachusetts, broken in health and spirit.

My strong suggestion, therefore, is that we *should* credit Peig with her authorship, however collaboratively exercised in conjunction with her son. Indeed, instead of trying to assign ownership to one or the other, we should attend more positively to the evident warmth of the collaboration between them. This is clear in the arresting photograph, taken about 1930, which shows them on either side of the fire, Maidhc with fountain-pen poised over a school copybook, his high laced boots covered in ash, and Peig with one hand laid serenely over the other, about to speak. Folklore and ethnography scholars are now considering that the Blasket autobiographies are perhaps the least mediated of all the narratives which came out of that traditional storytelling world. It is beginning to be acknowledged that the situation staged by the folklore collector, however much he might have felt himself to be paying homage at the undefiled shrine of immemorial tradition, was in fact a highly artificial one. The product, in the form of the orally performed tales, was very strongly influenced by the intrusive presence of that collector himself (it pretty well always *was* a him), and sometimes of his cumbersome recording equipment. Collectors valued some kinds of material over others (e.g., hero tales, magic tales); they came with a list – 'Do you know this one?' – and they tried to re-create, cold and usually one-to-one, an originally communal occasion.[7]

I turn now to the question of Peig's image and her readers' reactions to it. Often these, as we shall see, were older teenagers and unwilling conscripts. Two images of Peig Sayers are current in the Irish imagination, or rather two aspects of, or responses to, the same image; I believe we should move beyond both these views and seek to arrive at a fresh understanding of the material. The first is the quintessential holy Irish mother, who has suffered and is resigned. She has had her children snatched away by death or emigration; she endures femininely, emulating the Virgin Mary. She can be imaginatively assimilated also to the Mother Ireland figure which Pearse's work developed from the composite traditions of nationalist rhetoric, nineteenth-century ballad and Irish Revival drama. This, broadly, was the image offered to generations of 16- to 18-year-olds for whom the first volume (ed. Máire Ní Chinnéide) was a school Leaving Certificate textbook. From 1942/3, it was prescribed once every third or fourth year. During the 1970s, however, it was a much stronger presence, since it figured among a list of six prose texts, of which students had to be conversant with two; it was finally dropped in the late 1990s (Department of Education, *Rules and Programmes for Schools*). Peig was, as we might put it, promoted as a role model for girls, and her piety, purity and allegedly unquestioning acceptance of suffering agreed very well with the dominant ideology of the De Valera years. We might note that between the two volumes of the autobiography there appeared that other famous national document, the 1937 Constitution, with its well-known insistence on the essentially domestic function of women.[8]

I would, however, argue that this image of the writings Peig actually produced is quite misleading. For school use, the first volume was edited, removing, among other things, an episode of communal drunkenness (during a rare trip to Dingle), which is recounted humorously, without disapproval. Unfortunately, we do not know what the manuscripts of either of the first two volumes might have originally contained to shock the Dublin commissars of nationalist ideology, who were at their most stern in the 1930s. No part of a typescript or proof, still less a precious original manuscript, appears to survive.[9] The Government National Publications Office (An Gúm), which published the second volume, was notorious in these decades for its censoring zeal. Finally, in her later years at least, Peig had a rich fund of bawdy and earthy humour. According to a younger personal friend of Peig's, also a native speaker of Irish, who often visited her in the Dingle hospital, she was perfectly willing to mention (probably within the framework of quasi-humorous vocabulary discussion, a familiar genre in Gaeltacht conversation) the words in Irish for officially taboo topics involving sexual and physiological functions.[10]

Nevertheless, a version of Peig as a figure of lugubrious piety prevailed in Irish public consciousness, producing mainly negative effects. When in the 1980s and 1990s there set in an explicit reaction to this idealization, practitioners of *kulturkritik*, mainly from Dublin, systematically rejected this iconic, saintly Peig. Her alleged passivity and her whole mental world were criticized as classic examples of the imposition of sentimental, backward-looking and ruralist ideology upon the nation, and specifically upon adolescents, to whom the Great Blasket was as remote and irrelevant as a life led on Mars. A prominent instance occurs in a play by 'New Dublin Realist' Dermot Bolger.[11] It was as part of this continuing reaction that during the 1990s, a spoof website could be accessed in which 'Peig' proffered agony-aunt advice on everything; other such gestures of repudiation were much in evidence among younger adults, particularly in Irish cities and towns.

This revisionist move itself, however, produced a certain backlash in 1998. A controversy ensued in the *Irish Times* after a possibly mischievous sub-editor headlined as follows: 'A feminist Peig Sayers chafed at being a chattel', the report of a Blasket Commemoration lecture in which I had not anachronistically attributed feminism to poor Peig but had only suggested that a feminist *reading* should be made of her work.[12] A County Kerry priest began a public correspondence in which he sought to defend and preserve the traditional image of Peig; my own explanation of my views and expression of my admiration for her failed to allay his sense of profanation. This unlikely, sometimes hilarious, controversy over who owned Peig, who might think and write about her, and in what ways, generated national radio coverage, even on current-affairs programmes, besides widespread discussion on local radio stations all over Ireland. This contestation of her meaning makes clear that in the national psyche or cultural memory Peig Sayers crystallized the roles women might and might not be allowed to occupy in Ireland.

How do the Peig texts in fact represent women's lives in the Blasket and West Kerry communities? Further analysis is needed; I can only name here some of the main themes of this representation as they appear in the Peig texts. Most striking is the importance of mutual support and emotional closeness between girls and women. Examples are Peig's relationships with Cáit Jim, with her own mother and later with her kind and supportive mother-in-law. Also marked is the fellowship among the women on the island, with whom, the narrative relates, Peig gains a warm intimacy after an initial period of shyness and homesickness for the mainland. This fellowship of women is a dominant theme and is pursued throughout the texts: I see this as part of a consistent validation of women's social roles and their life experience as agents, which has not hitherto been thematized or much attended to.[13] The repertoire of feminine roles shown is also of great interest. These emphasize women's especial association with birth and death. We see the former in the deftly comic scene showing the chorus of old women round Peig's infant son when he is brought home to the island – 'his nose is too long', 'his chin sticks out' – which might be from Perrault (*Peig: A Scéal Féin*, chs. 19–21). There is also a vivid account of the old women's conducting of a wake, which I shall return to at the end.

Furthermore, Peig's texts are full of concrete social information. For instance, they provide a sharp insight from within about the 'surplus woman' problem among subsistence smallholders and tenants in Ireland in the late nineteenth century.[14] The wife of Peig's eldest brother, who 'marries in' to the Sayers household, resents the continuing presence of Peig as an extra mouth to feed. This painful experience is vividly rendered early in the autobiography, and is the impetus for her removal, at thirteen, from her home, to be sent into service. It is intriguing – and characteristic of the imaginative technique of these texts – that this topic is again treated, in a displaced way, in the *seanchas* or lore contained within the main autobiographical narrative, though demarcated from it. In this instance the second volume unfolds a story about a clever tailor who reconciles the in-laws old and young to one another in a situation of domestic conflict (*Machtnamh Sheana-Mhná*, ch. 4). During this anecdote, the man of the house is reproached for not establishing order and ending the constant disputes: a discreetly distanced reflection of Peig's sense of her own father's rather passive approach to the struggle in his household.

An insistent recurring theme is Peig's resentment at the lack of personal autonomy in her young life before her marriage. This focuses especially on her lack of income. Irish society was predicated upon communal existence, not upon the individual, and the norm was to hand over a servant girl's pay to her brother or father at season's or year's end. Boys who were hired out also had their wages paid over to their families until they became adults.[15] The narrative repeatedly rehearses Peig's bitterness, her chagrin, at this and at her disempowered situation when ill health forces her to return home, already a young woman, and live penniless again in her father's house (*Peig: A Scéal Féin*, ch. 11).

The insistence upon this discontent gives the lie to the image of a saintly all-enduring Peig, and the story does have its dark colourings. These are not only to do with the endurance of material deprivation and emotional loss (among instances of such loss that of Cáit Jim is central: the narrator repeatedly revisits it with a poignant sadness). There are also the two episodes of theft by the younger Peig, frankly enough recounted and painfully explored.

First is the little girl's stealing of a freshly baked half-griddle cake on her way to school. This is thematically echoed in the double theft of the salt fish and the weaver's duck by the young adult woman desperate to acquire goods so she can join in the other girls' party in the village. Both are markedly associated with the defiant desire for pleasure and gratification. The second, more bitter, instance deliberately recalls the first, innocent one, and they combine in signifying to the reader a personality capable not only of appetite but also of a resentment strong enough to induce rule-breaking.

The frustrated sense of a near-complete lack of individual agency in a demeaning economic situation is what motivates the second theft. The clarity with which this state of dependency is observed – and resisted – in Peig's story makes inappropriate an attack upon her from another, rather different, angle (Cathal Ó hÁinle, 'Peig, Aonghus Ó Dálaigh agus Macbeth'). This critiques the texts for an alleged lack of existential protest and subjective presence. Ó hÁinle unfavorably compares Peig's autobiography with some of the great autobiographical texts of Western tradition (all by men). This is questionable on several grounds. First, far from invariably evincing the kind of holy docility of which Ó hÁinle accuses her (from the vantage point of a changed Ireland), Peig *does* express her protest, and trenchantly, about this and the many other sorrows of her life. Ó hÁinle, adapting Marx, remarks patronizingly about the expressions of religious feeling that 'faith was the valium of the era', which is reductionist. He also inexplicably fails to notice some of the most painful and moving moments of the story when he doubts whether Peig ever experienced terror and fear of an existential or metaphysical kind. It should go without saying that no one in Peig Sayers's community had the kind of Augustinian, Montaignian or Sartrean freedom which permitted these great autobiographers of the past to elaborate the specifically philosophical discourses of subjectivity for which their writing is valued. Questions both of gender and of social structure and system are not irrelevant here: for a woman in the subsistence economy of the Blasket in the 1920s and 1930s, tormented individuality would probably have been about as much use as sun lotion in a rainstorm. Adequate interpretation always involves some sympathy with the character of a text. In the case of women's works, and indeed of works emerging from a social milieu in which community takes primacy over individuality, the role of connectedness or inter-relatedness in forming and expressing identity and experience will usually take precedence over an *angst*-ridden subjectivity. The expression of subjectivity in the Peig material is certainly different from the masculine and predominant Western model, in which heroism is shown precisely by the construction of an atomized selfhood, which then engages itself in competitive striving against others and against a patriarchal God.[16]

The texts do, however, offer a fascinating patchwork of attitudes towards the prevailing patriarchal ideology in Irish rural society. Equable and humorous citations of traditional anti-feminine sayings and attitudes coexist with a strong strand of feminine intelligence, wit and capacity to stand up for oneself. The lively chaffing between men and women in the boats rowing out of the island for the pilgrimage excursion to the holy well of Tobar na Molt is an example. Another is the comic passage where an agreeably, even brazenly, assertive Peig obliges the corpulent and self-important bourgeois from the town of Tralee to move his coat from the train seats so she and her female companions can sit down (*Machtnamh Sheana-Mhná*, ch. 10). In the '*caismirt na gcearc*' story (a dispute over the ownership of a hen), which represents women as quarrelsome and envious, the skills of verbal wit and verse-making by the participants are nevertheless savoured (ch. 14). Another chapter rehearses two stories about the sea mounting the land to threaten or annihilate young women who break religious taboos from pure high spirits and the desire for pleasure, in one instance by going to the strand to collect barnacles on Easter Monday. They are swept away by a great wave, but are seen by a kinswoman in an uncanny vision dancing a four-hand reel on the clifftop, with the brilliantly surreal touch of 'the fifth one playing the music' (ch. 24). The effect of such regulatory warnings is countered both by the storyteller's evident delight in this vivid tale, by Peig's emphasis on her own good sense and perfectly peaceful friendship and cooperation with other women, and by her ready enjoyment of small pleasures. This is also shown in the comic, quasi-picaresque episode of an adventurous expedition to Ballyferriter on the mainland to claim the pension for the first time.[17]

The Peig material must also be explored as an example of women's autobiography, a genre of which we are quite short in Ireland, especially outside the middle or upper classes. In this connection, it is important to get beyond the mere-transcription theory, which has so far dominated what few commentaries there are. We need to acknowledge the reflexivity and fictionality of Peig's narrations, to whatever extent they may be refracted through the pens or minds of the 'certain editors' said by scholar Máirín Nic Eoin to have 'come between us' and Peig.[18] The late-twentieth-century theoretical scholarship on autobiography as a genre emphasizes that all autobiography *is always already narrative,* and that as such it is both a work of creation and one of reflective understanding (Jerome Bruner and Susan Weisser, 'The Invention of Self'; Laura Marcus, *Auto/biographical Discourses*). There is no scope here to investigate Peig's subjective life as these texts construct it. But I would argue that the texts do evince such a life and that they could and should be discussed in the contexts of reflexivity, constructions of femininity and psychological self-development, as well as world view (see Linda Anderson, *Women and Autobiography*). To do this will require a greater degree of historical and social imagination and psychological tact than has been evident to date in the Irish reception of Peig.

I turn finally to discuss these texts as narratives and to argue that they do indeed offer the satisfactions *of* narrative. I have chosen passages which also touch on the thematic points made earlier about representations of women's lives.

The first moment is a famous one: the account of the death of Tomás in 1920 (*Peig: A Scéal Féin*, ch. 23). The chapter opens with Peig looking across the table at her late-adolescent son and mentioning the imminent departure of his older brother Pádraig for America. When Peig expresses her wish that Pádraig might stay one more year, Tomás reaches to take her hand and says, with shining eyes, that as long as his hand is strong he will never leave her to fend for herself. Then he races out over the threshold, the description emphasizing his strength and high spirits. That day he falls to his death over the island cliffs while reaching for a branch of furze. A direct link is made between his loss and the family's – indeed the whole community's – state of deprivation: there is no turf on the island in that season, hence this dangerous obligation to gather firewood even on the cliff's edge. The sea tosses his body up onto a flat rock, where it can be recovered, an eventuality much marvelled at and a source of some consolation (often the bodies of drowned fishermen were recovered months later or not at all). Finding the body is a social and psychological blessing, which enabled the bereaved to complete what, after Freud, we would call the work of mourning.

When Tomás's body is sighted, his hand is in his pocket. We should pause here to observe how skillfully this accurate detail of the *actual* event is woven into the narrative: the motif of the boy's hand, with its connotations both of filial love and of physical prowess and promise, is introduced in the first scene of the chapter so that it can sharpen the poignant description of the dead body. This skilful management of material for aesthetic and emotional effect is what narratologists call *discourse,* and is evidence of a highly developed narrative art beneath the apparent artlessness of the *story* (Mieke Bal, *Narratology*; Seymour Chatman, *Story and Discourse*).

Another important part of this narrated episode is the heartbroken mother's reaction when her son's battered body is brought home to her. Alone (according to the story) except for her now-invalided and bedridden husband, she must somehow find the strength to wash and lay out the corpse, whose skull is shattered. This she finally achieves, after several reprises, by setting the statue of the Virgin Mary beside her while she works.[19] Most people who have ever read this passage remember, even if they did first encounter it as rebellious urban teenagers, that the sense of sheer loss and religious feeling has an agonized intensity very far removed from the notional effects of valium. The isolation and dignity of the grieving woman tending to the broken body makes it a kind of Blasket Pietà, which draws upon a fundamental understanding of attachment and grief.

But the text has not yet done with these themes: after an intervening chapter Peig tells a story from the Famine era in West Kerry which resumes and emotionally transacts the motif of mothers with lost children (*Peig: A Scéal Féin*, ch. 25). This is the story of Bríde Liath, who is the sole survivor of her household. Her husband and all her children have died of Famine fever or starvation, and when the story opens, she must carry alone to the grave the body of her adult daughter, the last to die. She is offered food by a woman whose house she passes, carrying the corpse, and helped with the burial itself by four male neighbours. Then she stands by the common grave of all her loved ones and recites a prayer, a beautiful formal invocation of eternity and of an ultimate consolation. Both this passage and the earlier drowning episode draw upon the language of traditional songs and poems, especially love poetry. Here is Bríde Liath's prayer, spoken by the female figure, the last one left standing, face to face with death:

> Sleep peacefully in an eternal peace, o my children and my gentle husband. There's no danger you will be awakened until the sea comes down from the north and the black raven turns white. Don't be afraid, o my children, that you will suffer hunger or thirst. You have your fill of the Stream of Glory to quench your thirst today. I leave you sleeping in the grace of God until the Angel will sound the trumpet on the last day! (My translation).

This incantation acts as a crowning moment of aesthetic stasis which draws together the Bríde Liath material with the earlier account of Peig's own maternal grief and necessary fortitude. The text arranges these two narrative elements, with their evident thematic relation, in a delicate and intensely moving conjunction. The effect is to set up a typology which celebrates the self's powers of endurance and regeneration by spiritual insight and by hope. The notion of catharsis might be adapted here: pity at the loss of those so young and terror at the power of death in nature. But there is also a powerful sense of solace, achieved by calling upon the idea of a saving and benign eternity which can transcend both pity and terror; and this is imaginatively realized in the natural and vernacular figures of the ever-moving ocean and the black raven (see Angela Bourke, 'The Irish Traditional Lament and the Grieving Process').

Both the death of Tomás and the Bríde Liath story are markedly concerned with the link between women and death. This association in Irish traditional society is attested by folklorists and anthropologists (see Patricia Lysaght, 'Perspectives on Women', and Angela Bourke, 'More in Anger Than in Sorrow'): on a symbolic level it echoes women's equally strong, but more physically evident, association with birth. An intriguing example of the felt closeness of women to death is the custom that when someone died on the island and the *naomhóga* went out to the mainland to bring back the wake materials (whiskey, tobacco, the coffin), there must always be a woman in one of the boats.[20] The final passage I shall discuss concerns this closeness (*Machtnamh Sheana-Mhná*, ch. 7). In Dunquin during Peig's childhood, the miser Tomáisín Ó Gríofa dies. He has always stinted his wife, Big Nell, in everything, and so there is a degree of relief for her in his demise. The mood of this scene is different, recalling the comic and semi-grotesque *fabliau* atmosphere of Boccaccio and Chaucer. The little girl Peig and her great friend

Cáit Jim, the former bold and the latter fearful, hang around at the threshold of the death room. Cáit is terrified of seeing the dead person's face, while Peig, who has *saighdiúireacht* (a streak of bravery), wants to move up nearer and even announces she will touch him. Cáit tries to leave, but Peig threatens her with an alleged *piseog* [taboo]: that whoever leaves the wake house alone will be haunted forever by the dead person. Throughout the exchange, the child Peig is presented as the leader, the daring one, the tease. Eventually the older women who are in charge of things call the two girls up to the fire and give them white bread and jam, which, though a great luxury, barely relieves Cáit's terror at having to go nearer the corpse. The remainder of the scene relates the old women's busyness about the appropriate conduct of the wake, and notes their strong appetite for tea and tobacco, which clearly parallels the girls' enjoyment of the bread and jam. An unspoken but clear imaginative connection is made between the strength shown by young Peig, that of the capable older women who are in charge of the occasion and the specifically narrative authority possessed by old Peig as storyteller. The situation presents a *mise en abyme,* or effect of embedding, with, in sequence: (1) the reader, looking in upon the whole scene; (2) the narrator, whom we know as old Peig, telling the story; (3) the two little girls, looking on in their turn; (4) the old women, bustling about the conduct of the wake; and finally, at the inner heart of this *abyme,* (5) the dead body of Tomáisín, who, of course, can neither look nor speak nor lift a finger. This may implicitly suggest a silencing of men in the presence of death. But what is definite is that Peig's *saighdiúireacht,* her agency, is what has brought her to this controlling, storyteller's place, and that we are intentionally shown this at the meta-level of fictional signification.

Furthermore, the scene has ended in feasting: a feast set up and offered in the presence of the dead man – and therefore of death itself – and against death. We see in this and in many other ways that, for all their constant awareness of hardship, danger and mortality, these texts are turned towards life. The miasmatic gloom of the 1980s caricature is not their principal note, and nor is the docile conformity enjoined upon Irishwomen in our mothers' and grandmothers' generations, and even into our own. We saw earlier how Peig teases her friend; she also consoles her, with a speech that is touching and funny in equal measure: 'Our only problem is that we're children. A day will come, if we live to see it, when we won't be afraid.' There is a delicate poise and a heartbreaking poignancy in the narrator's recall of this hopeful moment. The little speech is, after all, constructed by the biographical Peig in her mid-sixties, in view – and in spite of – the life of loss and suffering, of chagrin and indeed of terror, which she now knows lay ahead to be lived through. The moment is a triumph of the narrative imagination over the constriction of actual circumstance, and should be recognized as such. Nabokov wrote that imagination is a form of memory, but it is also, as Proust showed, a transformative force. Peig Sayers deserves, then, to be reread for the power of her texts as social history from a woman's perspective and for the psychological insight they afford into feminine subjectivity in Irish traditional society. In what is, to be sure, a small compass, her writings also show the working of this transformative aesthetic imagination on the material of ordinary lives, however poor, culturally subaltern and geographically marginal the community where those lives were lived. Finally, on the subject of women's agency, let us recall how the chapter ends: with a delighted, ironic description of Big Nell's pleasure in spending the miser's hoarded wealth, happily lavishing hospitality on all comers.

*   *   *   *   *

Peig Sayers: biographical and critical contexts

Peig Sayers was born in Dunquin, West Kerry, in 1873. She left school at thirteen and was hired out for farm work, but illness forced her home again. After marriage to Pádraig Ó Gaoithín, she moved to the Great Blasket Islands and gave birth to ten children. Known for her fine oral storytelling, Sayers also produced autobiographical texts by dictating to others, including her son Micháil. Although she was literate in English, Sayers could neither read nor write Irish, which has raised questions about primary authorship of her work, addressed in this essay. Eventually she moved back to Dingle on the mainland, lost her sight and died in 1958. Long a staple of Irish exams, her work was used to exemplify the ideal and pious Irish mother, an image challenged in recent analyses.

Volumes IV and V of the *Field Day Anthology* (2002), on women's writing and traditions, have provided a fuller context for the study of Peig Sayers's life, times and works, in general terms, in that they offer a wealth of accompanying and background texts, and much information about women's lives, their roles in Irish culture, history and writing, and their creative contributions in both the languages of Ireland before and during the life of Peig Sayers herself. More specifically, those interested in Peig will find a short but useful discussion in the introduction by Bríona Nic Dhiarmada to the section 'Inscribing Voices: Twentieth-Century Irish-Language Memoirs' (vol. IV, pp. 1046–7). Also of interest is Caitriona Clear's introduction to the section 'Women of the House in Ireland, 1800–1950' (vol. V, pp. 589–96). The bilingual *Dictionary of Munster Women Writers, 1800–2000* (ed. Tina O'Toole), with its biographical and bibliographical listing of women writers, provides a specifically regional context for Sayers's literary autobiographies and oral narration.

Works cited

Almqvist, Bo, 'The Mysterious Micheál Ó Gaoithín, Boccaccio and the Blasket Tradition. Reflections occasioned by James Stewart's *Boccaccio in the Blaskets*', *Béaloideas* 58 (1990), pp. 75–140.

Anderson, Linda, *Women and Autobiography in the Twentieth Century: Remembered Futures* (London: Harvester Wheatsheaf, 1997).

Bal, Mieke, *Narratology: Introduction to the Theory of Narrative* (University of Toronto Press, 1985).

Benjamin, Jessica, *The Bonds of Love: Psychoanalysis, Feminism and the Problem of Domination* (London: Virago, 1990).

Bolger, Dermot, *In High Germany*, in *A Dublin Quartet* (London: Penguin, 1992), pp. 71–109.

Bourke, Angela, 'The Irish Traditional Lament and the Grieving Process', *Women's Studies International Forum* 11, 4 (1988), pp. 287–91.

——, 'Performing – Not Writing: The Reception of an Irish Woman's Lament', *Graph* 11 (Winter 1991–2), pp. 28–31. (Reprinted in Yopie Prins and Maeera Shreiber (eds.), *Dwelling in Possibility: Women Poets and Critics on Poetry* (Ithaca: Cornell University Press, 1997), pp. 132–46.

——, 'More in Anger Than in Sorrow: Irish Women's Lament Poetry', in Joan Newlon Radner (ed.), *Feminist Messages: Codings in Women's Folk Culture* (Urbana/Chicago: University of Illinois Press, 1993), pp. 160–82.

——, 'Language, Stories, Healing', in Anthony Bradley and Maryann Gialanella Valiulis (ed.), *Gender and Sexuality in Modern Ireland* (Amherst: University of Massachusetts Press, 1997), pp. 299–314.

Bourke, Joanna, *Husbandry to Housewifery: Women, Economic Change, and Housework in Ireland, 1890–1914* (Oxford: Clarendon Press, 1993).

Breatnach, Diarmuid and Máire Ní Mhurchú, *Beathaisnéis 5: 1881–1982* (Baile Átha Cliath: An Clóchomhar Tta, 1990).

Bruner, Jerome and Susan Weisser, 'The Invention of Self: Autobiography and its Forms', in David R. Olson and Nancy Torrance (eds.), *Literacy and Orality* (Cambridge University Press, 1991), pp. 129–48.

Chatman, Seymour. *Story and Discourse: Narrative Structure in Fiction and Film* (Ithaca: Cornell University Press, 1978).

Clear, Caitriona, Introduction, 'Women of the House in Ireland, 1800–1950', in Angela Bourke et al. (eds.), *The Field Day Anthology of Irish Writing Volumes IV & V: Irish Women's Writing and Traditions* (Cork University Press, 2002), pp. 589–96.

Coughlan, Patricia. 'An Léiriú ar Shaol na mBan i dTéacsanna Dírbheathaisnéise Pheig Sayers', in Máire Ni Chéilleachair (ed.), *Peig Sayers Scéalaí 1873–1958, Ceiliúradh an Bhlascaoid 3* (Baile Átha Cliath: Coiscéim, 1999), pp. 20–57.

Davidoff, Leonore and Catherine Hall, *Family Fortunes: Men and Women of the English Middle Class, 1780–1850* (University of Chicago Press, 1987).

Department of Education, *Rules and Programmes for Schools* (Dublin: Government Publications Office, 1943).

Ennis, Séamus (trans.), *An Old Woman's Reflections* (Oxford University Press, 1962).

Feirtéar, Breandán (dir.), *Blasket Roots, American Dreams*, television documentary (Dublin: RTÉ, 1997).

——, *Slán an Scéalaí*, television drama-documentary with English subtitles (Dublin: RTÉ, 1998).

Flower, Robin, *The Western Island* [1944] (Oxford University Press, 1978).

Gough, Julian, *Juno and Juliet* (London: Flamingo, 2002).

Inglis, Tom, *The Moral Monopoly: The Rise and Fall of the Catholic Church in Modern Ireland*, 2nd edn (Dublin: University College Dublin Press, 1998).

Lysaght, Patricia, 'Perspectives on Women during the Great Irish Famine from the Oral Tradition', *Béaloideas* 64–5 (1996–7), pp. 63–130.

Mac Conghail, Muiris, *The Blaskets: People and Literature* (1987; Dublin: Country House, 1994).

——, *Pat Kenny Show*, RTÉ, Radio 1, April 1998.

MacCurtain, Margaret, 'Fullness of Life: Defining Irish Spirituality in 20th-Century Ireland', in Maria Luddy and Clíona Murphy (eds.), *Women Surviving: Studies in Irish Women's History in the 19th and 20th Centuries* (Dublin: Poolbeg, 1989), pp. 237–9.

MacMahon, Bryan (trans.), *Peig: The Autobiography of Peig Sayers of the Blasket Island* (Dublin: Talbot Press, 1974).

McWilliams, John, 'The Rationale for "The American Romance"', in Donald Pease (ed.), *Revisionary Interventions into the Americanist Canon* (Durham, NC: Duke University Press, 1994), pp. 71–82.

Marcus, Laura, *Auto/biographical Discourses: Theory, Criticism, Practice* (Manchester University Press, 1994).

Matson, Leslie, *Méiní: The Blasket Nurse* (Cork: Mercier Press, 1996).

Miller, Kerby, *Emigrants and Exiles: Ireland and the Irish Exodus to North America* (New York: Oxford University Press, 1985).

Murphy, Maureen, 'The Fionnuala Factor: Irish Sibling Emigration at the Turn of the Century', in Anthony Bradley and Maryann Gialanella Valiulis (eds.), *Gender and Sexuality in Modern Ireland* (Amherst: University of Massachusetts Press, 1997), pp. 85–101.

Nic Dhiarmada, Bríona, Introduction, 'Inscribing Voices: Twentieth-Century Irish-Language Memoirs', in Angela Bourke et al. (eds.), *The Field Day Anthology of Irish Writing Volume V: Irish Women's Writing and Traditions* (Cork University Press, 2002), pp. 1046–7.

Ní Dhomhnaill, Nuala, *Selected Poems/Rogha Dánta*, trans. Michael Hartnett (Dublin: Raven Arts Press, 1988).

Ní Dhuinnshléibhe, Máirín, 'Saol na mBan', in Aogán Ó Muircheartaigh (ed.), *Oidhreacht an Bhlascaoid* (Baile Átha Cliath: Coiscéim, 1989), pp. 334–45.

Ní Shúilleabháin, Eibhlín, *Cín Lae Eibhlín Ní Shúilleabháin*, ed. Máiréad Ní Loingsigh (Baile Átha Cliath: Coiscéim, 2000).

Ní Shúilleabháin, Eibhlís, *Letters from the Great Blasket*, ed. Seán Ó Coileáin (Cork/Dublin: Mercier Press, 1978).

Ó Criomhthain, Tomás, *An tOileánach* (Baile Átha Cliath: Oifig an tSoláthair, 1929).

Ó Fiannachta, Pádraig, 'Micheál Ó Gaoithín, An File (1907–1974)', in Aogán Ó Muircheartaigh (ed.), *Oidhreacht an Bhlascaoid* (Baile Átha Cliath: Coiscéim, 1989), pp. 270–90.

—— (ed.), *Oileáin and Oileánaigh* (An Daingean: An Sagart, 1995).

Ó Gaoithín, Mícheál, *Diary* (1923), National Library of Ireland, Ms. G. 1021.

——, *Beatha Pheig Sayers* (Baile Átha Cliath: Foilseacháin Náisiúnta Tta, 1970).

Ó hÁinle, Cathal, 'Peig, Aonghus Ó Dálaigh agus Macbeth', in Aogán Ó Muircheartaigh (ed.), *Oidhreacht an Bhlascaoid* (Baile Átha Cliath: Coiscéim, 1989), pp. 253–69.

O'Toole, Tina (ed.), *Dictionary of Munster Women Writers, 1800–2000* (Cork University Press, 2005).

——, and Patricia Coughlan, 'Introduction', *Dictionary of Munster Women Writers, 1800–2000*. Cork University Press, 2005, pp. xv–xxxvi.

Radner, Joan Newlon, '"The Woman Who Went to Hell": Coded Values in Irish Folk Narrative', *Midwestern Folklore* 15, 2 (1989), pp. 109–17.

Russ, Joanna, *How to Suppress Women's Writing* (London: Women's Press, 1983).

Sayers, Peig, *Peig. A Scéal Féin* (Baile Átha Cliath: Clólucht an Talbóidigh, 1936).

——, *Machtnamh Sheana-Mhná* (Baile Átha Cliath: Oifig an tSoláthair, 1939).

——, *Peig. A Scéal Féin*, school edn, ed. Máire Ní Chinnéide (Baile Átha Cliath: Comhlucht Oideachais na hÉireann, n.d.).

——, *Peig: A Scéal Féin*, new edn, ed. Máire Ní Mhainnín and Liam P. Ó Murchú (An Daingean: An Sagart, 1998).

Scannell, Yvonne, 'The Constitution and the Role of Women', in Brian Farrell (ed.), *De Valera's Constitution and Ours* (Dublin: Gill & Macmillan, 1988), pp. 123–36.

Thomson, George, *The Blasket That Was: The Story of a Deserted Village* (Maynooth: An Sagart, 1982).

Valiulis, Maryann, 'Neither Feminist nor Flapper: The Ecclesiastical Construction of the Ideal Irish Woman', in Mary O'Dowd and Sabine Wichert (ed.), *Chattel, Servant, or Citizen: Women's Status in Church, State and Society* (Belfast: Institute of Irish Studies, 1995), pp. 168–86.

Chapter 5

'But Greek . . . usually knows Greek'

Recognizing Queer Sexuality in
Kate O'Brien's *Mary Lavelle*

Katherine O'Donnell

'Queer theory' was a term coined by Teresa de Lauretis in 1990 to describe how lesbian studies and gay studies were critiquing the discourses and methods by which reproductive heterosexuality is enforced as the dominant norm (what is awkwardly called heteronormativity) while all other sexualities are proscribed as deviant: queer ('Queer Theory'). It took de Lauretis just four years to distance her work from the term queer theory, describing it as a 'conceptually vacuous creature of the publishing industry' and to insist on the specificity of lesbian sexuality ('Habit Changes – Response', p. 316). On an ideological level, the difference between lesbian studies and queer theory is a profound one in that lesbian studies presumes either a lesbian subject, practice or desire and queer theory insists on the instability of all identities and critiques the processes by which sexual identities become socially recognized and regulated. However, the distinction between lesbian studies and queer theory is more one of object choice or perspective rather than method. The priority of lesbian studies is a focus on the formation and expression of erotic relations between those who are either gendered or sexed female while queer theory is alert to 'the existence and expression of a wide range of positions within culture that are "queer" or non-, anti-, or contra-straight' (Alexander Doty, *Making Things Perfectly Queer*, p. 3). It might be said that lesbian studies is a subset of queer theory but it is more accurate to say that queer theory is an offshoot or the fertile and ever-proliferating result of a meeting between lesbian studies and gay studies.

Lesbian studies as we have inherited it from other parts of the world and as it emerges in Ireland has come out of a feminist project which described heterosexuality as a primary site of women's oppression and sought to dismantle heterosexism. Lesbian studies has from the beginning been anti-heteronormative, critiquing the ways in which heterosexuality has been instituted as the compulsory norm, heterosexual privilege rewarded and sexual deviance punished: in this sense lesbian studies has always been queer. Like feminism, lesbian studies has always had a twin project – a combination of what might be termed a modernist quest for equality with a deconstructive project of dismantling (or at least disturbing) what Peggy McIntosh terms the 'unearned advantage' of privilege ('White Privilege', p. 264). Many of the key thinkers in the field (most notably perhaps, Judith Butler) understand themselves to be engaged also with feminism. Thinking lesbian and queer *within* feminist analysis alerts us to that dynamic of privilege and oppression which feminism can critique so well, but it is just as vital that lesbian and queer analysis think *against* feminist terms of reference – one of these tasks being the 'revelation of how heterosexual presumption structures some of the founding scenes of feminist inquiry' (Butler, 'Against Proper Objects', p. 24).

Given that I locate (my) lesbian and queer analysis within feminism, one of the effects of reading Irish literature through the lens of lesbian or queer studies is the necessary interrogation of feminist readings of texts. Gayle Rubin's 1983 article 'Thinking Sex: Notes for a Radical Theory of the Politics of Sexuality' is seen by the editors of *The Lesbian & Gay Studies Reader* (Henry Abelove, Michèle Aina Barale and David M. Halperin) as a foundational text in lesbian and gay studies in that it makes a constitutive break with feminism. In that article Rubin argued that feminism does not and cannot provide by itself a full explanation for the oppression of sexual minorities. However, the crucial point is that the feminism that Rubin was critiquing was the feminism then in ascendancy in America: that is, the feminist anti-porn movement with arguments characterized by Catharine MacKinnon, who saw sexual relations as being structured by relations of coerced subordination, where the social meaning of being a 'man' was constituted as being a sexual dominator, and the condition of coerced sexual subordination constituted the social meaning of being a 'woman.' Rubin's focus on oppression based on sexual conduct or illicit desire that was distinct from gender oppression sought not only to establish sexuality as a 'vector of persecution' ('"Sexual Traffic" Interview', p. 97); she succeeded in mapping the way for a generation of feminist scholars who wanted to shift the hetero-centric (if not heterosexist) perspectives of feminism and interrogate productively arguments which saw gender role as necessarily determining sexuality: femininity and females locked into a submissive relationship to masculinity and males.

Applying the insights of lesbian and queer theory approach to a reading of Kate O'Brien's third novel *Mary Lavelle* (1936) allows us not only to see a rich and intriguing text but also by contrasting a queer reading to feminist readings of *Mary Lavelle*, we can see how a queer reading can both develop and challenge a feminist approach to the text. The plot of this novel is relatively straightforward: the housebound and naïve Mary Lavelle leaves Mellick and her fiancé, John, to be a governess with the Areavaga family in Northern Spain. She falls in love with Spain and eventually has a brief affair with Juanito, the married son of her employers. Mary decides to return to Ireland to break with John and begin a more independent life. It is at the juncture where it is claimed that the depiction of female heterosexuality in the novels of Kate O'Brien is characterized as a sado-masochistic sexuality (in the manner of Catharine MacKinnon and Andrea Dworkin) that I wish to intervene to begin a queer reading of *Mary Lavelle*. Patricia Coughlan, in 'Kate O'Brien: Feminine Beauty, Feminist Writing and Sexual Role', argues that in her fiction in general, and in *Mary Lavelle* in particular, O'Brien appropriates 'the masculinist construction of women as aesthetic objects' (p. 75), that her depiction of heterosexual feminine beauty and sexual role inscribes 'domination-and-submission' (p. 68) and 'scopic, possessive, sado-masochistic sexualities' (p. 74). In addition to the essay by Patricia Coughlan, the matter of love between women in the novels of Kate O'Brien has received the attention of scholars such as Lorna Reynolds, Adele M. Dalsimer, Ailbhe Smyth, Anne Fogarty, Tina O'Toole, Emma Donoghue, Gerardine Meaney and Aintzane Legarreta-Mentxaha, and indeed we might consider O'Brien and Irish lesbian studies fortunate to have attracted such luminary critics. However, it is Coughlan alone who finds problematic the 'fetishistic and voyeur tendencies in the texts' description of women' (p. 73); she sees this 'tendency' as stemming from patriarchal misogyny, and she wonders how a lesbian author such as O'Brien could perpetuate such a discourse:

> Why does a woman novelist, and at that a writer of well-attested lesbian orientation in her own life – and therefore someone whom one might have expected to see women as active or desiring subjects on their own account – perpetuate the representation of women in this objectified way? (62)

Coughlan proposes:

> . . . that there is a moment of radical potential in 'sexual dissidence,' in which marginalised people can by virtue of their marginality gain insights probably obscured (maybe mercifully so) from the 'normal' masses. This would be a kind of compensatory privilege, helping to make bearable the subordination and concealment of the marginal state. (p. 78)

The suggestion that what makes being a lesbian 'bearable' is an outsider's insight into heterosexuality (an insight so grim that it is merciful that the normal heterosexuals are spared this view) is quite startling but Coughlan argues that even this 'compensatory privilege' is not evident in the work of the lesbian O'Brien. She insists that O'Brien's depiction of women's sexuality remains problematic: 'the feminine and sexual representations, the eroticism of the domination-and-submission, subject-and-object pattern is only occasionally and imperfectly shed in O'Brien's fictional thought' (p. 79).

Coughlan provides few references to support her assertion of 'scopic, possessive, sado-masochistic sexualities' and those quotations that she does provide are not compelling. For instance she offers Dr Curran's appreciation of Agnes Mulqueen in *The Ante-Room* as an example of the domineering male gaze: he admires the 'long, narrow lines of her body, the girlish thinness of her arms, the sweet young breast, the soft dark fall of hair, her profile, saved from perfection by too much length of bone' (*The Ante-Room*, p. 66). Dr Curran's gaze might be characterized in a number of ways, but admiring long bones is not the stereotypical scopic, possessive, masculinist view of feminine beauty that Coughlan claims. She builds her argument with reference more to a particular strand of early 1980s American feminism than to the novels. This is made clear in her declaration that 'employing the language of our own contemporary feminist critique of representations, we would say that the scopic representation of women as objects of the male gaze is very prevalent in O'Brien' ('Kate O'Brien', p. 61).

The point could be made and copiously demonstrated that O'Brien does not in general represent female heterosexuals as masculinist constructs, sexist love objects and masochists and the depiction of Mary Lavelle's beauty is not the caricature of feminine beauty that Coughlan proposes it to be. Like Agnes Mulqueen and O'Brien's other heroines, Mary is described as tall and thin and her stunning physical beauty is frequently described as boyish and androgynous. Her androgyny is praised by the voice of the omniscient narrator and by other characters, including men who fancy her, such as the father of the girls she is tutoring, Don Pablo, and his son, Juanito. Don Pablo describes her thus: 'Her hair, of goldish brown, was curly and clung to her head like a Greek boy's. Her blue eyes, boyish too, androgynous, were wide and shy . . . Her carriage of head, neck and breast most virginal and pagan' (*Mary Lavelle*, p. 67). Juanito sees her as: 'A slender girl, in tennis shoes and cotton dress, a girl with lightly curled short locks, with slender neck and sweetly springing virgin breasts; Greek headed, with grave features and white skin' (p. 146). He admires her 'slender body . . . Those features came unflawed – oh, impossible marvel! – from Greece's most exacting and fastidious time' (p. 167). Just before Mary takes it upon herself to kiss Juanito she is described thus: 'Her short, unsettled curls stirred softly. The dark blue, careless clothes and composed, braced attitude of meditation gave her for the moment the non-voluptuous, introverted air of a boy' (p. 248).

Besides the fact that Juanito and his father find Mary's boyishness sexually attractive, the accent on describing Mary Lavelle as a classical Greek boy has, of course, a queer valence: during the trials of Oscar Wilde, which ultimately led him to Reading Gaol, Wilde argued that the line penned by his lover, Lord Alfred Douglas – the 'Love that dares not speak its name' – referred to the sexual love between men appreciated by the classical Greeks (Richard Ellmann, *Oscar Wilde*, p. 435). Wilde was released from gaol in 1897, the year that O'Brien was born, and it was also in the 1890s that an unprecedented find of Sappho's poetry recorded on papyrus was made available to scholars and to a wider public through translation. This discovery was inspirational for many modernists but particularly for a generation of lesbian writers who found in Sappho of Lesbos not only a literary model but also a role model for the creation of lesbian society (Shari Benstock, *Women of the Left Bank*; Ruth Vanita, *Sappho and the Virgin Mary*). 'Greek love' was a phrase still current in 1936, when *Mary Lavelle* was published, to allude to male and female homosexuality – a euphemistic but positive term.

In distinction to Coughlan, I see the physical description of Mary's beauty as boyish, androgynous and 'Greek' to be a description in counterpoint (to take up Smyth's suggestive analysis) to the usual and normative descriptions of heterosexual feminine voluptuous beauty.[1] Mary Lavelle is beautiful, yes, but her beauty is decidedly queer, and nowhere is this more evident than in those pages where Mary first meets Juanito's wife, Luisa, passages that Coughlan dismisses as 'some of the novel's sillier passages' ('Kate O'Brien', p. 68).

But Greek, however unsuspecting and untried, usually knows Greek.

A reading attentive to the lesbian and queer erotics of *Mary Lavelle* will focus on the meeting between Mary and Luisa (the wife of Juanito, Mary's lover-to-be) as the central emotional encounter of the novel: '[Luisa's] eyes were green-gold and her skin had a gold bloom on its pallor . . . She was dramatic and enchanting to behold, so happily did she harmonize mondaine with eternal beauty' (p. 150). The golden Luisa of *Mary Lavelle* uncannily prefigures another Castilian Luisa, the brilliant and beautiful mezzo-soprano who is the lover of the Ballykerin girl, Clare Halvey, in O'Brien's last book *As Music and Splendour* (1958):[2]

> Had Luisa become more beautiful, or had she not remembered her exactly? She was thinner surely – and her skin had grown more gold; so had the gold-brown hair. Her eyes were the remembered green-gold, however, and shone when Clare's met them with sharp remembered sweetness. She has the sun all through her, Clare thought; she is sun-drenched, and if I touched her she would be warm like an apricot in the sun. (p. 242)

Mary Lavelle is astonished and excited on seeing Luisa:

> The untutored girl from Ireland saw in one glance the flawless outward glory of such extravagant endowment, but she felt too with a thrill of simple admiration its mighty inner power.
>   'How brave of him to marry her,' was her first clear thought. (*Mary Lavelle*, p. 150)

O'Brien describes that Mary's next thoughts go to her fiancé, John, who was waiting for her in Ireland, and his 'fantastic faith' in her physical beauty; she regarded his passion as a 'tender joke – no more. Nothing in her trembled to his sweet illusion, though lately she was faintly and uneasily aware that some nerve in her waited to be thus disturbed' (p. 151). It is in meeting the glorious

Luisa that her waiting nerve gets delightedly disturbed, and again she identifies herself as boyish and regards Juanito as audacious in proposing himself as a spouse to Luisa, for 'he seemed simple to her, boyish, young and untidy, a human being like her brothers and herself' (p. 152).

Luisa and Mary are described as opposites: Mary is 'startled at meeting a creature so unusual as almost to seem a different species' (p. 150). Luisa is fair, urban and sophisticated while Mary is dark, provincial and naive, but O'Brien describes the couple as sharing a profound affinity, a likeness that Mary recognizes as essential to herself, a reverberation that is described as 'Greek':

> [Luisa's] grooming, dress and manner were of a simplicity so perfect that they should have deceived as naïve a person as Mary, and had she not been by accident herself of formidable beauty, perhaps she would at first have missed the true ring of steel. But Greek, however unsuspecting and untried, usually knows Greek. (p. 151)

This odd, awkward phrase again prefigures one of O'Brien's most famous passages in her last book, As Music and Splendour. The Irishwoman, Clare, and her Spanish lover, Luisa, are singing the title roles in Gluck's opera Orphée et Eurydice:

> The music they both loved had carried them far tonight, together and above themselves. Their descent was slow and reluctant, and their hands did not fall apart when they paused in Clare's doorway.
> Still Orpheus and Eurydice, their brilliantly made-up eyes swept for each the other's face, as if to insist that this disguise of myth in which they stood was their mutual reality, their one true dress wherein they recognized each other, and were free of that full recognition and could sing it as if their very singing was a kind of Greek, immortal light, not singing at all. (p. 113)

For a number of pages at the heart of Mary Lavelle it appears that the central love affair is to be between Mary and Luisa: their meeting is dramatic, intense and immediately intimate. They sit together on a window seat and talk about Irish and Spanish politics, Luisa well informed and opinionated, Mary hesitant. Then they listen to flamenco music, the singer's voice 'superbly held against the passionate, low urge of the guitar. Then the zigzag, savage singing and the coaxing, sudden "Olé". Music that tore the air and seemed to burn it.' Mary confesses that she prefers the flamenco to traditional Irish music because 'it is so much more crazy'. Luisa looks at her thoughtfully. '"How beautifully you speak," she said after a pause' (p. 153). Mary becomes restless and fidgety after her conversation with Luisa: '. . . there was a sense that eyes were on her, and a restless inclination to use her own, to look about and fidget. It must be that grand and lovely creature, Dona Luisa, induced so odd a nervousness – and yet, when over there on the window-seat she had not felt it quite so much' (p. 157). 'Odd' was a word regularly used throughout the twentieth century as a code for lesbian (Lillian Faderman, Odd Girls and Twilight Lovers, p. 6; Terry

Castle, *The Apparitional Lesbian*, pp. 9–10). Mary worries about this odd nervousness and why she did not feel odd until after she had spoken with Luisa. She tells herself that she was 'under the spell of the other woman's good manners. She talked so well and simply that at close range she made one forget oneself and one's deficiencies, no doubt' (*Mary Lavelle*, p. 157). Then comes one of the most curious passages in the book:

> She looked across at Luisa now. The beautiful creature, bending forward, was whispering some joke to Doña Consuelo, and Mary, looking at her steadily, realized with a sinking heart – she could not imagine why – that her fear, her excitement did not come from there. And yet, what was new and alive in the atmosphere? As for this brother, he was so clearly the brother of the house, the son, so naturally one of them, and so boyish with his sweets and his wireless. Ah, God, what could there be to alarm her there? (p. 157)

Mary's heart sinks '– she could not imagine why – '; is it that she cannot imagine why her heart sinks at the notion that it is *not* Luisa who excites her, or that she cannot imagine *why* it is not Luisa who thrills her? In either sense, her sinking heart houses queer desires, perhaps the queer desires of the author who does not get to write the fulfillment of this scenario for another twenty-two years. This passage signals the start of the transfer of Mary's excited emotions from the 'beautiful creature' Luisa to her boyish husband, Juanito, a transfer that never quite rings true. Luisa leaves the house after just two nights, her last cryptic words to the childish Juanito noting how curious is it that the two most attractive rooms in the house are the schoolroom and the room they gave to Mary (p. 171).

In the film version of *Mary Lavelle*, entitled *Talk of Angels* (dir. Nick Hamm), the encounter between Luisa and Mary was radically redrawn. Luisa is characterized as a cold, haughty wife who sneers at Mary, but there is still not enough between Juanito and Mary to make their love affair a gripping romance, even with Vincent Perez and Polly Walker playing the roles. Online reviewers of the straight-to-video production bemoan the lack of chemistry between the pair.[3] The scene-stealers are Ruth McCabe as O'Toole, a fellow governess or 'Miss', and Oscar-winner Frances McDormand as another 'Miss', the lesbian Agatha Conlan. The film cannot leave behind the book's regard for Conlan's passion for Mary nor the focus on the colony of governesses, 'the Misses', which inspire some of the best passages in the book, their sexuality brilliantly depicted as being both simultaneously frustrated and excited by religious, national and class concerns (pp. 80–2, 92–4). Such warm concerns do not readily facilitate the straightforward narrative of heterosexual romance.

Indeed the novel's depiction of Mary Lavelle's transition from a stereotypical Irish governess, naive and dutiful, to adulterous lover of Juanito does not follow any of the conventional routes of straight romance. The odd nervousness felt by Mary after her conversation with Luisa is only one of a number of moments in Mary's winding path. As Adele M. Dalsimer points out in her ground-breaking study, it is in the transferring of affections from Ireland to Spain that Mary's sexual awakening begins (*Kate O'Brien*, pp. 35–6) and one of the foremost influences in Mary's falling in love with Spain is her astonishing 14-year-old charge, Milagros. Dalsimer writes: 'Mary's affection for Milagros functions in the novel as a symbol of the effect that Spain will have on her and as a measure of her alienation from her past' (p. 39). According to Dalsimer, this 'fourteen-year-old philosopher is one of Kate O'Brien's most unrealistic characters' (p. 38). In the eyes of Mary Lavelle, Milagros can do no wrong, and Mary thinks about how 'brainless and immature' she must appear to 'this grave, eloquent and comic child' (*Mary Lavelle*, p. 135). The lack of reality noted by Dalsimer lies in the fact that Milagros is wise, witty and charming, not only beyond the bounds of the capabilities of the average 14-year-old. She is wise, witty and charming to the point of perfection and she is also decidedly queer: questioning everything; resisting the norms of what might be expected of an upper-middle-class Spanish girl. Discussing her expected fate as a debutante, Milagros muses that perhaps she would not enter the marriage market, or perhaps she might be a nun (p. 15). Her mother, Doña Consuelo wonders what sort of husband they could find for 'the queer child' (p. 43), and her father, Don Pablo, finds himself 'wary with this child for he found her penetratively intelligent beyond her years' (p. 64). Joking that it was perhaps Milagros instead of Juanito who would become 'one of Spain's great men', the child responded delightedly that 'there's room for more than one' (p. 64).

Milagros's sister, Nieves, is a year older and is for the most part a shadowy figure in the book, but she echoes Milagros's queer relationship to her gender: 'Her chief day-dream was that she was an English boy at Eton. A Catholic, naturally, but at Eton' (p. 16). Remarkably, the only issue that Nieves must have resolved before she can attend Eton is religion rather than the more insurmountable one of gender. Milagros has a 'coltish awkwardness' (p. 17) and general disdain for the prescribed female gender role, which adds rather than detracts from her allure to the inexperienced Mary, who finds Milagros an 'astonishing child . . . [who] liked to examine every phenomenon that came her way, no matter how much might seem to others to threaten faith or morals' (pp. 129–30).

Milagros functions as more than a measure of how far Mary wanders from her Irish heritage, and the child's classroom recitation for Juanito and Mary of the sixteenth-century English poem 'Come live with me and be my love' is the event that suddenly sparks the love between Juanito and Mary (p. 179).[4] Mary admires and loves Milagros utterly, she is captivated by her lectures on Spanish literature, painting, music, philosophy and bull-fighting, and it is through Milagros that Mary begins to understand and fall in love with Spain. Milagros' insightful, personal and witty lectures sound distinctly like the warm, ironic voice of O'Brien herself in the intimate travelogue, *Farewell Spain,* which she published a year after *Mary Lavelle*, which O'Brien described as 'almost autobiographical' (José María de Areilza, 'Kate O'Brien', p. 38). It is in the travelogue (particularly the chapter 'Mainly Personal', which revisits when and where she herself was a 'Miss') that we get an insight into O'Brien's view of Spain that illuminates the passions of *Mary Lavelle:*

> Fatal attraction between persons is an old poets' notion that some of us still believe is possible and occasional, though not probable – and Spain seems to me to be the *femme fatale* among countries. Though many claim that for lovely France. For me, however, it has been Spain. So true is this that I have hardly seen any other countries. Always I go back over the Pyrenees. My love has been long and slow – lazy and selfish too, but I know that wherever I go henceforward and whatever I see I shall never again be able to love an earthly scene as I have loved the Spanish. Except some bits of Ireland, bits of home. But that is different. Though Ireland is as beautiful as any country on earth, I am native to her, and therefore cannot feel the novel thrill of her attraction. One does not mix up the love one feels for a parent with the infatuations of adult life. And with Spain I am once and for all infatuated. With curious fidelity – for I am fickle. (*Farewell Spain*, p. 227)

By loving Milagros and loving Spain, Mary moves further from her dutiful obedience to her fiancé and it is in her attendance at the bullfight, despite John's warnings, that Mary is completely overcome in her last resistance to the charms of Spain. (The fact that sexual awakening occurs outside Ireland is perhaps a theme worth exploring in the work of other Irish writers.) The tumult of feelings stirred in Mary by the bullfight is analogous to the emotions experienced in sexual transgression. The chapter entitled 'A Corrida' ('At the Bullfight') opens with a startling passage:

> She had never felt so much ashamed of herself as she was feeling now. She was acutely frightened too and her confused emotional state was inducing physical misery. . . . 'Oh God!' she prayed, 'Oh God, forgive me, please!' (*Mary Lavelle*, p. 102)

The language of sexual temptation is continued throughout the chapter: 'This liking [of Spanish people] was one reason why she sat at a bullfight, in a condition of shame and terror' (p. 105). The actual killing of the bull is depicted as explicitly (homo)erotic: 'The matador [Pronceda] drew his enemy to his breast, and past it, on the gentle lure; brought him back along his thigh as if for sheer love; let him go and drew him home again' (p. 114). When Mary's companion at the bullfight, the Irish Miss, Agatha Conlan, wonders why the Church doesn't make it a sin to go to the bullfight, Mary states that she thinks it is a sin (p. 119).

The passage in *Farewell Spain* where O'Brien describes her love for Spain as falling for a *femme fatale* has an analogy in *Mary Lavelle*, where Mary's falling in love with Spain is also described in sexual terms: 'But the wound of the bullfight was in fact – though she tried to ignore and forget it – the gateway through which Spain had entered in and taken her. She did not know how much an afternoon in the bullring had changed her' (p. 129). Spain, not only in O'Brien's lexicon, but also in general terms, is conventionally described as feminine. Spain, that *femme fatale*, 'entering and taking' Mary through her experience of the bullfight described in such masculine homoerotic terms is a queer relationship indeed.

This uniting of the bullfight, love of Spain and Spanish art, and sexual passion has its ultimate dénouement in the sex between Mary and Juanito, but the weight of these analogies is too much to bear and the crude links between the bullfight and a sex act that is physically painful for Mary make for passages that border on the ridiculous. Mary is the instigator of the kisses, embraces and sex, she contemplates 'taking' Juanito (pp. 248, 258, 306–7) but for the climactic scenes O'Brien makes a clumsy attempt to reinsert Juanito as the partner in control:

> He took her quickly and bravely. The pain made her cry out and writhe in shock, but he held her hard against him and in great love compelled her to endure it. He felt the sweat of pain break over all the silk of her body . . . saw her set teeth and quivering nostril, beating eyelids, flowing, flowing tears. (308–9)

This passage continues with the lines: 'The curls were clammy on her forehead now, as on that day when she came into Luisa's drawing-room from the bullfight. She was no longer Aphrodite, but a broken, tortured Christian, a wounded Saint Sebastian' (p. 309). These lines make clear the links between the bullfight and loving Spain and loving Juanito, but while they ostensibly proclaim a robust conventional heterosexuality, they are among the queerest lines in the novel. Images of the pierced naked body of the young Saint Sebastian have a long queer genealogy, both as icon and fetish, in Christian Europe. (Oscar Wilde adopted the pseudonym Sebastian Melmoth on his release from prison.) But most surprising of all is how Luisa is recalled in the middle of the heterosexual scene. The recalled event of Mary's visit to Luisa's drawing-room in Madrid is the second and last time we see them together; Mary had been nervous at seeing Juanito again, but as before she becomes completely captivated by Luisa and feels quite at ease with Juanito. We hear again her refrain: 'How brave of him to marry such a miracle!' (p. 233). Luisa's haunting of Mary's (and O'Brien's) consciousness is not as the wife of Juanito but as a spectral vision of loveliness. Her role is reminiscent of that described by Terry Castle as the apparitional lesbian:

> Nowhere has the work of ghosting been carried on more intensely than in the realm of literature and popular fantasy. Western writing over the centuries is from one angle a kind of derealization machine: insert the lesbian and watch her disappear . . . the very frequency with which the lesbian has been 'apparition-alized' in the Western imagination also testifies to her peculiar cultural power.

> Only something very palpable – at a deeper level – has the capacity to 'haunt'
> us so thoroughly. (*The Apparitional Lesbian*, pp. 6–7)

The relationship of boyish Mary and Juanito is reminiscent of the homoerotic triangles described by Eve Kosofsky Sedgwick in *Between Men*, where men's desires for each other are bonded and contained through the bodies of women. Mary initially sees Juanito as no better than herself or her brothers and hence brave or lucky to marry Luisa. This rivalry or a common desire for Luisa brings them together in a sex scene reminiscent of the male homoerotics of the bullfight. This queer erotic triangle, where a man becomes the medium for the expression of lesbian desire, is explicitly stated in the last pages of *As Music and Splendour*:

> Clare looked diffidently towards Iago's face, and thought how perverse and
> strange it would be to kiss a mouth that Luisa had known and kissed – had
> kissed by habit and goodwill even when she was Clare's sworn lover. Would I
> find her there, the villain? Would I find any trace of you, Luisa, in so wrong a
> place? (p. 334)

'It's a very ancient and terrible vice'

O'Brien's wonderfully-realized lesbian character, Agatha Conlan, is probably one of the prime reasons why *Mary Lavelle* was banned in Ireland. Emma Donoghue gives a rich analysis of Agatha's role in her article '"Out of Order": Kate O'Brien's Lesbian Fictions'; she points to the significance of the fact that it is Agatha, 'whose passion for heroic, bloody Spain Mary finds so disturbing and attractive' (p. 43), and who takes Mary to her first bullfight (Milagros takes her to the second).[5] Donoghue elaborates on how 'Agatha has a key place in the moral web of *Mary Lavelle*' (p. 44) and how O'Brien's depiction of lesbian passion is remarkable for its honesty, complexity and sympathy, particularly given the literary and political contexts in which it was composed (pp. 44–8). On the one hand Agatha is described in terms that are conventional to the late-nineteenth- and early-twentieth-century depictions of lesbian. Like Beaudelaire's *Fleurs de mals,* she is a gaunt, spectral, vampirish, 'hungry' and 'starved' being the adjectives of choice, (*Mary Lavelle*, pp. 85, 117, 200, 210, 343). But there are some significant moments where this conventional description is undercut and her love for Mary is treated ultimately with great sensitivity.

A cacophony of Misses' voices herald Agatha's first appearance: she is described for Mary as the: 'worst-tempered woman in Spain . . . She's just not like the rest of us . . . One of her sort is quite enough.' Mary replies: 'She sounds queer.' O'Toole announces, 'Talk of angels – !' and Agatha enters the novel (p. 84). She is described as 'a very hungry-looking woman . . . She had a pale, fanatical face, nobly planned but faltering below the large eccentric nose to a too mobile, too bitter mouth. "What beautiful eyes!" Mary thought' (p. 85).

In this remarkable passage, Mary's voice is a counterpoint to the omniscient voice of the narrator who is describing the novel's lesbian in the canonical Gothic mode as an evil vampire, a 'stinking lily', while Mary sees a woman with beautiful eyes, full of light. Mary's observation might be read as innocent and naive but it also succeeds in unsettling the generic depiction. At the bullfight, there is another moment where Agatha is described through Mary's eyes as beautiful *and* queer: 'Mary looked at Conlan. Her blue eyes were shining . . . "You might take her for a boy just now," Mary thought' (p. 117). O'Brien gives her own, rather more personal signals to highlight Agatha's lesbianism. O'Brien was fascinated with the passionate Carmelite Teresa of Avila, who struggled with her lesbian desires, and Agatha prays in a Carmelite convent. 'Only a few old women go to the Carmelites, and then there are just the nuns behind the grill. You can pray in a place like that' (p. 200).[6] A further register is Agatha's love of Castile. It is her proposal that she and Mary go on a holiday to Avila (p. 283) that precipitates her declaration of love for Mary and her new-found knowledge that according to her confessor her passion is a 'very ancient and terrible vice' (p. 285).

Coughlan claims that 'Conlan is left in blank, isolated misery, O'Brien herself remaining true to her vision in giving no hint of a possible moral rehabilitation of Conlan in her own eyes' ('Kate O'Brien', p. 76). However, I follow Dalsimer and Donoghue in seeing Agatha's coming out as lesbian as a positive experience both for the character and reader. Mary and Agatha become closer, 'not so much because Agatha fantastically and perversely loved *her* but because, like her, she was fantastically and perversely in love' (*Mary Lavelle*, p. 296). O'Brien makes the queer argument (an argument that she is to articulate again in *As Music and Splendour*) that Mary's adulterous love and Agatha's lesbian love are similar and equivalent. She has Mary watching the swinging of the church door as people go in to pray incessantly: 'Agatha did so often, as she did, as Juanito too, perhaps, seeking strength against the perversions of their hearts and escape from fantastic longings' (p. 285).

Moreover, Mary's contemplation on the people praying in San Geronimo imagines herself, Agatha and Juanito '[s]eeking mercy, explanation and forgiveness because they are so vicious as to love each other . . . Oh, Lord have pity! Help us to have pity on each other, to make some sense sometime out of this tangle of our longings!' (pp. 285–6). As Donoghue puts it, O'Brien argues lyrically for 'divine help with the human project of mutual mercy' ('"Out of Order"', p. 46). Agatha's intelligence, self-awareness, her appreciation of the bullfight, her honesty, integrity and loyalty, even her brittle sarcasm, mark her as an attractive character, certainly compared with the rest of the colony of 'Misses'.

'This threat in his breast'

A feminist psychoanalytic reading of *Mary Lavelle* was undertaken in 1990 by Rose Quiello, whose formulation of Mary Lavelle as an 'hysteric' points the way to understanding Mary as 'queer' although ultimately the article is more revealing about feminist psychoanalysis than it is about the novel. Another feminist psychoanalytic article written before the full flowering of queer theory is Anne Fogarty's insightful article, '"The Business of Attachment": Romance and Desire in the Novels of Kate O'Brien', in which she states that in relation to the chief protagonists of O'Brien's novels '[t]he plot of desire never releases them from the story of family romance' (p. 104). Fogarty claims that Mary reinstates a Freudian family romance in the Spanish household:

> [T]he forceful and sexually aggressive Juanito provides a counterweight to her feeble and asexual Irish lover. Moreover, the death of Don Pablo who passes away while Mary makes love to Juanito may be constructed as a revenge fantasy . . . . Even the benign patriarch, Don Pablo, must be jettisoned to make way for her new-found passion. (p. 112)

However, Juanito/little John is not the forceful character that Fogarty depicts: he is described and depicted as 'boyish' to the point of tedium; certainly compared to the 'brown, lively forthright handsomeness of John' in Mellick with his pipe and dog and talk of shaking Mary (*Mary Lavelle*, p. 103), Juanito is 'little John' indeed. The Areavaga family is also not quite the Freudian model that Fogarty proposes. There is only one person in the household who might be described as conventionally heterosexual and that is Pilár, whose delighted anticipation of her 'coming out' onto the marriage market is roundly mocked in the novel. Pilár's two sisters like to think of themselves as boys or potential men; her parents have been celibate for over fourteen years; her father is feminized; her mother has never known sexual passion; her brother is childlike and her music teacher, Don Jorge, a priest, is a lecherous, molesting, vindictive creep.

A straight Freudian paradigm would insist that 'the benign patriarch, Don Pablo, must be jettisoned' to make way for Mary's passion, but the triangle that is formed by Don Pablo, Mary and Juanito does not fit the straight Freudian paradigm or the conventional anthropological triangle of compulsory heterosexuality where the woman is the basis for exchange between men.[7] Mary often remarks on Juanito's resemblance to his father (pp. 176, 331) but Juanito, the child, and his gentle, sick, sad father are not the epitome of the patriarch. It is the gentle, defeated and childlike natures of both men that Mary finds attractive: in the classroom, before Milagros makes her fateful poetic recitation, Mary notices that Juanito's eyes 'were upon her, and half-closed, more grave than she had ever seen them, grave and unhappy as his father's. There was something helpless in his look . . . "He's very young," she thought wearily' (p. 180). The first physical encounter between Mary and Juanito ends not in sex but in tears, they cry together: 'quiet and miserable as children . . . It was one kind of consummation' (p. 256). Don Pablo, too, tends to think of Mary and Juanito as his children: after her first bullfight Don Pablo is startled by Mary's 'childish searching, and was reminded oddly of his son, Juanito' (p. 120). 'These two whom he loved were the victims [of love] now. These two, his darlings' (p. 320).

The Freudian family romance is in motion to a certain extent when Don Pablo learns of the love between the two and understands Juanito to be his surrogate: 'She would be his since Juanito, so much loved and understood of him, was not only his flesh but spiritually him enhanced, corrected' (p. 321). Don Pablo has 'angina pectoris, seizures of which are induced by great emotional or physical excitement' (p. 337). He finds an incriminating souvenir postcard from Juanito to Mary, which he put in his breast pocket. The vile Don Jorge confirms his apprehensions and he begins to suffer from the heart attack that will kill him, his 'anticlimax' occurring as Mary and Juanito have a sexual 'climax' (p. 339):

> Did he grudge her to Juanito? And Juanito to her? . . . . Was he jealous and going crazy? . . . . He was ill and much agitated, afraid of death and pain, afraid of life and over-indulgent of sick fantasies. . . . . This threat in his breast – all his folly came from that. (p. 322)

So to a certain extent the romance in a blatant if not clumsy way fits the Freudian model: 'Within one little hour, when he was at his most sick and inadequate, a whole undreamt-of story of his son's love, loss and woe were flung at him, in three quick jerks' (p. 326). However, I cannot subscribe to Fogarty's tenet that '[t]he plot of desire never releases them from the story of family romance' ('"The Business of Attachment"', p. 104). In the case of *Mary Lavelle*, I would argue that it is the plot of desires that queers the family romance. Nowhere is this more evident than in Mary and Juanito's shared understanding that Don Pablo would have been on their side (pp. 327, 339–40): 'He would actually have understood . . . He could have forgiven the unforgivable' (p. 339). His death is a blow to their chances of being together: '"Hasta luego," [Juanito] said and broke into childish sobbing. Mary hurried away and left him to his [dead] father' (p. 342). Don Pablo, Juanito and Mary form a very queer triangle indeed even aside from the triangles of Agatha, Juanito and Mary; Milagros, Mary and Juanito; and, of course, Juanito, Mary and Luisa.

Lesbian studies, queer theory and Irish feminist literary studies: 'When . . . all the world seems bright and gay'

A lesbian and queer theory analysis of Irish literature is an analysis that I find works well in my teaching of women's studies. This approach is useful in terms of illustrating feminist theory: the students are able to put behind them that tired binary of essentialism/constructionism, to paraphrase Valerie Traub (*The Renaissance of Lesbianism*, p. 357), and to experience how concerns of identity politics (be it feminist and/or lesbian) can be addressed through postmodern readings. Many students find the lesbian and queer theory engagement with the heterosexual presumptions of psychoanalysis to be a helpful introduction to the field.

Approaching Irish literature through the lens of queer theory and lesbian studies has proved to be a wonderful introduction to reading literature for those who have no background in literary studies. Students quickly appreciate that contexts determine meaning, and they see that their readings are greatly enriched by information on the historical contexts in which the text was produced (be it social, political, biographical, cultural, economic, religious or legal). Reading from the perspective of queer theory demands all the literary skills involved in close reading, and as someone who has probably wandered too far away from the boundaries of an English department to ever find her way back, it is a thrill to teach those skills and see that students find reading literature to be frankly enjoyable. I have a suspicion that many of us trained in literary studies feel slightly embarrassed about the fact that we earn our money reading and talking about stories and poetry. Our discipline is relatively new and seems never to have established a coherent alibi; why else do we wander off in such great numbers into interdisciplinary territories demarcated by region or era or under such grand banners as 'women' or 'culture' or 'postcolonial'? Teaching lesbian and queer analysis of Irish literature in a women's studies department provides me with a range of grand political alibis, but, perhaps perversely, my experience of this teaching affirms my inarticulate but profound hunch that the enjoyment of reading stories and poetry and conversations on that reading can provide some of life's best educational experiences.

A queer reading, such as the reading above of *Mary Lavelle,* shows that, if readings are alert to the complex and myriad possibilities of same-sex and queer desire, our understanding and appreciation of certain texts can be enhanced. Gender and sexuality can be seen to be distinct though related performances and, perhaps more importantly, this lens of lesbian studies and queer theory can enable us to understand how – when it comes to gender and sexuality – knowledges and silences in their many guises (disavowal, science, secrets, code, religion, aphasia, law, lies, amnesia, etc.) work to structure and regulate our interior psyches and social relationships. Irish national identity (worldwide) and Irish social institutions are structured and maintained through profound homophobia. The anxious defence of heterosexuality as the cherished, protected and enforced norm damages us all, and reading *Mary Lavelle*, we are reminded that an unwitting acceptance of heterosexuality and heterosexism as the unmarked norm can inhibit, at the very least, our pleasure in the text. It's a truism among academic feminists that if we are not working in response to or with a wider feminist movement for social change, our work is at best irrelevant, or at worst part of the problem for the feminist movement. Of course, this makes our work both exhilarating and impossible to fully accomplish as there are so many issues that affect women that must be addressed: classism, racism and ableism, to name a few. But as I am committed to working for a non-homophobic society, I hope this academic analysis and pedagogy provides at least a small measure of information, support and ideas for all those working for this change.

*   *   *   *   *

Kate O'Brien: Biographical and critical contexts

Kate O'Brien was born in 1897 into an upper-middle-class Catholic family in Limerick. Kate's mother died when she was five, and as she was the youngest girl, she was sent to join her sisters in boarding school at Laurel Hill before she went to University College Dublin. After college, O'Brien worked for the foreign page of the *Manchester Guardian* newspaper. Taking up a bet, O'Brien wrote a play in under a month, and *The Distinguished Villa* was a critical and commercial success. Her first novel, *Without My Cloak* (1932) was awarded both the James Tait Black Memorial Prize and the Hawthornden Prize, and its sequel, *The Ante-Room* (1934) was also a bestseller. Over the course of three decades, living variously in Spain, Dublin, Connemara, London and Kent, she wrote nine novels, a travel book on Spain and one on Ireland, a short biography of Teresa of Avila, a memoir of her aunts who were Presentation nuns in Limerick and an occasional column for *The Irish Times*. She wrote book reviews for *The Spectator,* and was an excellent critic, one of the few who early recognized Beckett's genius. Her novels continued to be commercial and critical successes; in particular, her novel *That Lady* (1946) was an international hit. Two of her novels, however, *Mary Lavelle* (1936) and *The Land of Spices* (1941), were banned as obscene by the Irish Censorship Board.

O'Brien was one of the first writers to be 'rediscovered' by feminists: the feminist publishing press, Arlen House, instituted the 'Kate O'Brien Weekends' in Limerick in the 1980s, which continue to be held every February and which showcase academic and writers' reflections on her work. Her novels, out of print in the 1980s, began to be reprinted by Arlen House in Ireland and later Virago Press in England. The benchmark academic book on O'Brien's work remains Adele M. Dalsimer's *Kate O'Brien: A Critical Study* (1990), while a valuable collection of essays on her work can be found in *Ordinary People Dancing* (1993), edited by Eibhear Walshe. Her writings continue to be analysed, largely by feminists and very much within the context of Irish studies, as exemplified by Gerardine Meaney's 2005 essay on O'Brien in the collection entitled *The UCD Aesthetic*, edited by Anthony Roche. Eibhear Walshe's forthcoming biography of O'Brien promises to make more available other contexts for understanding her work, particularly the network in England of other Catholic lesbian authors of which she was part.

Works cited

Abelove, Henry, Michèle Aina Barale and David M. Halperin (eds.), *The Lesbian & Gay Studies Reader* (New York: Routledge, 1993).

Areilza, José María de, 'Kate O'Brien: A Personal and Literary Portrait', in John Logan (ed.), *With Warmest Love: Lectures for Kate O'Brien, 1984–1993* (Limerick: Mellick Press), pp. 33–42.

Benstock, Shari, *Women of the Left Bank, Paris, 1900–1940* (Austin: University of Texas Press, 1986).

Brown, Wendy, 'At the Edge', *Political Theory* 30:4 (2002), pp. 556–76.

Butler, Judith, 'Against Proper Objects', in Elizabeth Weed and Naomi Schor (eds.), *Feminism Meets Queer Theory* (Bloomington/Indianapolis: Indiana University Press, 1997), pp. 1–30.

Castle, Terry, *The Apparitional Lesbian: Female Homosexuality and Modern Culture* (New York: Columbia University Press, 1993).

Coughlan, Patricia, 'Kate O'Brien: Feminine Beauty, Feminist Writing and Sexual Role', in Eibhear Walshe (ed.), *Ordinary People Dancing: Essays on Kate O'Brien* (Cork University Press, 1993), pp. 59–84.

Dalsimer, Adele M., *Kate O'Brien: A Critical Study* (Dublin: Gill & Macmillan; Boston: Twayne Publishers, 1990).

Donoghue, Emma, '"Out of Order": Kate O'Brien's Lesbian Fictions', in Eibhear Walshe (ed.), *Ordinary People Dancing: Essays on Kate O'Brien* (Cork University Press, 1993), pp. 36–58.

Doty, Alexander, *Making Things Perfectly Queer: Interpreting Mass Culture* (Minneapolis: University of Minnesota Press, 1993).

Ellmann, Richard, *Oscar Wilde* (Harmondsworth: Penguin, 1987).

Faderman, Lillian, *Odd Girls and Twilight Lovers: A History of Lesbian Life in Twentieth-Century America* (New York: Columbia University Press, 1991).

Fogarty, Anne, '"The Business of Attachment": Romance and Desire in the Novels of Kate O'Brien', in Eibhear Walshe (ed.), *Ordinary People Dancing: Essays on Kate O'Brien* (Cork University Press, 1993), pp. 101–19.

Hamm, Nick (dir.), *Talk of Angels* (Buena Vista Home Video, 1998).

Lauretis, Teresa de, 'Queer Theory: Lesbian and Gay Sexualities: An Introduction', special issue, *Differences: A Journal of Feminist Cultural Studies* 3: 2 (1991), pp. iii–xviii.

——, 'Habit Changes–Response', in Elizabeth Weed and Naomi Schor (ed.), *Feminism Meets Queer Theory* (Bloomington/Indianapolis: Indiana University Press, 1997), pp. 315–33.

McIntosh, Peggy, 'White Privilege: Unpacking the Invisible Backpack', in Amy Kesselman, Lily D. McNair and Nancy Schniedewind (ed.), *Women: Images and Realities: A Multicultural Reader* (Mountain View, CA: Mayfield Publishing Co., 1995), pp. 264–7.

MacKinnon, Catharine, 'Marxism, Feminism, Method and the State: An Agenda for Theory', *Signs* 7.3 (1982), pp. 515–44.

——, 'Marxism, Feminism, Method and the State: Toward Feminist Jurisprudence', *Signs* 8.4 (1983), pp. 635–58.

Meaney, Gerardine, 'Kate O'Brien', in Anthony Roche (ed.), *The UCD Aesthetic: Celebrating 150 Years of UCD Writers* (Dublin: New Island, 2005).

O'Brien, Kate, *The Ante-Room* (London: Heinemann, 1934).

——, *Mary Lavelle* (London/Toronto: Heinemann, 1936).

——, *Farewell Spain,* illustrated with drawings by Mary O'Neill (London/Toronto: Heinemann, 1937).

——, *The Land of Spices* (London: Heinemann, 1941).

——, *Teresa of Avila* (New York: Sheed & Ward, 1951).

——, *As Music and Splendour* (London/Melbourne/Toronto: Heinemann, 1958).

Quiello, Rose, 'Disturbed Desires: The Hysteric in Mary Lavelle', *Éire-Ireland* 25.3 (1990), pp. 46–57.

Reynolds, Lorna, *Kate O'Brien: A Literary Portrait,* Irish Literary Studies No. 25 (Gerrards Cross, Bucks: Colin Smythe, 1987).

Rubin, Gayle, 'The Traffic in Women: Notes toward a Political Economy of Sex', in Rayna Reiter (ed.), *Toward an Anthropology of Women* (New York: Monthly Review Press, 1975).

——, 'Thinking Sex: Notes for a Radical Theory of the Politics of Sexuality', in Carole S Vance (ed.), *Pleasure and Danger: Exploring Female Sexuality* (London: Routledge, 1984), pp. 267–319.

Rubin, Gayle, with Judith Butler, '"Sexual Traffic" Interview', in Elizabeth Weed and Naomi Schor (ed.), *Feminism Meets Queer Theory* (Bloomington/Indianapolis: Indiana University Press, 1997), pp. 68–108.

Sedgwick, Eve Kosofsky, *Between Men: English Literature and Male Homosocial Desire* (New York: Columbia University Press, 1985).

Smyth, Ailbhe, 'Counterpoints: A Note (or Two) on Feminism and Kate O'Brien', in Eibhear Walshe (ed.), *Ordinary People Dancing: Essays on Kate O'Brien* (Cork University Press, 1993), pp. 24–35.

Traub, Valerie, *The Renaissance of Lesbianism in Early Modern England*, Cambridge Studies in Renaissance Literature and Culture, vol. 42 (Cambridge University Press, 2002).

Vanita, Ruth, *Sappho and the Virgin Mary: Same-Sex Love and the English Literary Imagination* (New York: Columbia University Press, 1996).

Walshe, Eibhear, *Ordinary People Dancing: Essays on Kate O'Brien* (Cork University Press, 1993).

Chapter 6

Feminist Meanings of Presence and Performance in Theatre

Marina Carr's *Portia Coughlan*

Cathy Leeney

Playwriting is the powerful business of putting words in people's mouths. Within the frame of performance on stage, the imaginings of the playwright become actions and conversations taking place in real time, before witnesses. In theatre, story becomes experience, at one remove for the performer and at a second remove for the audience. My argument has two stages: firstly, that certain performance aspects of theatre have the power to disrupt, overthrow and overwhelm narrative or story; secondly, that where women characters are concerned, this dynamic relationship between narrative and performance can create a space where representations of woman may escape the bonds of narrative and gain access to subjectivity outside narrative's limits. Thus, stories in which women are defeated, silenced, destroyed even, may, under certain performance conditions, impress upon an audience not defeat, silence or obliteration but thrilling, moving, exhilarating life.

In this twenty-first century, theatre in the western world still negotiates with the realist tradition. Established in Europe at the end of the nineteenth century, realist theatre asserts its power by proposing the stage as the mirror of life: one image, one truth. For women, or indeed for any oppressed category, this poses a problem. If the stage is a mirror, all that can appear on stage must reflect the limits and restraints suffered in life outside the theatre; if women are oppressed and demeaned as persons in life, women characters in realist theatre must reflect that oppression and humiliation.

The mirror function of realism appeals to its witnesses (the audience) as a recognizable version of their lived experience. But theatre is not only about reflecting a truth; it is also about transformative processes, about proposing possibilities, about rehearsing risky ventures, and about feeding and changing our reality through intellect, imagination and dream (Bert O. States, *Great Reckonings*).[1]

Representations on stage, in their power as a recognizable version of 'real life', may veer from being reflections to being confirmations of one version of the truth, excluding all others. Realist theatre is, arguably, deeply conservative in this way, asserting societal and cultural values as though they were eternal truths. My argument here is that realist theatre, in performance, need not always be so conservative. It may, especially in its contemporary form of neorealism, accommodate disturbing, transgressive and radical images which relate obliquely but powerfully to the real life of the witness. I will examine such possibilities in relation to a recent play by Marina Carr, *Portia Coughlan*, and look at issues including genre, use of stage space, and the tendons connecting character and language to expose how Carr disrupts the narrative of her heroine both structurally and performatively.

All texts are battlegrounds for meaning; as Catherine Belsey argues, a text 'constitutes a possible place from which to begin an analysis of what it means to be a person, a man or a woman, at a specific historical moment' (*The Subject of Tragedy*, p. 5). When the text is a play (and especially when it is a realist or neorealist play), this statement deepens in an exciting and challenging way. The text in performance becomes a double analysis, first by the performer, then by the audience; and these analyses involve the (re)creation of the person, the man or the woman in the double time of theatre: the fictional moment on stage and the actual moment of live performance. Theatre, then, is always already a battleground and a battle. Theatre texts are, *sui generis,* radically incomplete until performed. They exemplify issues of interpretation and contests for meaning which apply to all texts.

When it comes to feminist approaches to theatre, and to texts generally, a play's openness to interpretive fulfilment creates disturbance, and paradoxical insight. In the double time of theatre, the experience of the audience in the present moment of performance by live actors has the potential to disrupt the authority of narrative and its relation to history, and to disrupt the mirror function of realist representations as the inevitable reflection of eternal and unquestionable truths. Paradoxical insights may lie in the gap between the narrative fate of the character and the psychic, physical and emotional power of the performer representing that character in the play. In other words, the power of the narrative may be disrupted and overthrown by the actual embodied power of performance.

In the tradition of realist theatre, representations of women have been a crucial site where the conventions of realism's mirror function have been extended and challenged. Coinciding with the rise of women's suffrage movements in Europe, at the end of the nineteenth century, canonical realist plays such as Henrik Ibsen's *A Doll's House* (1879) and *Hedda Gabler* (1890) struggle to contain within their forms, their spaces and their dramatic conventions the energies and desires of their respective heroines, Nora and Hedda.

The sense in which dramatic characters may be imprisoned within dramatic narratives or forms, and may struggle to overcome them, is embodied in one of Ibsen's remarkable heroines. Hedda Gabler is a representation of subjectivity on stage which continues to fascinate performers and audiences. Yet to trace her progress through the play that bears her name is to see her lurch from petty snobbery to social cowardice, to malicious destructiveness and finally to a most unheroic suicide; hardly an attractive narrative path. At the end, the play itself seems not to have any room for her.[2] As Tesman and Mrs Elvsted require more space for their reanimation of Lovborg's manuscript, and Judge Brack outlines his cosy trap, Hedda retreats onto the stage within the stage, into the curtained chamber off the drawing room. When she shoots herself, she escapes not only from the story of her foolish marriage, her pregnancy and her guilty connection with Lovborg's death; she also escapes the play itself, and its realist structure which has imprisoned her. She has been at odds with the play from the start, and spends the entire second half trying to make it go her way, and failing. Hedda's glory lies not in the narrative of her nightmarishly squalid last days, cooped up in the chintzy den of her drawing room. No. It is her presence on stage, the monstrous power of her blind frustration, her twisted humour and desires that capture performers, audiences and readers. The opportunities offered by the part have made it one of the ambitions of every major female performer in the European theatrical tradition. Hedda Gabler is a site where we may excavate the strictures, both social and theatrical, of nineteenth-century bourgeois life, placed on women then, and still current now.

Portia Coughlan is a play of epic emotional tragedy, dominated by its anti-heroine, as Ibsen's play is. The story is set in a narrow, tribally parochial location and linguistic contour. It is about a 30-year-old Irish woman who finds her life as wife, mother, daughter and lover unbearable, and who is haunted by the ghost of her dead twin, Gabriel, drowned fifteen years earlier in the river which also (eventually) claims her life. Marina Carr wrote the play in 1995/6, a commission from the National Maternity Hospital in Dublin, an ironic connection, since Portia is one of the most unmaternal figures ever to take to the European, never mind the Irish stage, rivalling Hedda or even Medea.

Since 1996, and its first performance as part of the Abbey Theatre programme, *Portia Coughlan* has been played in the United Kingdom, in North America and in Continental Europe. The name part is a hugely attractive one for a performer; Portia dominates the play both physically (she is off stage only during the brief span of Act Two) and psychically. Her speech is a shattering expression of rage, frustrated love and idealism, and pure hatred. No other character in the play can understand her, although some do love her. Gabriel, the ghost who sings for her and the audience's ears exclusively, is the only one immune from her furious distress. As a character, she is spectacularly unsympathetic. She is placed in a recognizable, and indeed very specifically delineated, geographical and cultural location. Yet she is also a monster. The play, constructing a socially recognizable context, is haunted not only by the ghost of Gabriel, but also by the mythic connotations of the landscape in which it is set. It bears uneasily many realist characteristics, but bears them only to twist them, turn them inside out and throw them back into the face of the audience.

The feminist performer, critic, teacher or audience member often confronts powerful negative representations of the female and the womanly as weak, hysterical, self-hating, masochistic, inarticulate and defeated. If women in plays do appear as powerful or violent, they are likely to be abhorred as manipulative or immoral. More often, women on-stage are minor characters who are not allowed to say very much, and who are present only to serve the function of the play's narrative or structure. Inversely, women playwrights are sometimes burdened – by feminist critics and commentators – with the duty of positive representation of women's lives. The grim patriarchal landscape of mainstream theatre, as in fiction, film and other media, is dominated by male writers' images of the female and the womanly. It is understandable then, that where the author is female, contrasting images of women protagonists as heroic, admirable, inspired or inspiring might be proposed. But this is not the case in *Portia Coughlan*. Rather, Portia embodies the epitome of the unwomanly woman; she is self-absorbed, promiscuous, violent, foul-mouthed, unloving, self-destructive and perhaps worst of all, a bad housekeeper. As a representation of Irish womanhood in the 1990s she challenges audiences to examine their expectations of the feminine.

In a number of ways, Portia represents the acme of a psychoanalytic figuring of woman as lack, lacking the phallus, failing to qualify for entry into the symbolic order and hence failing to attain full individuation, independence and maturity. In her analysis of desire, Rachel Bowlby examines 'the implications for women of the forms of female desire constructed by patriarchy' and suggests that 'one of these is the representation of women as the victims of a limitless "longing or lacking"' (quoted in Catherine Belsey and Jane Moore, 'The Story So Far', p. 11). With Portia, the sense of separation, isolation and incompleteness that this implies is traced back to the moment of her birth. But it is not, significantly, separation from the mother, but from her male twin, Gabriel, that characterizes Portia's wound of longing: 'Times I close my eyes and I feel a rush of water around me and above we hear the thumpin' of me mother's heart, and we're atwined, his foot on my head, mine on his foetal arm, and we don't know which of us is the other and we don't want to [. . .] and all the world is Portia and Gabriel packed for ever in a tight hot womb' (*Portia Coughlan*, p. 254). Portia's despair at her incompleteness, and her narcissistic (and incestuous) desire for reunion with the male version of herself, is offset against her vigorous refusal of the feminine role. Her abject failure as a mother, wife and daughter, her anger, promiscuity and slovenliness, are thrown down like challenges to the audience to condemn her. But all of these aspects of Portia are fundamentally irrelevant to her, and, if we travel with her, to us. Thus Carr creates a radical representation of woman in the face of a searing rejection of all the categories traditionally used to define woman. The category of gender as a source of identity is interrogated and found wanting. In performance Portia explodes gender assumptions and carries the audience beyond the narrative of her own destruction.

Contemporary neo-realist playwriting maintains the notion of the stage as a recognizable reflection of a social reality, but also accommodates, to a far greater degree, the social instability and confusions attendant on the media overload which characterize our postmodern world. Defining what is 'real' or recognizable has, in itself, become part of the drama. The neorealist playwright manipulates the theatrical vocabulary of realism. Domestic spaces, the structure of the narrative, dramatic language, modes of character representation, the invitation to the audience to feel empathy, all are disrupted, re-formed or shattered altogether as the contest for subjectivity is fought out in the relationship between the performance and the audience. Gender identity proves to be central to testing realist limits. The female or homosexual subject on stage unsettles the assertion of a unitary masculine, heterosexual hegemony as it is materialized in the domestic prison-house of realism's fourth-wall interiors. As the category of gender is challenged, so by association are those of class, race and nationality. In performance, the audience read the signs of these conflicts in unease and disturbance, in the failure to tie up loose ends, in disruption of narrative expectation and in what may appear as inappropriate behaviour on the part of certain characters. There are certain production and performance choices which acknowledge and celebrate these traits rather than whitewashing or disguising them, thus creating opportunities or spaces where the female subject on stage is made powerful.

First, though, it helps if the play invites such opportunities. I will look at genre, use of stage space, and the relationship between character and language as three areas in *Portia Coughlan* where the certainties of realism may break down, and where performance before an audience creates the potential to threaten or overthrow the power of narrative in the text. If the form of a play is hybrid, mixing genres, comedy interrupting tragedy, for example, or displaying discontinuities or fractures, it is more likely to make space for the female. The notorious well-made play that we have inherited from the nineteenth-century European tradition is a confining and often numbing form for feminist spectators. The crushing confinements of this form reflect and even assert the bourgeois patriarchal value system out of which it grew. To challenge narrative coherence, and to disrupt the seemingly inevitable progress from premise, through conflict, reversals of fortune and revelation of secrets, to resolution, is tantamount to challenging representations of women and men required by a patriarchal gender hierarchy.

In two crucial ways, Marina Carr resists the certainties of realist form. She structures *Portia Coughlan* so that the heroine's suicide occurs at the beginning of Act Two, and the third act is a flashback to her last day alive. The (inevitable) suicide of the heroine is confronted midstream and the play is effectively hauled out of a slough of melodrama that might otherwise threaten to engulf it. In Act Three, then, a space is opened up for an intense and unremitting examination of Portia's pain, freed from the exigencies of structure and narrative.

Although Carr's work is often found to be bound in blood with Greek classical forms (Dido in the case of *Portia Coughlan*, Medea in Carr's later play *By the Bog of Cats*), the tragedy under scrutiny here is more Ibsenite than Greek, more modern than classical. George Steiner's analysis of modern tragedy is exemplified through reference back to early Ibsen, whose 'dramas presuppose the withdrawal of God from human affairs . . . [A]ssaults on reason and life come not from without, as in Greek . . . tragedy. They arise in the unstable soul' (*The Death of Tragedy*, p. 293). Ruin, in the play, lies embedded within the psychology of Portia. There is no escape from herself. This idea is extended in Carr's structuring of the action. Although we understand that the story ends with Portia's death, the play allows her to come to life again, as it were, in Act Three. The image of defeat that death carries, say in *Hedda Gabler*, is usurped by Portia's ability, dramaturgically, to live beyond it. And this ontological excess of Portia's is reinforced by the ghost twin's presence to her and the audience throughout. In *Portia Coughlan*, the stage represents an image beyond the realist limits of environment, psychology and mortality.

Part of the power of this play in performance is its exhilarating black comedy, impacting on the audience simultaneously with the brutal grotesquery of the language and action. The spectators are not permitted to settle into a mood of appalled awe without them breaking it with unexpected laughter, irresistibly fuelled by the wild vitality being acted out. Stage and audience are bound in a volatile tension that unsettles reassuring binaries such as man/woman, weak/powerful, good/bad, life/death.

The certainties of realist form are likewise resisted by Carr in the way she toys with the theatrical process of exposition, whereby the audience is (usually) given the background information necessary to understand situations and predict the fates of characters. In *Portia Coughlan*, there is a proliferation of expositional information, often contradictory, always complicated by a plethora of potentially significant reference points. Will the story of the heroine's famous namesake in *The Merchant of Venice* explicate her motivations and passions? Is Gabriel's angelic naming to be taken at face value, or is he rather the devil opposite to Portia's husband, who also bears an angel's name (Raphael)? Definitive answers are not available. Contradictory accounts of Gabriel's death are given by different characters, and we do not know what to believe. The play manipulates our expectation of narrative clarity, of cause and effect, and denies us satisfaction. Environment and heredity, the standbys of realist theatre, are not neglected. In Act One it is explained that Portia's mother and father are half-brother and -sister: 'Young Gabriel . . . was insane from too much inbreedin' and I'd swear he walked into the Belmont River be accident'

(*Portia Coughlan*, p. 145). This shadow of doom hangs over all that remains of the play, but explains nothing. It invites critical approaches based on analysis of the play as a critique of unhealthy social practices, but this is a false trail. Portia's furious intensity leaves behind all the reasons offered for it, all the narratives of causality, and thereby leaves behind realism's mirror function.

The unsteady ground underlying *Portia Coughlan* is, as critic Fintan O'Toole has identified, unstable and mutable. Carr opens the action in both Portia's living room and '*at the bank of the Belmont River*' (p. 193). Distinctions break down, opposites are blurred, 'borders between the living and the dead, between male and female, between the born and the unborn, between the past and the present dissolve in the [Belmont] river's interminable flow' (O'Toole, 'Figures on a Dark Landscape', p. 10). This breakdown of borders and limits is expressed in the division of the stage space between the chaotic domesticity of Portia's house, or, in some scenes, the High Chaparral Bar in the local town, and the river itself. Portia moves fluidly between the two, reflecting her inability to escape the impact of Gabriel's death by drowning, finally succumbing to his ghosting by drowning herself. The stage at once divides and connects inside (the house/the bar) and outside (the river), society and nature. Portia's failure to define one against the other, her deep absorption in the landscape, memories and myths of the river, are her passion and her undoing. The Heraclitean flow of the water, always necessarily imagined on a stage, asserts history as endlessly changing, the past as irretrievably but hauntingly lost. The stage space expresses the failure to maintain binary opposites, narrative stability or the boundaries of identity, and signals a crisis in the representation of 'woman'.

When it comes to dramatic language, the images it presents may invite the audience to imagine beyond the everyday; dialogue may lead us to question the nature of our conversations with one another, to search for what is inexpressible within certain social, economic, emotional or gender borders. The language of a play may create an alien world on stage which dares the audience to step outside their familiar linguistic territory, naming secrets, proposing lies, revealing the life of possible truths. If the language of a play brings us to the borderlines of language itself, it may also point to those zones where music or silence take over as the word falters.

To speak on-stage is to enter into a power struggle for control of the action. Women on stage frequently are allowed less to say than men, or are silenced altogether. In terms of the history of western theatre, even today, it is culturally significant when a female figure (played by a female performer) dominates through her speech. Strangely enough, the myth that women never shut up has not penetrated the practice of male playwrights, even realist ones, who would purport to give an accurate reflection of the world. The question 'who is speaking?' is obviously a layered one in the theatre, and a female character may speak as the ventriloquist's doll of the playwright. Where the playwright herself is a woman there is a higher expectation of speech as an authentic expression of women's oft-theorized, problematic relationship with language, or of her appropriation of its powers in the physical act of performance.

The Irish actress Olwen Fouéré, who has played in the world premieres of Carr's *The Mai* (1994), and *By the Bog of Cats* (1998), has described the remarkable power of language in this playwright's work: 'At times I feel [Carr] is actually articulating the female rage of the nation' ('Journeys in Performance', p. 169). *Portia Coughlan* teems with verbal energy, live and dangerous in intensity. The first edition was written in an idiomatic form of English to reflect the accent of Carr's native Co. Offaly,[3] but Carr rewrote the play in more standard English for its republication in her collected *Plays 1*. Even with the changes, however, the force of the verbal expression has a physical impact on performers and audiences. It is perhaps in its insults that the language most effectively gives an impression of its power when taken out of context, as it must be here. For example, Portia attacks her hapless husband in Act One: 'The problem's not Gabriel's, I'm over him this years! The problem's you! . . . Moochin' up to me with your slick theories of what's wrong of me! Ye haven't a fuckin' clue, ye ignorant auld fuckin' cripple ye! I can't bear the sight of you hobblin' around me in your custom-made cowboy boots' (*Portia Coughlan*, 221).

Portia Coughlan exemplifies the self-expressive mode of performance that Bert O. States defines as writing designed to be a 'vehicle . . . for the release of the actor's power' (*Great Reckonings*, p. 161). To an extent this applies across the cast of Carr's play, but to Portia falls the overwhelming array of spoken fireworks. Of self-expressive forms of theatre, States says, 'Whatever they are *about* is always less important than what they display' (p. 162). His view draws attention to the way the play is so much more than the individual circumstances of Portia's life and death, or even than the embittered, gnarled community and family surrounding her. In the moment of performance, the heroine, embodied by the actor, creates the possibility of theatre as an act of imagination between stage and audience. When the ghost Gabriel sings, Carr marks the borders between the guttural writhings of speech and a territory that breathes only in silence or music. The intricacies of locale, the details of family history and the burdens of social conditions are held in tensile opposition to a numinous resistance and an assertion of the possibility to imagine otherwise. Elin Diamond has pointed out that '[f]eminism, whose empirical, historical project continues to be the recovery and analysis of women's texts and experiences, has a stake in truth' (*Unmaking Mimesis*, p. vii). Through performance, the notion of truth may be extended beyond history as narrative, to include the imaginative present moment, not for its own sake but as the haven of the future, of the possibility of change that lies waiting to be roused.

I have suggested that manipulations, and instabilities of form, stage space, and dramatic language, when they characterize a play text, open possibilities for the overturning of narrative power and reflect crises in representation. They provide peculiarly fertile conditions for challenges to the regulation of women's subjectivity on stage, and of gender identity. All of the above, as potential sites of transgression, point to ways in which a play creates and controls the relationship of empathy between audience and performer. The playwright organizes the action of the play, the dramatic space, and the language in order to invite the audience to empathize, or to discourage empathy and to alienate the audience from this seductive response. As Augusto Boal points out, empathy may be seen as the coercion of the 'real' audience by the 'fictitious' character, so that the former relinquishes their power to 'the image' (*Theatre of the Oppressed*, p. 113). However, what if the empathic character is already a representation poised at the limits of representability (such as the unwomanly woman or the unmanly man)? Then the playwright (in creating the character) and the performer (in embodying the character) may invite the audience to extend, through their empathy, their imaginative engagement with possibility, outside the borders of conservative models of behaviour, outside the limits of choices as they are presented in society. Empathy may serve the feminist spectator to assert the validity of a woman's 'imaginary', shared between stage and audience. As the playwright and performer offer and withdraw the dramatic preconditions of an empathic response, so the audience is thrown from affirmation (through identification) to alienation, interrogation and imagination. This dynamic flow between performance and audience is focused on performers. The presence of the performer (representing the character) becomes the site of identification and, crucially, in a feminist context, becomes a way into women's experience and history, but also into the dreamt life and possibilities of the imagination.

*   *   *   *   *

Marina Carr: biographical and critical contexts

Marina Carr was born in Co. Offaly, educated at University College Dublin, and has lived and worked in Ireland, Europe and the United States. Her many plays include *Low in the Dark*, *This Love Thing*, *The Deer's Surrender*, *The Mai*, *Portia Coughlan*, *By the Bog of Cats*, and *Ariel*. She has been awarded several commissions, writing residencies and fellowships, and her plays have been translated into a number of languages and have been produced around the world.

Critical interest in her work springs from its remarkable scale, power and depth. In the context of Irish theatre at the beginning of the twenty-first century, Carr is the most visible of her generation of women playwrights. Her work is thus a focus for discussion of and research into the role of Irish women writers in theatre and new representations of women's lives on the contemporary Irish stage.

Works cited

Belsey, Catherine, *The Subject of Tragedy* (London: Routledge, 1993).

Belsey, Catherine and Jane Moore, 'Introduction: The Story So Far', in Catherine Belsey and Jane Moore (eds.), *The Feminist Reader* (London: Macmillan, 1989), pp. 1–20.

Boal, Augusto, *Theatre of the Oppressed* (London: Pluto Press, 1979).

Carr, Marina, *By the Bog of Cats* (Loughcrew, Oldcastle, Co. Meath: Gallery Press, 1998).

——, *Portia Coughlan*, in *Plays 1* (London: Faber & Faber, 1999), pp. 187–255.

Diamond, Elin, *Unmaking Mimesis: Essays on Feminism and Theater* (London: Routledge, 1997).

Fouéré, Olwen, 'Journeys in Performance', in Cathy Leeney and Anna McMullan (eds.), *The Theatre of Marina Carr: 'Before Rules Was Made'* (Dublin; Carysfort Press, 2003).

McGuinness, Frank (ed.), *The Dazzling Dark: New Irish Plays* (London: Faber & Faber, 1996).

O'Toole, Fintan, 'Figures on a Dark Landscape', *Irish Times*, 2 April 1996.

Solomon, Alisa, *Re-Dressing the Canon: Essays on Theater and Gender* (London: Routledge, 1997).

States, Bert O., *Great Reckonings in Little Rooms* (Berkeley: University of California Press, 1985).

Steiner, George, *The Death of Tragedy* (London: Faber & Faber, 1961).

Chapter 7

'Wide open . . . to mirth and wonder'

Sheela-Na-Gigs as Multiple Signifiers of the Female Body in Ireland

Luz Mar González Arias

. . . the guilt of knowledge
of the surfeit
of our embarrassing fertility
and power.
Katie Donovan, 'Underneath Our Skirts' (p. 34)

I'm not your muse, not that creature
in the painting, with the beautiful body,
Venus on the half-shell.
Paula Meehan, 'Not Your Muse' (p. 24)

The stone images known as Sheela-na-gigs are medieval carvings to be found on the walls of some Irish churches and castles.[1] Although positions and shape vary – some are seated, others stand – the so-called 'exhibitionist' figures are always naked bodies characterized by their display of female genitalia, much exaggerated in size. Some controversy has developed over whether the Sheela-na-gigs were originally meant to represent actual women. The absence of breasts, sometimes only insinuated, sometimes totally absent, and the schematic features many of them present seem to support the theory that they were devised as some kind of 'arcane symbolism' (Joanne McMahon and Jack Roberts, *The Sheela-Na-Gigs of Ireland and Great Britain*, p. 12). However, even though we cannot assume that they were carved as naturalistic reproductions of particular women, the gender dimension of these figures should not be underestimated, since they explicitly exhibit the vulva, as opposed to the male exhibitionist figures that occur more regularly on the Continent. Actually, the Sheelas' out-of-proportion vaginas become their defining feature and necessarily forefront issues of female sexuality.

According to archaeological evidence, the earliest examples of Irish Sheela-na-gigs date back to the eleventh century, but most of them were carved between the Norman invasion of the island in 1169 and the sixteenth or seventeenth centuries, which indicates that they are a product of medieval Christianity, at least in terms of date. The cultural and religious developments that took place during this prolonged period are responsible for the differences in the carvings. While the earliest examples are rather schematic in their facial and bodily characteristics, later Sheelas are more explicit and elaborate. The Sheela-na-gig found in a monastery in Liathmor (Leighmore), Co. Tipperary (Figure 1), exemplifies the first case. This figure is most probably a twelfth-century creation. She is lying on her side but could be described as standing; her breasts are insinuated but do not seem to have been very important in the composition; the head is triangular, quite simple; and the hands are joined around the genital area, which is clearly indicated and slightly bigger than expected. The Sheela found on a section of the fourteenth-century town wall in Fethard, Co. Tipperary (Figure 2), is a more complex composition. Popping eyes with staring pupils, grim teeth and incised ribs confer to this figure an emaciated look that strikes and even scares the viewer. The breasts are, again, absent, but the hands join below the thighs and draw attention to the vulva, which is held open by the fingers.[2]

Figure 1: Liathmor (Leighmore), Co. Tipperary

Sheela-na-gigs started attracting the attention of antiquarians and historians in the 1840s, but there is no agreement on their ultimate origin or functions, and the figures have remained controversial. However, interpretations have not been scant, frequently reflecting prejudices against female corporeality as much as serious research on the role these exhibitionist figures may have played at the time they were created. In the nineteenth century, for instance, the Sheelas' displayed vaginas were sometimes perceived

Figure 2: Fethard, Co. Tipperary

as hearts opening to the world, an image much more compatible with the Victorian ideal of femininity than that of a vulva.

It was not until the second half of the twentieth century that the most committed studies on the Sheela-na-gigs were undertaken. One of the plausible theories on the carvings sees them as examples of negative attitudes towards the female body as articulated by early Irish Christianity. In medieval times, representations of lust and death in the shape of a woman are not infrequent, probably associated with Eve's supposed original sin. For the patriarchal ideologies of the Christian west, female corporeality was perceived as volatile, its processes and orifices turning it into a penetrable entity, as opposed to the normative body of males and virgins: compact, complete, self-contained and under control. According to Margaret R. Miles, these different conceptualizations of male and female physicality account for the fear of women's sexuality and the need to keep its difference under control. In her wonderful study on female nakedness and religious meanings, Miles concludes that grotesque representations of the vagina were the main means patriarchy devised to alleviate this fear of womanhood, so that the disturbing figure could be managed and dominated (*Carnal Knowing*, p. 147). Sheela-na-gigs perfectly exemplify the grotesque figuration of women's genitalia through caricature. While massive male sexual organs are to be admired, the extreme example of female genitalia:

> . . . inevitably discloses what it is that society aims to prevent . . . Caricature
> isolates and fetishizes parts of the body. In theological and medical discourse

as well as in the popular arts of the Christian West, the breasts, vagina, and uterus have frequently been objects of caricature, in both explicit and covert ways. (p. 155)

Instead of explicitly exploring the gender implications of the Sheela-na-gigs as Miles does, Jorgen Andersen's *The Witch on the Wall*, Anthony Weir and Jim Jerman's *Images of Lust* or Eamonn P. Kelly's *Sheela-Na-Gigs: Origins and Functions* use religion as their main interpretative framework and connect the Sheela-na-gigs to the developments of Romanesque art on the Continent. For these scholars, the changes in the carvings over time – from less to more overtly sexual – and the fact that they began to be placed in secular buildings imply a change in their function. Sheelas from the later Middle Ages are frequently found at vulnerable parts of castles and towers and would play the role of apotropaic or protective icons against evil: ugly and explicit representations of the much-feared vulva would turn the female sex into a demonic figure able to prevent other demons from approaching.

Apart from these generally accepted theories, a number of researchers (mostly women) have linked the Sheelas to pagan fertility rites in which female corporeality was perceived as reminiscent of goddess imagery. While in most cases these interpretations cannot be supported with archaeological evidence, they reveal deep suspicion towards patriarchal scholarship and reflect an interesting dimension of these erotic images. Barbara Walker, for instance, relates the Sheela-na-gigs to the yonic statues of Kali in India and refers to the life-giving powers of both icons (*The Woman's Encyclopedia of Myths and Secrets*, p. 931); for Ann Pearson, Irish exhibitionist figures fit into the model of the Egyptian goddesses that represent the most pleasurable side of women's sexuality ('Reclaiming the Sheela-Na-Gigs', p. 20). Within the Irish mythological traditions, the Sheelas have also been perceived as heiresses of a long list of Celtic gods, sovereignty goddesses, women warriors and queens (Helen L. Wood, 'Women in Myths'; Etienne Rynne, 'A Pagan Celtic Background for Sheela-Na-Gigs?'). Heroines like Queen Medbh, from the *Ulster Cycle,* or the Irish territorial goddesses present themselves as overtly sexual and politically powerful, so that in general they become friendlier models of women's corporeality than later Christian and Catholic icons. In this light, Sheela-na-gigs are regarded as medieval derivations of the sexual and creative possibilities of pre-Christian concepts of femininity.

In 2004, two new publications brought to light further analysis on the original functions of the Irish Sheela-na-gigs. In *The Sacred Whore: Sheela Goddess of the Celts,* Maureen Concannon contends that Sheela-na-gigs represented 'an aspect of the Goddess of the land, worshipped by the indigenous people of Ireland and adopted by the Celts when they settled on this island' (p. 2). Following Marija Gimbutas (*The Civilization of the Goddess*) in her belief that archaeology must be analysed from the point of view of ideology, Concannon uses an interdisciplinary approach – mainly mythology, history and psychology – to account for the roles these medieval icons may fulfil in the contemporary world. Her main contribution to previous studies of the Sheelas lies in her understanding of the stone image as a 'psychopomp' or symbol to assist in the psychological developments of humanity after centuries of neglected feminine spirituality. *Sheela-Na-Gigs: Unravelling an Enigma* is Barbara Freitag's most recent contribution to the Sheela question. In her study, Freitag includes a comprehensive catalogue of Sheela-na-gigs and is suspicious of theories that present the Sheelas as warnings against lust and female sexuality because, she maintains, this interpretation implies imposing a biased academic view onto a rural peasant background. For Freitag the 'Sheela-na-gig belongs to the realm of folk deities and as such is associated with life-giving powers, birth and death and the renewal of life' (p. 2). According to this investigation, the Sheela-na-gig must be placed in its medieval social context and perceived as an important icon in the assistance of women at childbirth.

From another perspective, Cheryl Herr, in her article 'The Erotics of Irishness', suggests that alternative methodologies need to be found in order to explore Irish culture, and she proposes the corporeal as a useful starting point. Since the neutralization of the body has been pervasive in the culture of the island, and seems to be especially virulent in recent times, Herr argues that finding the meanings of this longstanding somatophobia and the relationship between Irish bodies and Irish minds would help researchers in their attempts to analyse Irish culture today (pp. 5–6).

The need to articulate an intellectual basis inclusive of the corporeal has characterized feminist debates all over the world, Ireland being no exception in this respect. The specificity of the Irish historical, socio-political and artistic contexts and the importance the female body has played in the evolution of these contexts make it impossible to claim total homogeneity between feminist projects in Ireland and elsewhere. And yet it is worth noting that Nira Yuval-Davis, in her extensive study of the gender implications of nationalist movements globally (*Gender & Nation*), states that women invariably play the roles of biological, cultural and symbolic reproducers of the nation to which they belong. In this respect, then, Ireland does fit a larger pattern, as its nationalist movements used women's bodies as allegorical representations either of the land colonized, penetrated, raped – Hibernia – or else as an icon for the national cause – Dark Rosaleen, Cathleen Ní Houlihan, Mother Ireland.

The dynamics of the interaction between gender and nation are clearly exemplified in the Irish consciousness, where women have always represented something else. They became abstract icons, silent muses, while real flesh-and-blood women were edited out of the public arena. As Ailbhe Smyth has written in her influential article 'The Floozie in the Jacuzzi', women's function is merely iconic in Ireland: '"Woman" always stands for something else. "Woman" is an empty signifier, or to put it another way, can be construed to mean whatever "we" want it to mean' (pp. 8–9). Nationalism and Catholicism formed a strong nexus that simplified women under the image of a Mother

Ireland reminiscent of Mother Mary: maternal, non-sexual, non-corporeal. The most insidious consequence of this process was the total erasure of the female body both from political discourses – the 1937 Constitution is a clear instance of this – and also from representation – where women tended to be invoked merely as political muses. Far from remaining in the realm of abstraction, in Ireland these issues are constantly translated into a repressive defence of institutionalized versions of motherhood and the family. Since the beginning of the 1980s, the history of the country abounds in stories where the legislation against women's access to their own corporeality has resulted in amazing accounts of moving statues of the Virgin Mary, clandestine abortions, lonely deaths in childbirth and bizarrely misinterpreted infanticide.

In this context, the recuperation of the medieval Sheela-na-gigs, with their uninhibited display of female physicality, unquestionably moves beyond the merely aesthetic to acquire an ethical dimension in one of the most critical feminist debates on the island. These carvings illustrate the kind of methodology Herr devised: their theoretical and artistic implications, both in their original shape and in the contemporary texts, make it possible for the female body to claim a space of its own in the creation and transformation of Irish culture. In the literary and visual texts of the Irish women artists who pay attention to the Sheela-na-gigs, feminist and/or postcolonial vindications are carried out by placing special emphasis on the pagan dimension of the icons. Bodies and voices are constantly referred to in these new re-creations; both the mouth, in particular the tongue, and the vagina become signifiers whose meaning keeps changing over time but whose articulatory possibilities cannot be denied.

A number of Irish women poets and visual artists are recovering the Sheela-na-gigs in their work, thus participating in the debates on the functions these female bodies may fulfil in contemporary Ireland. Susan Connolly, Anne Le Marquand Hartigan, Louise C. Callaghan and the Irish-American Nuala Archer are among the women who have used this part of the Irish archaeological heritage in their poetry.[3] The visible quality of the female sex in these carvings is one of the reasons why many people, still today, find them repellent, even disgusting. The visual dimension of the Sheelas, however, illustrates many of the debates in Ireland on the so-called 'body issue', attracting the attention of a number of contemporary artists. The paintings and lithographs of Carmel Benson and the tapestries of Monica Bates are particularly relevant in this respect.[4] The medieval carvings become extraordinary means to counteract the deep somatophobia that has characterized Irish political and cultural discourses and, at the same time, as we will see, they fit into a global feminist recuperation of the body as an active participant in the creation of culture.

The poetry of Susan Connolly exemplifies the treatment given to the Sheela-na-gigs in contemporary Irish literature and contributes to the creation of new interpretative frameworks for the female body. In 1992, Connolly participated in the creation of *Brigid's Place/Áit Bhríde,* a chapbook published with few resources by the marginal Cailleach Press. This book contained poems exclusively by women, a statement against Ireland's male publishing policies, which have systematically omitted women from anthologies and literary histories; it also included self-identified lesbian writers, a further challenge to the privilege traditionally accorded to Irish male perspectives. *Brigid's Place* included five poems on the Sheela-na-gigs: 'Síle na Gig' by Íde O'Carroll (translated by Louise Hermana),[5] 'Female Figure' by Susan Connolly,[6] 'Sheela' by Louise Hermana, 'Síle na Gig' by Rita Dowling and 'Stone Activist' by Hernan Turner.

Connolly's 'Female Figure' opens with a physical description of the stone image, as if it were one of the descriptive texts written by nineteenth-century antiquarians and historians. The poem focuses on the face, in particular the mouth, and the vagina as the most characteristic, and actually defining, features of the icon. This time, however, the object of the description is turned into the subject of its own narrative and draws the audience's attention to the relationship that exists between the organs of speech and the female sex. In the poem, the discourse of the Sheela is influenced by the rhythms of her body, which participates actively in her self-definition. By intertwining the facial and vaginal lips, Connolly endows the female body with articulatory possibilities, so that this Sheela-na-gig can acquire a voice and some sexual visibility in a cultural tradition full of silent, non-sexual muses: 'Mouth fixed / in a wide grin, / puffed-out / cheeks / fingers to lips – / am I saying something bad?'[7] Immediately after describing her body, the Sheela questions her own self, no doubt influenced by the misogyny and somatophobia that has characterized Irish Catholic and nationalist movements. However, the protagonist of these lines finds reassurance in her own speech and in the fact that finally she is able to give her own interpretation of her unquestionably female corporeality: 'am I saying / something bad? / No! after / centuries of / darkness / I tell / the truth.'

The grotesque aspect of the figure, which may have been intended as a warning against women's 'dangerous propensities' to sin, is now turned into a symbol of strength for the narrator. Her startling – even frightening – appearance does not fit into the physical stereotypes of femininity sanctioned by the patriarchal establishments. The ideal of Irish womanhood has traditionally been constructed around the qualities of chastity, passivity and submissiveness; now, as these fade, these characteristics are replaced by an exaggerated emphasis on beauty, so much so that women's bodies remain imprisoned in models altogether impossible to fulfil. Female corporeality, too, often a mere object of desire for the male gaze, changes in Connolly's poem through the device of the display of massive sexual organs. The physicality of this Sheela-na-gig becomes a source of knowledge for her. At the same time, the Sheela's grotesque body can also arouse a kind of desire, primarily same-sex, that does not involve her reification: 'Women – / you look at me / and talk about / your / 'desire-need'. / I hear a babble, / then your / wisdom. /

Fingers to / lips I speak / my need of / you.' The female narrator acknowledges she has been paralysed in history by male definitions of her own self, but at the same time triumphantly declares: 'I laugh – / witness / and survivor.' The Sheela-na-gig concludes her poem by celebrating a community of women and her hope in the articulatory possibilities of the corporeal. Although '[c]aught in stone', she is happy to participate in an incipient language that challenges phallocratic discourses and that eventually will allow her to express alternative versions of femininity:

> Caught in stone
> I celebrate
> all who tell
> the truth –
> over centuries
> of darkness.

For the purposes of a feminist interpretation of the text, one of the most interesting aspects of 'Female Figure' is the parallelism established between the Sheela's genitalia and her organs of speech. In lines like '[f]ingers to lips – / am I saying something bad?' or 'fingers to / lips I speak / my need of / you', Connolly skilfully manages to intertwine body and word. This verbal aspect of the Sheela's corporeality – and the same could be said about the medieval stones – contributes to the inscription of the body into a cultural tradition that has systematically omitted it from public visibility. At the same time, this type of iconography illustrates the vindications carried out in the name of 'corporeal feminisms' on both sides of the Atlantic, since there is now a general tendency towards conceptualizing the corporeal as a meaningful entity, as the shifting product of the interaction between culture and nature.

The term 'corporeal feminism' was introduced by Elizabeth Grosz in an early article for the journal *Australian Feminist Studies* (1987), in which she sketched a methodology towards constructing a much needed theoretical framework from which to proffer a healthy conceptualization of the (female) body. In her study, Grosz concluded that for a very long time feminists had been reluctant to incorporate women's physicality in their theoretical and/or artistic projects, as they had uncritically adopted philosophical assumptions on the role of the body. Cartesian dualist thought, together with religious discourses, triggered the conceptualization of the body as mere matter, passive and non-signifying, a hindrance for the mind and for the soul on their way to a supposedly more transcendental existence.

Previous to this relatively recent interest in making the body visible, Simone de Beauvoir's 1949 pioneering treatise *The Second Sex* had already defined the corporeal as signifying matter. In the chapter entitled 'The Data of Biology', Beauvoir states that the body 'is not a *thing*, it is a situation, as viewed in the perspective I am adopting – that of Heidegger, Sartre, and Merleau-Ponty; it is the instrument of our grasp upon the world, a limiting factor for our projects' (p. 34). From the existentialist perspective that underpins all of Beauvoir's work, the material dimension of the body is not denied, but its cultural value must also be acknowledged. Beauvoir's body is a *situated* one, a *lived* body that is always immersed in a never-ending process of *becoming*. It is a body that cannot be perceived as a neutral and compact whole upon which culture would impose its gender roles, but as an incomplete and situational material that will always have to negotiate its identity with the outside.[8]

In the 1970s, the sex/gender distinction had been used to counteract nineteenth-century biological determinism and to denounce the social practices that led to the marginalization of women. It soon became evident, however, that such a binary also had the disadvantage of perceiving the body as innocent, passive and prediscursive.[9] The different 'corporeal theories' that are part of the international agenda of contemporary feminism share an interest in the body as an active agent of culture. Physicality is no longer perceived as pre-given, as a passive tabula rasa upon which gender is projected. Judith Butler's *Gender Trouble* and *Bodies That Matter*, together with Elizabeth Grosz's *Volatile Bodies*, summarize the main lines of investigation adopted by feminist theorists working on the body. In these works, the same as in Beauvoir's study, words like 'sex' or 'body' are turned into hybrid categories in which the realms of biology and culture are fused. In the words of Judith Butler, the 'construct called 'sex' is as culturally constructed as gender' (*Gender Trouble*, p. 7). Once the discursive values of the body are acknowledged, its 'fall from grace', to use Grosz's phraseology (*Volatile Bodies*, p. 3), is challenged, since the corporeal goes beyond the merely physical to generate meanings. Studies on the body have been produced at an amazing speed and the label 'corporeal feminism' stands for a most varied set of complex theories. In spite of their different approaches, what they have in common is the conceptualization of the (female) body as both signifying and signified, and this perspective has come to supersede previous discourses on physicality.[10]

Like Susan Connolly's 'Female Figure', which presents the reader with a new understanding of the Irish body and exemplifies the theoretical frameworks that endow the corporeal with creative and verbal functions, Carmel Benson's *Crouching Sheela* (Figure 3)[11] can function as a visual illustration of this subject. This lithograph represents a huge shape that almost surpasses the limits of the frame assigned to it. Instead of a compact and clear-cut body, Benson's Sheela displays an out-of-proportion vagina, which is held open by her own hands. As in the poem, the facial and vaginal lips of the Sheela are linked, this time by their common colour and striking size, in an attempt to reclaim the articulatory dimension of what was previously perceived as pre-discursive (and sinful) material. Benson's work rescues the damaged carvings of medieval times from oblivion and presents the viewer with a gigantic and colourful body. Most contemporary versions of the Sheela-na-gigs are fluid, their shapes never fixed, never stable but permanently suspended in the possibilities of change and growth.

In *The Serpent and the Goddess*, Mary Condren explains that honouring the serpent was a common characteristic of pre-Christian religions. The serpent would ultimately symbolize the Goddess and the intimate connection between life and death. For Condren, 'crushing the serpent in the Hebrew Bible was a mythical act of cosmic significance'(p. 23), since immortality would be introduced then, together with a patriarchal monotheism and the inevitable displacement of female spirituality. Since women academics began to write on religion, especially from the 1970s onwards, the connection between paganism and femininity has been frequently referred to in order to denounce the dominant iconography of a powerful male God. A celebration of goddess imagery would imply a rejection of the phallocentric ideology characteristic of most cultures in which religion is still highly operative as an interpretative framework. Carmel Benson sees in the Sheela-na-gigs a Celtic connection that eventually manages to trigger 'a resurrection of the old primitive female qualities and a rejection of the passivity imposed by the male' (González Arias, 'Beyond Categorizations', p. 95).

In 'Sheela-Na-Gig',[12] a poem published in her 1993 collection *For the Stranger*, Connolly develops these questions further. This time the poet

Figure 3: Carmel Benson, Crouching Sheela

strengthens the links between the naked icon and the pagan tradition of fertility goddesses, with the effect of counteracting Christian discourses on the female sex. The poem explicitly bypasses the repressive effects that the new iconography imposed on female corporeality and makes the Sheela go back to her supposedly original pre-Christian Ireland. The poem is divided into eight brief stanzas, with each alluding to the signifying aspect of the body:

> Her thighs
> widely-splayed,
> her enlarged
> vagina
> wide-open
> place-of-the-snake (p. 51)

The description of this grotesque carving is completed in the second stanza with a reference to her organs of speech and birth-giving powers. For Barbara Walker, giving birth was the condition most truly identified with the divine in primitive belief, as 'usurpation of the feminine power of birth-giving seems to have been the distinguishing mark of the earlier gods' (*Women's Encyclopedia of Myths and Secrets*, p. 106). As monotheism gained a space of its own in different cultures, maternity was reduced to a negative biological burden, responsible for women's seclusion in the private sphere, while it continued to be used as a metaphor for male creativity in the public arena. Susan Connolly's Sheela, however, imagines back to a matrilineal Ireland where female sexuality and maternity had not yet been institutionalized. Once more, the mouth and the vulva form a nexus that reclaim what had remained in the margins of representation for too long. The Sheela's grotesqueness is translated into the activity and strength necessary to reassert herself:

> Face distorted,
> deeply-furrowed
> brow,
> tip of her tongue
> protruding
> from a big wide
> mouth;
> both hands
> clutch her cunt
> womb-of-the-mother (p. 52)

The procreative dimension of this 'womb-of-the-mother' does not deny the creative possibilities of the Sheela-na-gig, whose tongue keeps sticking out. However, the attempts to ignore patriarchal discourses face the difficulty of deconstructing generations of reification and simplification. The icon acknowledges that everything about her has been 'wide-open . . . / to mirth / and wonder' and cannot help feeling sad at the thought of being 'so exposed'. In traditional psychoanalytical theories, the visible quality of the male sexual organs justified the conceptualization of the male body as normative and labelled women's corporeality as 'lack'. At the same time, the dynamics of the gaze turned women's bodies into objects to be looked at, described and defined by a patriarchal voyeur. Connolly's Sheela-na-gig is aware of the dangers inherent in the politics of the visual when it comes to constructing her self-definition. After being the object of much misinterpretation, the icon struggles to find an identity of her own: she knows she is a 'stone image' but 'image . . . / of what?' she wonders. This question is the Sheela's realization that every representation is presided over by an ideological agenda whose power to create cultural stereotypes should not be underestimated. Once more, her grotesque ugliness is not in contradiction to the arousal of desire and becomes a perfect means to counteract the traditional reification of the female body:

> Sex-hunger
> the fast
> and the slow
> of arousal,
> sudden
> seductive-power
> lying-down-together
> again and again (p. 53)

In the final lines of the poem, the carving is presented as descendant and embodiment of the Goddess, her overt sexuality a threat to the Virgin iconography that has pervaded Irish cultural discourses: 'Clutching / her vagina / with both hands / place-of-the-snake / womb-of-the-mother / mother-of-us-all / sheela-na-gig' (p. 53).

Like Susan Connolly, Carmel Benson has also underlined a pagan origin for the Sheela-na-gigs in her visual work. In the painting *Seir-Kieran Sheela-Na-Gig Travels* (Figure 4) – from Benson's 2003 collection 'Into the Pattern' – a Sheela is placed against the background of contemporary North African textile work. This time the icon leaves its original setting, the Irish countryside, to acquire a multicultural dimension. From its new location, the corporeality of the Sheela resists any fixed interpretation and instead represents a multiplicity of voices. In Benson's painting, the pagan influences that many authors have seen in the medieval Sheela-na-gigs are brought in contact with the work of anonymous African women, who also articulate some kind of female spirituality in their orderly patterns.

As mentioned above, other writers and visual artists working with Sheela icons also trace their origins back to pagan times. This seems to be now the general tendency, even though a pagan origin for the Sheela-na-gigs is hard to prove from a purely archaeological point of view. It could be argued that such a perspective may easily turn into the biological reductionism that feminist theories on the body are trying to avoid. In these works, an emphasis on the corporeal and its discursive, creative possibilities may involve the dangerous

Figure 4: Carmel Benson, Seir-Kieran Sheela-Na-Gig Travels

assumption that biology is destiny and that the female body hides some kind of universal 'truth' to be rescued from invisibility and oblivion. Goddess imagery can also mislead us to believe that, in the remote past, women had all the power over the systems of representation in a matriarchal Ireland whose existence, again, is difficult to prove historically. In general, the simplifications that can derive from the celebration of pagan myths have also been the subject of feminist criticism and artistic revisions.[13] However, the deep influence that Christianity (in particular Catholicism) has played in the construction of 'Irish womanhood' turns pre-Christian myths into appropriate vehicles to resist non-corporeal representations for the women of Ireland and, although a product of Christianity, the pagan side of the Sheelas becomes a most interesting and powerful means to make visible what was previously hidden and/or misinterpreted.

In the context of Ireland, the iconic feminine implicit in nationalist discourses produced a homogeneous image of Woman (upper-case, singular) that excluded the explicitly corporeal, as well as the homosexual, the racially different or the ethnic. This exclusive iconography – together with anti-abortion and anti-divorce legislation – is partly responsible for the rhythm of the women's movement in Ireland. For too long a time, notions of 'Irishness' have depended on problematic constructions of the female body. Irish feminists have been investing their energies in the necessary struggle for women's access to their own bodies and self-definitions. But however necessary and noble, debates on nationalist iconography and/or reproductive rights insist on the body as a site occupied, penetrated, politically invaded or physically controlled by either a patriarchal order – be it colonial or nationalist – or by women themselves. Instead of being conceptualized as a signifying entity, the passivity of female corporeality is underlined in these basic struggles. And so, although debates on the female body may already have gained some space of their own in an international feminist agenda, they may not be so evident and still demand constant attention in the case of the Irish nation-state.

This situation is beginning to change, albeit slowly, in aesthetic representation as well as in social practice. As a reaction to misogynist representations and public invisibility, the body has gradually acquired thematic weight in the work of Irish women academics, writers and visual artists, who have started flooding their texts with women's physicality. Women are now represented as concrete realities no longer denied sexual needs and physical dimensions. One of the great achievements of the last generation of women writers in Ireland is making the difficult move from being the objects of the disembodied Irish text to being the 'embodied' subjects of their own representations. In the words of Eavan Boland, Irish women are slowly, but confidently, turning 'from poems into poets' (A Kind of Scar, p. 92), and it is in this artistic and social project that the recuperation of the medieval Sheela-na-gigs is especially illuminating.

As we have seen, the Irish Sheela-na-gigs are also relevant in the international debates on the female body, since their corporeality is 'volatile', shifting, immersed in a never-ending process of 'becoming' meaningful, both signifying and signified. A focus on their fluid dimension seems to be particularly pertinent here, as these icons have been signifiers whose meaning is plural and has changed over time depending on the cultural needs of specific contexts. And so, in Connolly's 'Female Figure', the grotesque aspect of the carving is used to counteract the contemporary reification of women, forced by a patriarchal establishment to fit into extremely beautiful and slim bodies. Connolly's Sheela-na-gig is protected from this process and becomes the subject of her own description. In 'Sheela-na-gig', the articulatory possibilities of the corporeal are revealed when the icon presents her facial and vaginal lips as organs that spell a new message, however repressed or rooted back in time. The protagonist of this poem rescues the voices of those female bodies that had been hidden since the end of female spirituality in Ireland. Connolly's Sheela-na-gigs also express the existence of other kinds of desire, mainly lesbian desire, and give a voice to women who have been discriminated against in a phallocentric, Catholic, heterosexist Irish nation-state.

Sheela-na-gigs are, above all, female erotic representations and, therefore, powerful bodies ignored by patriarchal ideologies. They are bodies that speak and, from their language, resist cultural invisibility for the women of Ireland. The Sheelas we have seen celebrate the plural dimension of the label 'womanhood' and express the need to do away with strict and exclusive definitions of Irishness. Ultimately, these female bodies coming from the early Middles Ages, re-created in and for our time, encourage contemporary women to stop perceiving their own corporeality as a heavy, awkward and shameful burden of guilt.

*   *   *   *   *

Susan Connolly: biographical and critical contexts

Susan Connolly was born in Drogheda, Co. Louth, in 1956 and lives there today. She studied music and Italian at University College Dublin, and her poetry has appeared in a number of magazines throughout Ireland and the UK and in anthologies such as *Ireland's Women: Writings Past and Present* (ed. Katie Donovan, A. Norman Jeffares and Brendan Kennelly, 1994). In much of her work, Connolly has engaged with mythological figures from the Celtic tradition as a means to locate contemporary Irish women within the specific socio-political framework of the island. In the series 'Boann and Other Poems', published in the collection *How High the Moon* (1991), Connolly explored the legends of Boann, The Banshee, Badb, Fedelm and the Sheela-na-gigs. In 1992, she contributed to a chapbook entitled *Brigid's Place/Áit Bhríde*, which included texts on the Sheela-na-gigs by a number of women poets. In 1995, Connolly's treatment of female Celtic figures attracted the attention of novelist and critic Lia Mills in her ground-breaking article '"I Won't Go Back to It": Irish Women Poets and the Iconic Feminine'. Connolly's first solo collection of poetry, *For the Stranger* (1993), was followed by two co-publications with Anne-Marie Moroney, *Stone and Tree Sheltering Water: An Exploration of Sacred and Secular Wells in Co. Louth* (1998), then *Ogham: Ancestors Remembered in Stone* (2000), among other publications. In 2001, she was awarded the Patrick and Katherine Kavanagh Fellowship in poetry.

Works cited

Andersen, Jorgen, *The Witch on the Wall: Medieval Erotic Sculpture in the British Isles* (London: Allen & Unwin, 1977).

Benson, Carmel, *Crouching Sheela*, solo exhibition, Graphic Studio Gallery, Dublin, 1990.

——, *Seir Kieran Sheela-na-gig Travels*, Into the Pattern, solo exhibition, Hallward Gallery, Dublin, 2003.

Beauvoir, Simone de, *The Second Sex* [1949], trans. H.M. Parshley (New York: Vintage Books, 1989).

Boland, Eavan, *A Kind of Scar: The Woman Poet in a National Tradition*, LIP pamphlet (Dublin: Attic Press, 1989).

Butler, Judith, 'Sex and Gender in Simone de Beauvoir's *Second Sex*', *Yale French Studies* 72 (1986), pp. 35–49.

——, *Gender Trouble: Feminism and the Subversion of Identity* (New York: Routledge, 1990).

——, *Bodies That Matter: On the Discursive Limits of 'Sex'* (New York: Routledge, 1993).

Concannon, Maureen, *The Sacred Whore: Sheela, Goddess of the Celts* (Cork: Collins, 2004).

Condren, Mary, *The Serpent and the Goddess: Women, Religion, and Power in Celtic Ireland* (New York: Harper & Row, 1989).

Connolly, Susan, *For the Stranger* (Dublin: Dedalus Press, 1993).

Connolly, Susan et al., *Brigid's Place/Áit Bhríde*, a chapbook (Dublin: Cailleach Press, 1992).

Connolly, Susan and Catherine Phil MacCarthy, *How High the Moon: Boann and Other Poems* (Dublin: Poetry Ireland, 1991).

Connolly, Susan and Anne-Marie Moroney, *Stone and Tree Sheltering Water: An Exploration of Sacred and Secular Wells in Co. Louth* (Drogheda: Flax Mills Publications, 1998).

——, *Ogham: Ancestors Remembered in Stone* (Drogheda: Flax Mills Publications, 2000).

Donovan, Katie, 'Underneath Our Skirts', in *Watermelon Man* (Newcastle-upon-Tyne: Bloodaxe Books, 1993).

Donovan, Katie, A. Norman Jeffares and Brendan Kennelly, *Ireland's Women: Writings Past and Present* (Dublin: Gill & Macmillan, 1994).

Freitag, Barbara, *Sheela-Na-Gigs: Unravelling an Enigma* (New York: Routledge, 2004).

Gatens, Moira, *Imaginary Bodies: Ethics, Power and Corporeality* (New York: Routledge, 1996).

Gimbutas, Marija, *The Civilization of the Goddess: The World of Old Europe*, ed. Joan Marler (San Francisco: HarperSanFrancisco: 1991).

González Arias, Luz Mar, 'Beyond Categorisations: A Conversation with Carmel Benson', *Women's Studies Review* 8 (2002), pp. 91–5.

Grosz, Elizabeth. 'Notes Towards a Corporeal Feminism', *Australian Feminist Studies* 5 (1987), pp. 1–16.

——. *Volatile Bodies: Toward a Corporeal Feminism* (Bloomington: Indiana University Press, 1994).

Heaney, Seamus, *Station Island* (London/Boston: Faber & Faber, 1984).

Herr, Cheryl, 'The Erotics of Irishness', *Critical Inquiry* 17.1 (1990), pp. 1–34.

Kelly, Eamonn P., *Sheela-Na-Gigs: Origins and Functions* (Dublin: County House and the National Museum of Ireland, 1996).

Longley, Michael, *The Ghost Orchid* (London: Cape Poetry, 1995).

McMahon, Joanne and Jack Roberts, *The Sheela-Na-Gigs of Ireland and Britain: The Divine Hag of the Christian Celts – An Illustrated Guide* (Dublin: Mercier Press, 2001).

Meehan, Paula, 'Not Your Muse', in *Pillow Talk* (Oldcastle, Co. Meath: Gallery Books, 1994).

Miles, Margaret R., *Carnal Knowing: Female Nakedness and Religious Meaning in the Christian West* (Kent: Burns & Oates, 1992).

Mills, Lia, '"I Won't Go Back to It": Irish Women Poets and the Iconic Feminine', *Feminist Review* 50 (1995), pp. 69–88.

Ní Dhomhnaill, Nuala, *Selected Poems/Rogha Dánta*, trans. Michael Hartnett (Dublin: Raven Arts Press, 1991).

Pearson, Ann, 'Reclaiming the Sheela-Na-Gigs: Goddess Imagery in Medieval Sculptures of Ireland', *Canadian Woman Studies/Les cahiers de la femme* 17. 3 (1997), pp. 20–4.

Rynne, Etienne, 'A Pagan Celtic Background for the Sheela-na-Gigs?', in Etienne Rynne (ed.), *Figures from the Past: Studies on Figurative Art in Christian Ireland* (Dun Laoghaire: The Glendale Press, 1987), pp. 189–202.

Smyth, Ailbhe, 'The Floozie in the Jacuzzi', *The Irish Review* 6 (1989), pp. 7–24.

Walker, Barbara, *The Woman's Encyclopedia of Myths and Secrets* (London: Pandora, 1983).

Weir, Anthony and Jim Jerman, *Images of Lust: Sexual Carvings on Medieval Churches* (London: Batsford, 1986).

Wood, Helen L., 'Women in Myths and Early Depictions', in Eiléan Ní Chuilleanáin (ed.), *Irish Women – Image and Achievement: Women in Irish Culture from Earliest Times* (Dublin: Arlen House, 1995), pp. 13–24.

Yuval-Davis, Nira, *Gender & Nation* (London: Sage, 1997).

Chapter 8

All of Their Own Making

Contemporary Women's Poetry from Northern Ireland

Rebecca Pelan

Markings on the inside of a book from my early teens tell me a great deal about my sense of identity at the time. My name is followed by my street address, then: 'Belfast. Northern Ireland. The World. The Universe.' I recall this as a common habit of the day, but what strikes me as remarkable now is that, at the time, only Northern Ireland stood between me, the rest of the world and the entire universe. I knew other countries existed, of course; I even had relatives in some of them. But with a sense of belonging and certainty now long gone, they had no bearing on my place in the world. Belfast and Northern Ireland were as much a part of me as my name and the house I lived in. Its language, sectarianism, violence (though not then of the scale experienced later) and industrial darkness – evident in the regular pea-soup fogs of winter and black city buildings – were an unproblematic and uninterrogated part of who I was.

In my mid teens I left Belfast, not voluntarily but with parents who, reluctant to witness another bout of madness, formed part of that mass exodus of Northerners in the late 1960s. With the move away, my certainties as to who I was and where I belonged went the way of all childish things. When I return these days, Belfast is a different place from that which exists in my memory: the darkness has largely vanished along with the fuels that caused it, the buildings are clean, American fast-food outlets have proliferated, there are nightclubs and good restaurants aplenty in the city, and if you stay away from 'hot spots' in East, West and North Belfast (and don't listen to local news broadcasts), then you can pretend it's just like any other place. But it's not. Over thirty years of war mean that Belfast and Northern Ireland have been appropriated almost entirely by sectarianism and, as a result, everything 'belongs' to one side or the other. One result of this is that identity in the North *seems* much less complex than in other places where the whole notion of 'who we are' has been under the microscope for some time. For many people in the

North, knowing who they are embodies certainties that have all but vanished elsewhere.

When in the North these days, I am acutely aware of walking a very careful line between one 'side' and the other – no doubt a result of my own altered perspective, but equally because I am so uncertain of precisely the same things that both sides in this dispute seem so sure of. Outsiders, of course, will be forgiven anything, but I'm not an outsider, just someone who wasn't there to take my corner when doing so was a strategy of survival. And so, I move between one community and the other, as my family always did, making sure that I take none of the cultural markers with me into either camp: symbols, certain books, colours or particular types of music that might indicate a political sympathy or leaning. I do this not only because I don't want to offend, but also because I don't want to be claimed by either side in a war that isn't mine. To avoid appropriation, however, above all else I watch my language, because in a place where tribal differences are not overtly marked – either by skin colour or physical features – then other means of differentiation develop, and in the North, it is most often language which acts as an important marker of who you are, where you come from and, ostensibly at least, which side you belong to.

Language offers Northern Irish people a highly coded way of finding out things about each other, and it is an acknowledged fact that Northerners speak differently depending on whose company we are in: one way when we are in our own community, another when in the company of the 'other' community, and yet another when we are uncertain of the company. There are the obvious markers of name, address, school attended or sporting team/code supported, all of which provide a wealth of information relating to religious tradition, class and, often, political affiliation. Names, of course, provide the most immediate form of cultural identification in many countries, and Northern Ireland is no exception. There is, for example, no mistaking the denominational differences that mark the nicknames for 'William': a Protestant Billy would not substitute for Catholic Liam.

But apart from the personal forms of identification, there are less obvious examples that live in the wider language of the North: 'Northern Ireland' (geographically a misnomer) is the official term for the British Province, but republicans prefer 'the Six Counties'; similarly, for republicans the term 'the Troubles' represents little more than a euphemism for 'war'; unionists (Protestants) use 'Londonderry' while nationalists (Catholics) prefer 'Derry' (even though two prominent loyalist (Protestant) songs – 'The Sash' and 'Derry's Walls' – both use 'Derry'); Protestants say 'aitch', Catholics 'haitch' (for the letter 'h'), reflecting distinctions in the education system; if you talk of collecting for Barnardos as a child, then it means attendance at a Protestant school, since that organization did not operate in Catholic schools; and in the darkest days of civil strife it was important to remember which area you were in when using one of the many (paramilitary controlled) black taxis, since there were ways of asking to be let out at the next stop that were peculiar to both communities. This is Heaney's 'land of password, handgrip, wink and nod, / Of open minds as open as a trap', where people manoeuvre to find out those small but all important indicators of identity, one's name or school, what Heaney calls 'subtle discrimination by addresses' ('Whatever You Say, Say Nothing', p. 79). Saying something meaningful outside these complex codes becomes not only incredibly difficult, but an act of great political dexterity.[1]

But the ability to use language strategically is even more difficult for women in the North since the society as a whole has remained so astonishingly gender-blind and since, despite the fact that the concept of identity has always been central to Irish politics, an interrogation of the whole notion of identity rarely extends beyond the most conventional categories of Irish/British, nationalist/unionist, republican/loyalist, and so on. This means that women, in particular, have not only had to choose between such binaries in terms of their personal politics, but have also been represented as confined within these political categories, and so have become trapped by the binaries themselves, or are discussed in terms of conforming to one or the other. This situation is not only the result of Northern Ireland being dominated by the so-called 'major' political issues – which happen not to include, to any great degree, questions of, say, gender equality, discrimination or domestic violence – but also because those politics and the accompanying war have precluded other political movements, such as the Women's Movement, from gaining the foothold they have elsewhere. And so, the North continues as a strictly gendered society in terms of roles and politics and, as a consequence, women and their concerns continue to be secondary to the dominant politics of the region. Even on the most fundamental level of sexist language, the North is markedly different from the rest of the industrialized world. When spokes*men* for the various political groups were responding to an IRA apology for non-combatant lives lost during the Troubles, their consistent references were to 'IRA *men*, UDA *men* and ordinary, working *men*' (BBC Northern Ireland, 17 July 2002). Not only does this belie the fact that a proportion of the 'non-combatants' killed over the past thirty years in the North have been women (and children of both sexes), but it also suggests that the continued use of such sexist language is of no great concern to those with the power to change things. The fact that women from both communities have played central roles both in contributing to and resisting sectarianism has never altered the dominant representation of the Troubles as a man's war with male victims.

However, despite the fact that gender too often gets overlooked as a political and critical alternative to the binaries that have become central to contemporary Northern Irish politics, it is precisely a gendered perspective that has provided Northern women with a consistently important means of *creatively* critiquing various aspects of dominant Northern ideologies – nationalist, unionist, capitalist and patriarchal – without forfeiting their sense of identity as women and/or Northern Irish. This perspective is most evident throughout a wealth of contemporary women's creative practices, which most often expose the many ways in which the Troubles and women's lives have intersected, not by juxtaposing terrorist and state (the familiar, if formulaic basis of the popular thriller) – or by setting state ideology against family values (as happened in much women's writing from the Republic) – but, instead, by confronting and exploiting the Troubles as a backdrop against which dominant political ideologies are interrogated to reveal their impact upon women and their worlds.

What I hope to do here is show that when we examine the three major genres of women's creative writing – fiction, drama and poetry – we can see that they developed in very distinct ways and had quite different influences on both sides of the border. Women writers in the Republic of Ireland, for instance, most successfully challenged their inherited traditions and images predominantly via the genres of realist fiction and poetry. By contrast, Northern women have been less prolific novelists, and though they have tended to use both poetry and drama as a means of confronting aspects of their respective communities, it has been in the production of poetry that Northern women writers have been able to most consistently oppose the singular and simplistic binaries, or 'double vision', that is so much a part of Northern Ireland. For analytical purposes, then, Northern women's poetry represents one important strand of women's oppositional cultural and creative practices, but, like any other example of cultural production, it needs to be seen as part of a much larger whole. As a result, I'm going to briefly look at the contexts of women's publishing generally, as well as the divergence in the development of prose and drama, before moving on to a closer examination of some samples of women's poetry from contemporary Northern Ireland.

Women's writing and publishing in the Republic flourished, in fact, during the 1970s and 1980s and continued to grow at a significant rate until the late 1990s, when it seemed to level out somewhat. But there was a time – somewhere between the mid 1980s and mid 1990s – when writing by women in the Republic seemed to be everywhere. We were spoiled for choice, not just in terms of volume, but also genre: short stories, novels, plays, poetry, journalism, comics, feminist fairy tales. And all seemed to have one aim: to change the way women had been represented in Ireland, in political, social and literary contexts.

In 1985, for instance, Irish publishing (in other words, books written by Irish writers, non-gender specific, published in the Republic of Ireland) accounted for 33 per cent of the total book market in the Republic and annual sales amounted to £16.3 million. By 1997, Irish publishing had consistently retained 40 per cent of the total market in the Republic for a period of four years, with sales of £39.3 million. Statistics on the influence specifically of women in Irish publishing remain sketchy during this period of intense growth, but we can assume that it was substantial, given that for a considerable length of time the Republic had two highly influential women's presses: Arlen House and Attic Press.

What we do know about women in Irish publishing suggests that they have had a significant impact on the infrastructure of the industry. In 1983, for instance, a Women in Publishing survey revealed that 11 per cent of all books published in the Republic in that year were written by women (Patricia Ferriera, 'Claiming and Transforming an "Entirely Gentlemanly Artifact"', p. 99) while a 1991 publication survey conducted by Cork-based poetry magazine *The Steeple* further suggested that, *excluding Attic Press*, women's writing had been taken up by most of the mainstream presses in the Republic. By 1993, 5 per cent of Dedalus Press, 16 per cent of Gallery Books, 11 per cent of Raven Arts Press and 45 per cent of Salmon Publishing books were written by women. In 2001, those presses mentioned that are still in existence estimated that between 14 and 20 per cent of their published writers are now women. These figures, of course, do not include the significant influence that journals and magazines also had in publishing women's writing during that entire period.

Although the percentages of women's writing in the Republic still lag significantly, in contrast to Northern Ireland they are stellar. Northern Ireland has never had a women's press and so women's writing and publishing did not undergo the same changes that occurred in the Republic. In the Introduction to *The Female Line* (1985), the first substantial published collection of writings by Northern Irish women writers, its editor, Ruth Hooley (now Ruth Carr), celebrated the arrival of the 1980s as a decade in which the setting up and expansion of women-only publishing houses throughout the world heralded the arrival of a 'whole new commercial apparatus' which allowed women's voices to be heard as never before. But she stated that:

> Here in Northern Ireland there is little evidence of any such revolution . . . Few female authors stare out from the covers of locally published fiction and poetry. (For instance, The Blackstaff Press's ratio of single-author poetry books is in the region of two female to fifteen male poets.) (p. 1)

Sadly, too little has changed, although the ratio today is five female to eighteen male poets in Blackstaff's current list, and Kate and Joan Newmann's Summer Palace Press, founded in 1999, has published a significant number of volumes by Northern women poets, among others. Carr believes that most women writers in Northern Ireland in the contemporary period produce poetry that is being published in magazines, because few other places exist that will accept it. But these magazines tend to be UK based, rather than Irish or Northern Irish, which means that Northern women tend to get lumped in with British women writers and are often pressured into writing about the same kinds of issues as they do rather than those issues that specifically relate to life in the North. Carr also believes, however, that there is a North/South divide which excludes particularly Northern women writers and that these writers face the regular complaint that Northern women do not include 'the Troubles' in their poetry, despite the fact that they very often write 'troubled' poetry (Carr, interview with the author).

Blackstaff, as the major publisher of women's writing in Northern Ireland, has always claimed a particular interest in local women's writing. However, its recently retired editor, Ann Tannehill, has stated that the press's inability to focus exclusively on women's writing or even to develop a specific feminist programme has much more to do with what is submitted for consideration than with any bias from within the press itself. According to Tannehill, they simply do not receive a sufficient number of manuscripts from Northern women writers to be able to concentrate on women's writing, yet they receive a great many submissions (often of poor quality) from Northern men. Tannehill blames the paucity of Northern women's writing, at least partially, on a lack of confidence (Carr, interview with the author), although by 2006 this is clearly changing with the recent emergence of such strong women poets as Sinead Morrissey, Moyra Donaldson, Jean Bleakney, Leontia Flynn and Colette Bryce. But in considering these issues, we also need to take account of the fact that contemporary Northern women's fiction has had to compete with the most popular form of writing to come out of the North, namely the largely male-produced thriller, in which women are either non-existent or appallingly stereotyped.

In drama, also, there are significant differences in development. In the Republic of Ireland during the 1980s, for instance, a significant number of women became involved at an administrative level both in the major theatre companies and in the setting up of new groups, and since that time the production of feminist drama there has generally lagged behind that of women's fiction and poetry. Interestingly, this largely administrative path evident in the Republic is one more often associated with those geographic areas less troubled by questions of identity and regionalism, such as the south of England. By contrast, women's drama in Northern Ireland followed the path of both regional and indigenous theatre by producing plays that interrogate identity politics through the local and contingent: something Elaine Aston refers to as an 'identity politics of regionalism' (*An Introduction to Feminism and Theatre*, p. 76) or, more generally, drama that reflects economically or otherwise divided societies.

Northern women's drama throughout the 1980s and most of the 1990s was greatly influenced by the work of Marie Jones (as chief scriptwriter for Charabanc Theatre), and by Christina Reid and Anne Devlin, and, like the poetry produced by women in the North, much of this drama was community based. Much evidence exists suggesting that drama came to represent to Northern women writers a genre that allowed a head-on confrontation with Northern politics. All the playwrights mentioned set many of their plays within the confines of sectarian settings in order to examine the position and representation of women within those communities. But with the demise of Charabanc in 1995 and the shift in interest of writers like Jones, Devlin and

Reid, Northern women's drama is no longer particularly in evidence and is certainly no longer visibly connected to anything resembling a feminist cultural practice – possibly, again, precisely as a direct result of its extraordinarily localized nature. Yet in the politically repressive environment of Northern Ireland, where the women's movement did not have the same radical effect, where women's publishing did not undergo the same degree of radical change and where women's writing in both fiction and drama had a brilliant though short-lived effect, poetry has consistently remained a radical genre in the hands of Northern women, crucially, from both communities.

Critic Jacqueline McCurry has suggested that while Northern Ireland's new poets throughout the 1960s and 1970s were exclusively male, since the early 1980s women poets from Northern Ireland 'have begun to raise their voices in poetry and in protest' and are proving to be more revolutionary than their male counterparts since their work 'consistently realigns our perspectives on the politics of sexuality and on the sexuality of politics' ('"Our Lady, Dispossessed"', p. 4). McCurry is just one feminist critic to argue convincingly that the revolutionary aspect of contemporary Northern women's poetry lies in its deconstruction, rather than inversion, of age-old literary/political images:

> Ulster's young women poets question sexual assumptions, realign religious perspectives and undermine the foundations of male sectarian politics. Preoccupied with the basis of all conflict, McGuckian, Hooley and Shepperson seek not revolt but revolution – and perhaps their 'dispossession' signals a new freedom from history and a movement towards autonomy. (p. 7)

Clair Wills also notes that the ways in which forms of sexuality in this poetry deemed 'improper' or at the very least impolite – maternal sexuality, prostitution, homosexuality, explicit sex – become ways of questioning the propriety of political processes, nationalist and unionist concepts of community and the very basis of the idea of home (*Improprieties*, p. 5). The subversive component to this poetry has clearly prevailed, and can be traced in the work of Northern women poets from *The Female Line* in 1985 to the most recent volumes of Northern women's poetry, such as that from the Word of Mouth collective in 1996 (ed. Ruth Carr et al.), from which I am using most of my examples, principally because it is easily available in print for anyone who would like to read more. The very names of the collections, of course, reveal a great deal about the subversive content and intent of the writing.

This subversive component is also embodied in the work of the best known of the Northern women poets, Medbh McGuckian, a writer more often associated with the creation of a new language – causing one critic to coin the term 'Medbhspeak' (Kimberley S. Bohman, 'Borders or Frontiers?', p. 119) – and a new reality, leading her poetic style to be described as one that interrogates rather than describes the world. In a 1990 interview, McGuckian said: 'I just take an assortment of words, though not exactly at random and I fuse them. It's like embroidery. It's very feminine, I guess. They are very intricate, my poems, a weaving of patterns of ins and outs and contradictions, one thing playing off another' (Rebecca Wilson, 'Medbh McGuckian', p. 4). But being the best known and most stylistically challenging Northern woman poet does not set McGuckian so very much apart when her poetry is read beside that of other, lesser-known Northern women poets rather than in the company of the 'big' names of Irish poetry, Yeats, Heaney or Durcan, or in the style of international literary movements, which is where (largely male) critics more regularly chose to place her work. When she is read as part of that body of work produced by contemporary Northern women, McGuckian can be seen to share with her compatriots many things, including a consistent challenge to the traditional systems of binary opposites: male/female, culture/nature, centre/margin,   domestic/political,   private/public,   reason/intuition, concrete/abstract, I/you – as well as a challenge to the many binaries, already mentioned, that dominate Northern politics.

So, while there is much about McGuckian that is unique, she shares with many Northern women poets a privileging of those things associated with the worlds of women: images of flowers/seeds/fruits as symbols of germination and new hope; houses with doors and windows that are always being opened and closed; windows leading into rooms; beds, closets, perfumes, stitching, sketching, images of birth/life/death; colours (especially blue – the Virgin's colour and that of neutrality/androgyny); the sea, the tide, the moon, which, for McGuckian, hold great importance in pointing to one of the major differences between men and women. The latter are used extensively by others too: Eilish Martin's 'Of earth and air,' Ann Zell's 'Water rites', Mary Twomey's 'Trout' and 'Sea walk', Kate Newmann's 'Mother earth mother goddess', 'My mother and I painting Galway Bay', and her 'Seahorses', which encapsulates so much of this fluid imagery, as well as the symbolically androgynous nature of the animal itself:

> 'I wish you could make me pregnant'
> He said
> I see us bellying in the green
> Growing tentacles like plants
> To disguise our extraordinary beings
> Living to the irresistible pull
> Of moon and tide
> Beyond the flux
> We do not ebb and flow
> Ours a more essential urge
> Rippling into thousands of lunar young
> Cocooned in a paternal pouch
> Released, effortless, fully formed
> Relinquished at once to fend for themselves
> To respond to the rhythms

Which for now
Lull us into peace
Nerve ends still as the seaweed
We have partially become. (*Word of Mouth*, p. 92)

The female body itself has a crucial place in this poetry, though it is by no means always represented in the same way. Work centred on the maternal body is very evident and incorporates, for instance, the erotic, the fluid (literally and metaphorically), as well as the humorous. As a consequence, the internal female voice of the poetry is often pitched against an external world of struggle, and not just in Northern Ireland. In Gráinne Tobin's light-hearted prayer in 'Eight months gone', the 'ham fisted insomniac guest' of her womb becomes a secretive stranger, a fugitive with disorderly behaviour, keeping her up at night hiccupping, stretching, to whom she suggests a period of 'peaceful co-existence' until they eventually meet (*Word of Mouth*, p. 22). Or Ruth Carr's 'Community relation' which sets the arrival of a child against the arrival of a new political era:

Who is this urgent, longed-for creature
tugging the milk from my body
who dreamed nine months in my inner sea
tumbling, kicking, hiccupping
while ceasefires were declared
in the world that she will absorb
like litmus paper? (*There Is a House*, p. 48)

But many of the women deal with the relationship between the internal and external worlds quite differently. Sally Wheeler, for instance, uses both the ancient past and the present refugee crisis to say something about her narrator's life in 'Trojan women', in which the threatening 'far-off murmur which grows out in the street' (*Word of Mouth*, p. 65) makes Trojan women of all women who survive in troubled societies. Ann Zell uses humour, in 'Nature Programme', to trivialize the existence of the ubiquitous helicopters, so much a part of life in the North: 'Before there were helicopters there were dragonflies, And will be, after' (*Word of Mouth*, p. 45).

Nature, fecundity, birds, water, ghosts (literary as well as spiritual), angels (an amazing number of them), mothers and daughters, the list goes on and on. But it is not just a list, of course. It is, rather, in its entirety, an overall working of certain crucial aspects of women's business and crucial determinants of women's lives, both old and new, into a symbolic hybridity which, as a whole, presents us with a uniquely Northern and female version and vision of life.

Some of the most powerful examples of this poetry also, of course, confront the Troubles head on, not through anger or bitterness or taking sides in an 'us' and 'them' dispute, and certainly not by centralizing the violence itself, but rather by providing a close-up of the mundane, the domestic, the ordinary events in life which are always and inevitably touched in some way by the violence. Ruth Carr's 'Your Blue Norwegian Cap', for example, contrasts images of innocence with those of evil to capture a mother's fear for her child's future in a Northern Ireland where women and children share their everyday lives and spaces with violent men, and yet the entire narrative rests on a simple bus journey for a mother and child.

Carr juxtaposes the captured scene on the brim of the child's Christmas hat with a moment in time in which the mother herself is frozen by the ghostly and recurring thought of who has sat in the same seats as her and her child:

> I feel his shadow falling every time.
> Is this the seat he sat in on his mission,
> staring out the window, maybe humming
> to himself, stroking the metal toy that rests
> so easy on his knee in the plastic bag? (*Word of Mouth*, p. 98)

The vibrating bells, dancing deer and 'steaming breath that hangs like thoughts / we don't have language for' on the child's hat contrast starkly with the foulness of the sinister breath she detects behind her:

> Or is he one behind, his breath on my neck
> curdling with mine? I hear the rabid humour:
> *Our hero, Rambo Stone. Next time you go*
> *To Milltown, take a tank* . . . (p. 98)

The reference here is to Michael Stone, a Protestant paramilitary who was imprisoned for murder after opening fire on a group of mourners at a republican funeral in Milltown Cemetery, just outside Belfast. But the specificity of the reference is secondary to the overwhelming fear of violence generally and, specifically, to the predatory nature of Northern paramilitary violence for future generations, all of which is poignantly depicted in the poem at the level of diction and in the form itself, whereby the two short, light stanzas which open and close the poem and which deal with the tableaux on the cap enclose the longer, central stanza of horrible reality. Recoiling from the awfulness of her own imagination, the mother retreats into a world of child-like pretence:

> I pull your cap down tight
> around your ears. Let's pretend
> that we are somewhere far,
> you in your red-painted sleigh
> me a dark-eyed doe
> that has not smelt the lust of dogs
> bearing you away. (p. 98)

Carr is acutely aware of her place as a woman poet in a specifically Northern Irish context where, on the one hand, there is a tremendous expectation that writers will deal with the Troubles almost to the exclusion of all else in their lives; while on the other hand, the writers know if they do engage too directly with the day-to-day reality of life and politics in the North, their work will be seen as too parochial, unpoetic or, even, opportunistic:

> All our hidden hierarchies that we have, that we're brought up with, that we learn through our institutions – all those hidden hierarchies really close our minds or predetermine how we see things. Here [in Northern Ireland] we seem to be riddled with them and I would see poetry as something that would allow an unpicking because it's trying to find ways to address the complexities of our lives. . . . It essentially goes back to the very words in the language where you're not taking anything for granted – or at least trying not to – or you're aware that you're always going to, but trying not to. . . . I think of poetry like a river which carries things for some people, and carries things to other people. (Carr, interview with the author)

In a familiar pattern of struggle between the politics of gender and something as dominant as war, women writers in Northern Ireland generally failed to flourish to the extent they did in many other places. But it becomes clear in any analysis of their writing makes clear, and that they have nevertheless found ways to articulate creatively how the dominant politics of Northern Ireland and women's lives have intersected. They have done so by exploiting the problems in Northern Ireland as a backdrop against which dominant political ideologies are critiqued *through* their impact on women and, by extension, their worlds, including the family: not necessarily as Protestant/Catholic, unionist/nationalist, loyalist/republican women but as women who live in a particular place at a particular time. By making women and their lives central to the writing, Northern women not only merge feminist and nationalist discourses, but also capture and portray a much greater complexity of life than is offered in much popular Northern men's writing. And by placing women and their worlds and concerns central to their narratives, they also, of course, offer alternatives to the entrenched and polarized sectarian perspectives that dominate Northern society and language. Northern women continue to write in a political and social environment that is very different from and still much more constrained and insular than that which exists in the Republic. In addition, there remains a disparity in the volume of women's publishing North and South, and a significant divergence in the way various genres have developed. As a result, if we choose always to talk of 'Irish women's writing' as homogeneous and not to take time to see the specifics of how and where that writing is produced, then we do Northern women a great disservice since, without a close examination of their work within the specifics of its production, their creativity not only looks impoverished, but more often than not looks conservative or, worse, regressive.

This essay began with a personal introduction of my own background as someone born into a working-class family in Northern Ireland, who has experienced being part of the educated diaspora *and* is also a returning emigrant, as well as being someone who comfortably moves between communities, all of which makes me acutely aware of my own language use, particularly when I am in Northern Ireland. But these things also make me aware of my own gendered speaking position – not only in general, but also within the two highly patriarchal political ideologies of nationalism and unionism. I have often felt that feminist criticism is something I 'learned' elsewhere (in Australia and in academe) and usefully deploy as an 'outside' or imported tool to interrogate something inside Ireland. At other times, I use feminist criticism as a means of interrogating various ideologies without forfeiting any notion of my identity as Northern Irish. I think this is also a regular feature of women's creative writing from Northern Ireland, whereby gender is used as a 'third position', which offers an alternative to the existing and entrenched polarizations. But this is quite different from the self-consciously 'neutral' position so often offered and utilized selectively as a means of avoiding confrontation with the Troubles, such as those discussed by Goldring, for instance, who suggests that wherever there is conflict there are always places, usually for those with a 'better' standard of living, which provide a shelter, and he cites the universities, the trade unions and the minority of integrated schools as Northern Irish examples. But Goldring rightly points out that the essential precondition on which these places bring together people from different denominations is that religion, cultural background and guns are checked at the door, since these are places where it is considered bad manners to talk of politics, to talk of the war, since they exist precisely to enable people to forget about the storm outside:

> And this is where my doubts creep in – the metaphorical guns are still in the cloakroom, and when leaving the Crown, Queen's University or the Linen Hall Library, people don't forget to pick up their guns any more than they leave behind their raincoats and umbrellas. (*Belfast*, p. 146)

By contrast, the ability to resist utter appropriation in the face of violence and the toys of war, though extraordinarily difficult for women writers in Northern Ireland, has led them to creatively find a 'third space' from which they interrogate the existing divisions in Northern Irish society.

We may well ask why it is that poetry in particular has played a more consistent role than either prose fiction or drama in the life of Northern women writers. I cannot offer a definitive answer, of course, but a few things come to mind, not least something that Dublin writer Evelyn Conlon has spoken about. When she first began writing in the very early 1970s, Conlon wrote short stories, but she moved to writing poetry for much of the first ten years of her life as a writer, only returning to fiction when she realized that poetry was, for her, a way of allowing her not to confront what she really wanted to say. Now I am not suggesting that every writer of poetry is actually a writer of fiction who really wants to say something controversial, but has not the courage to do so. Anyone familiar with contemporary women's poetry knows how ridiculous that would be. But it does suggest that poetry sometimes offers to writers who have something difficult to say in a hostile environment – and especially writers with limited opportunities and confidence – the opportunity to express themselves symbolically, perhaps in the tradition of Emily Dickinson's suggestion to 'tell the truth, but tell it slant'. It would, of course, be nice to think that the days of women having to tell anything 'slant' were gone. And in some places they are. But as in most troubled places, words still need to be carefully watched in the North. Language still means very different things to different people and can be used to hurt and damage or, worse still from the writer's point of view, to appropriate words for one side or the other. For Ruth Carr, however, poetry represents something quite different again:

> I'm totally in agreement with 'tell it, but tell it slant' – but, for me, it's not so much that you can't say it outright but when you're confronted with so many different realities you realize that it's more complex than can be told in one story – I think that poetry is very well suited to giving voice to external realities and inner truths which often may contradict each other. (Carr, interview with the author)

Perhaps above all else, however, women writers on both sides of the border have responded to the dominant medium *and* worked within the available outlets of their particular place and time, as writers have always done. Poetry in the North has been a creative force for a long time, but one that has been male dominated. And so, just as women in the Republic set about reimagining the roles and images of women within their own dominant literary traditions, so Northern women have done the same within theirs. Whatever the reasons, Northern women poets have continued to weave their quiet revolution in words and images and, in the process, created and fostered a whole new female tradition that has an extraordinary consistency of purpose and vision.

*   *   *   *   *

Ruth Carr: biographical and critical contexts

Ruth Carr, formerly Hooley, was born in Belfast in 1953. In 1986 her Revue was staged in Belfast and Cookstown, and a monologue, *What the Eye Doesn't See*, was commissioned and performed by Point Fields Theatre Company in Belfast and Glasgow. She works as an associate lecturer for the Belfast Institute of Further and Higher Education and has been generously involved in producing publications of students' work for many years. She edited *The Female Line* (1985), which was the first anthology of poetry by women to come out of Northern Ireland. She also compiled the section on contemporary women's fiction in *The Field Day Anthology of Irish Writing,*

Volumes IV & V: Women's Writing and Traditions (2002). A founder member of the Word of Mouth poetry collective, Ruth has had a number of her poems published in journals and anthologies. She was a co-editor of *HU* poetry magazine for about fifteen years, and compiled its last issue (2003) in commemoration of its founding editor, James Simmons. Ruth's first poetry collection, *There is a House,* was published by Summer Palace Press in 1999. The *Word of Mouth Anthology* (1996), which she co-edited with Gráinne Tobin, Sally Wheeler and Ann Zell, has been translated into Russian and was launched in St Petersburg in November 2005. Ruth is currently on the executive of the Creative Writers' Network and is working on her second collection of poetry.

Works cited

Aretxaga, Begoña, *Shattering Silence: Women, Nationalism, and Political Subjectivity in Northern Ireland* (Princeton University Press, 1997).

Aston, Elaine, *An Introduction to Feminism and Theatre* (London: Routledge, 1995).

Bohman, Kimberly S., 'Borders or Frontiers? Gender Roles and Gender Politics in McGuckian's Unconscious Realm', *Irish Journal of Feminist Studies* 1.1 (Spring 1996), pp. 119–32.

Carr, Ruth, *There is a House* (Kilcar, Co. Donegal: Summer Palace Press, 1999).

——, interview with the author, Belfast, Northern Ireland, 22 July 2002.

Carr, Ruth et al. (eds.), *Word of Mouth Anthology* (Belfast: The Blackstaff Press, 1996).

Ferriera, Patricia, 'Claiming and Transforming an "Entirely Gentlemanly Artifact": Ireland's Attic Press', *The Canadian Journal of Irish Studies* 19.1 (1993), pp. 97–109.

Goldring, Maurice, *Belfast: From Loyalty to Rebellion* (London: Lawrence & Wishart, 1991).

Heaney, Seamus, 'Whatever You Say, Say Nothing', in *New Selected Poems 1966–1987* (London: Faber & Faber, 1990).

Hooley, Ruth (ed.), *The Female Line* (Belfast: The Northern Ireland Women's Rights Association, 1985).

Martin, Eilish, *Slitting the Tongues of Jackdaws* (Kilcar, Co. Donegal: Summer Palace Press, 1999).

McCurry, Jacqueline, '"Our Lady, Dispossessed": Female Ulster Poets and Sexual Politics', *Colby Quarterly* 27.1 (March 1991), pp. 4–8.

McGuckian, Medbh, 'An Attitude of Compassions', interview with Kathleen McCracken, *Irish Literary Supplement* 9.2 (Fall 1990), pp. 20–1.

Newmann, Kate, *The Blind Woman in the Blue House* (Kilcar, Co. Donegal: Summer Palace Press, 2001).

Tobin, Grainne, *Banjaxed* (Donegal: Summer Palace Press, 2002).

Wills, Clair, *Improprieties: Politics and Sexuality in Northern Ireland Poetry* (Oxford: Clarendon Press, 1993).

Wilson, Rebecca, 'Medbh McGuckian', in *Sleeping with Monsters: Conversations with Scottish and Irish Women Poets* (Dublin: Wolfhound Press, 1990).

Zell, Ann, *Weathering* (Clare: Salmon Press, 1998).

Chapter 9

'Diving into the Wreck'[1]

Mary Morrissy's *Mother of Pearl*

Ann Owens Weekes

Writing this essay on an Irish novel probably set in the 1950s, I was reminded of the attitudes of many young women today and haunted by a sense of déjà vu. Contemporary Ireland of course differs enormously from its mid-century predecessor, but important behavioural patterns or attitudes persist, in and out of Ireland, and I believe these need to be addressed. One of the most dangerous patterns may be the human tendency to ignore history and to take contemporary conditions as a given, for our own and future lives. Back in the 1960s, for example, as feminism reawoke across much of the western world, young women, exposed for the first time to feminist theoretical and psychological texts, suddenly became aware that the privileging of their brothers, which they had always resented but whose origins they had never questioned, was not in fact natural but cultural. They realized too that this privileging not only enforced women's social, economic and psychological repression, but also that the repression of women was a necessary foundation for the fantasy of male superiority and consequently for male domination.

Fortunately, as we know, the plethora of women's groups which sprang up in the 1960s raised women's consciousness and planned strategies that did change lives. As I write this, I realize how completely the brief summary conceals the harsh and long battles so many institutions and groups waged against these reformers, the most bitter often waged by their own families. Although discriminations remain in private and public life today, feminist philosophical, psychological, Marxist and post-structuralist discourses now affect most areas of scholarship, and some academic insights have been translated into legal, economic and gender role changes. Of course, these changes do little to address injustice on a universal scale. But the advances have been such that many contemporary, privileged western women are uninterested in feminism; some see critical theory as purely academic, while others accept the changes in perceptions, of men as well as women, effected by activists and academics since the 1960s, as 'natural', and thus as unremarkable and unchangeable as the privileging of the male child in the 1960s. The ease with which the contemporary situation is accepted, the injustices of the present as well as the fierce battles of the past ignored, may be a tribute to human adaptability, but it is also dangerous, as the following discussion of unquestioning acceptance illustrates. In this, as in so many areas, feminist criticism is essential, in that it interrogates gender assumptions, exposes injustice and performs the salutary and necessary task of locating women's history.

The text I wish to discuss is Mary Morrissy's *Mother of Pearl,* published in 1996. As the text is not well known outside Europe, I will summarize. Organized into four sections, *Mother of Pearl* is set in an unnamed city in Ireland, in an unspecified period; the city, divided in two by a national border, closely parallels contemporary Ireland (although no actual city is thus separated), but the first section opens in a sanatorium, a ubiquitous feature not of the 1990s but of the 1950s, when tuberculosis was prevalent in the country. The reader familiar with the politics of Ireland is alerted to some connection the writer wishes to establish between the divided country and the sanatoria. In the first section, Irene Rivers, a tuberculosis patient rejected by her family, is treated and recovers in Granitefield Sanatorium.[2] From the city's south-side herself, Irene meets and marries Stanley Godwin and moves with him to his home on the north side of the political divide. Stanley is impotent, so Irene steals a baby from a southside hospital, a baby she and Stanley come to adore. Section two is devoted to Rita Golden, the biological mother of the baby. Barely more than a child herself, Rita becomes pregnant on her first date with her idol, Mel Spain. Although she had not desired the baby initially, she is shattered when the child disappears from the hospital and offers God to trade husband for baby, marriage having failed to fulfill her expectations. The third section is the baby's: christened Pearl by Irene and Mary by Rita, Pearl is discovered after four years, shortly after Stanley's (the adoptive father's) death, and returned to her birth mother. Because she distrusts and shuns the northside, Rita tells the four-year-old Pearl that her first-born died and insists that Pearl has always lived with herself, Rita and Rita's father. Later, Pearl, upset at finding no evidence of the 'dead' baby, creates an imagined life for this sister she calls Jewel. When she herself marries, Pearl, surprised by pregnancy, believes her duty is to her first 'child', Jewel, and induces an abortion, which cuts her off from both husband and mother. In the fourth section, Irene, whom we last saw on the way to prison, is released, returns to the sanatorium, now an old people's home, and awaits the arrival of Pearl, who she believes is out there somewhere.

Missing from this summary is the richness, humour and engaging prose of the text. The familiar in Morrissy is everywhere charged with originality; imaginative and actual doublings abound; and the novel is layered with allusions, so colloquial as to appear 'natural', yet all implying dark, gendered origins. Funny, yet terrible, the story catches the imagination. Although my responses were varied and even conflicting, I saw the disjunction between the characters' psychic and/or emotional responses and their words and physical behaviour as most compelling. Despite their desires, most of which are not consciously formulated, the characters' actions seem governed/determined by some invisible or hidden codes. These codes mandate women's economic and social dependence on men, and motherhood as the goal of their lives; they reify in fact the 1950s ubiquitous western myth of maternal desire. While the myth is almost universal, specific religious and Irish national traditions also invoke motherhood as the sole end of female development and promote images of the selfless woman who devotes herself entirely to her children. Genesis, as is common knowledge today, in both the Irish Catholic and the Presbyterian Churches, as in many others, was widely interpreted to explain women's role as that of mother, a punishment for her sinfulness, and also, without any trace of irony, the source of maternal desire (which, according to the interpretation, enables women alone to nurture children). In addition, early-twentieth-century Irish nationalists, in attempting to promote an ideology distinct from that of British colonists, depicted Irish women as guardians of purity and culture, dedicated to assisting the male fight for national independence, as emotional and physical supports and as mothers willing to sacrifice their sons. Ironically, of course, this ideology borrowed rather than differed from colonizing dogmas. After the division of the country into two states in 1922, Northern Ireland generally followed British practices, but the Free State and later the Republic continued to advocate limited roles for women, the 1937 Constitution of the Free State declaring the nuclear family to be the basic unit of the state, and women's role to be daughters and mothers in that family.[3]

Surprisingly little has changed in the western world with respect to mothers. It's not simply that the novel is set in the 1950s: reporting on the situation in 1992, a psychologist remarks that a mother is 'expected to be unselfish – indeed not to have a "self" at all but to be there to meet the needs of her children'.[4] Obviously little has changed in these codes since the 1950s, or indeed since the nineteenth century. In *Mother of Pearl,* the codes that govern the women in both the northern Protestant and southern Catholic states tear individuals apart, a splitting and division that echoes the pervasive familial as well as national and religious divisions. Many feminist theories would have served to address these ideas, but two seem most apt and gird the entire paper. They are Adrienne Rich's 'Compulsory Heterosexuality and Lesbian Existence' (1980), which helps to explain the social phenomenon of women's acceptance of marriage, motherhood[5] and male dominance, and Jessica Benjamin's work on psychic dependence, 'The Omnipotent Mother: A Psychoanalytical Study of Fantasy and Reality' (1994), which helps to explain the characters' apparently illogical and destructive actions.

In her essay, Rich notes that 'compulsory heterosexuality was named as one of the "crimes against women" by the Brussels Tribunal on Crimes against Women in 1976' (p. 653).[6] The Tribunal dealt with the forcible imposition of heterosexuality through psychological and physical means on lesbian women; Rich examines the repression of lesbian history, the origins of heterosexuality and the ways in which male power is used to enforce it. Critical of the failure to include lesbian existence in mainstream feminist analysis, Rich argues that 'heterosexuality, like motherhood, needs to be recognized and studied as a *political institution*'. As women are the first and most constant sources of nurturing and caring, Rich asks 'whether the search for love and tenderness in both sexes does not originally lead towards women', and questions the Freudian presumption of women's wish to redirect that search (p. 637). 'Societal forces,' she concludes, 'wrench women's emotional and erotic energies away from themselves and other women and from woman-identified values' (pp. 637–8). So pervasive is the assumption of heterosexuality, Rich notes, that even feminist texts presume it unnecessary to explain why women turn aside from attraction to their first source of love, the mother, to a source which many identify as economically, emotionally, and physically less attractive. On the contrary, 'lesbian sexuality . . . is seen as requiring explanation' (p. 637). Critics' and societies' taking of heterosexuality for granted parallels Morrissy's characters' unquestioning acceptance of unspoken codes. The danger lies in the hidden nature of these assumptions and codes; a concealment which continues, a recent critic notes, as contemporary representations depict the heterosexual as 'unmarked', the lesbian or gay as 'marked', a designation I apply to the codes determining female behaviour in Morrissy's novel.[7]

Rich itemizes the characteristics of male power which in the past, and still frequently today, make marriage and identification almost essential to many women's survival. The extent of these characteristics 'ranging from physical brutality to control of consciousness . . . suggests that an enormous potential counterforce [attraction to women] is having to be restrained' (p. 640). Among those pertinent to *Mother of Pearl,* apparent in the reading and needing no further comment, are: the forcing of male sexuality on women; the assumption of 'father right'; the forced economic dependence of wives; the restriction of female fulfillment to marriage and motherhood; the 'idealization of heterosexual romance in art, literature, media, advertising', and the erasure of alternative lifestyles (p. 639). Rich dismisses claims of 'the uncontrollability of the male sexual drive' and of men's fear of women's 'sexual appetites' (pp. 645, 643) as bases of male need to control, concluding that whatever the origins of compulsory heterosexuality, it ensures 'male right of physical, economical, and emotional access' to women (p. 647).

Rich's work illustrates the economic, physical and cultural underpinnings of compulsory heterosexuality and the concurrent dominance of men and denigration of women. Contemporary psychological theory discusses the psychic integration of negative omnipotent fantasies of the other and negative self-images. Jessica Benjamin, in her essay, responds to the theory that 'men's social subjugation of women' is the result of their 'psychic dread of the mother's power' by examining the 'fantasies' of omnipotence that fuel this notion and 'the psychological forces that might counteract it' (p. 131). The young child has the 'capacity to recognize the mother as another subject and [simultaneously to entertain] the fantasy of maternal omnipotence', she notes (p. 132); problems emerge when the tension between the two modes breaks down, and the child lapses totally into fantasy. The fantasy of omnipotence is more than an inability to distinguish self from other: 'it is a defensive reaction to disappointment. The wish says, in effect, I wish I could control everything as I once did (thought I did) when mother did everything I wanted; or if only mother would make everything perfect, which she could do if she wished.' Benjamin concludes with the important point: 'Once the cognitive capacity for distinguishing wish and reality begins to develop, mental omnipotence is a dynamic psychic matter, not an inability to differentiate' (n. 134).

In struggles between the mother and child's desires, Benjamin notes: 'if the mother is unable both to set a clear boundary for the child and to recognize the child's intentions and will, to insist on her own separateness and respect that of the child, the child does not really "get" that mother is also a person, a subject in her own right. Instead, the child continues to see her as all-powerful, either omnipotently controlling or engulfingly weak' (p. 135). In this breakdown of the tension between the fantasy and recognition of mother's subjectivity, the child projects his/her feelings onto the mother. 'All that is bad and dreaded is projectively placed on the other; all the anxiety is seen as the product of external attack rather than one's own subject state.' This psychic repudiation intensifies 'the fear of the other's omnipotence and the need to retaliate with assertion of one's own omnipotence' (p. 133). A pattern of complementary power relations, rather than the optimal one of mutuality, ensues. This pattern of 'doer and done-to', Benjamin asserts, is retained in the oedipal rejection of the mother, as the child dismisses as 'nothing' all that he is not. The young woman is equally chauvinistic, but male control of power allows the hegemony of male chauvinism (p. 140).

Female psyche is also affected by the omnipotent fantasy. The mother's temptation is to believe she can be ideal, 'always there, ready to sacrifice herself', capable of providing 'a perfect world for her child' (pp. 142, 135). This fantasy of the ideal, as well as 'the social reality that mothers are almost exclusively responsible for their children', causes mothers to believe that their children will suffer if they engage in autonomous activities (p. 143). Early feminist scholarship, Benjamin suggests, which substituted images of nurturing mothers for those of powerful fathers, ran the danger of reversing rather than dissolving power relations (p. 142). Ironically then, these early texts actually buttressed the multitude already available and reinforced the internalized image of the perfect mother and the ensuing psychic guilt when the ideal is, as it must be, unattainable. This image of the ideal is an added burden in a patriarchal society, which encourages the young woman only to identify with the mother 'by taking on her devalued status and her servicing role to men'.[8] Her psychic development thus involves the denial of her own needs and the adoption of those that will win approval from those in power. This results in uncertainty, unease with verbalizing and/or inability to verbalize and so recognize her own needs.[9] The overwhelming guilt Morrissy's characters feel, as well as their fantasies and uncertainties regarding their own desires, manifest their psychic development not only as a result of their relationship with their mothers, but also as a result of their and their mothers' enculturation in compulsory heterosexuality and the myth of maternal desire, with the attendant lesson of female inferiority.

Family is the pervasive metaphor that overshadows *Mother of Pearl,* and this essay reads family through the critical lenses above. When Irene is diagnosed with tuberculosis, her mother, in a brutalizing marriage herself, treats the disease as a disgrace, implying 'poverty, a lack of hygiene,' evicts Irene and forces her brothers to scour her room and to burn her possessions (*Mother of Pearl,* p. 4). When her husband inquires as to Irene's whereabouts, she implies the departure is connected to 'an unwanted child'. 'How else could she be?' she taunts, '*Your* daughter' (p. 6). The unmarked story reverberating for both wife and husband is the Irish Catholic misreading of Genesis, emphasizing female culpability and inherited sin.[10] This story is so deeply enshrined that it automatically, intuitively, silently informs Morrissy's characters. Irene daydreams a devoted mother figure coming to reclaim her, despite the fact that she, like the rest of the patients, never receives a visit or letter from home.[11] Her yearning to be nurtured, 'mothered', is pre-eminently human, but the figure she creates, drawn perhaps from popular fiction as well as Irish Catholic concepts of mother, corresponds to the 'demand' of 'conventions',[12] and resembles the psychic creations Benjamin discusses ('The Omnipotent Mother', p. 132) in that it bears no resemblance to any actual mother Irene encounters.

Sanatorium and divided city underscore the family metaphor. Given the pervasiveness and fatality rate of tuberculosis in the 1950s, we would expect the sanatorium to be a place of fear, and Irene experiences the loss of her ribs, a thorocoplasty, the traditional method for treatment of advanced tuberculosis, as a rape of sorts. Morrissy acknowledges her debt to Dr Noel Browne's autobiography for her knowledge of sanatoria and the treatment of tuberculosis. Dr Browne, who experienced these institutions as student, patient and doctor, depicts Irish sanatoria as leper colonies, administered by 'drunks, dope addicts, or simply lazy bastards' (*Against the Tide,* pp. 71, 85). But Morrissy's sanatorium is modelled not on Irish but on British institutions, her chief physician, Dr Clemens, following the practices of an enlightened British doctor in Browne's autobiography (p. 79). It is the abandonment by family, by all the patients' families, not simply the grim situation, that victimizes the patients.

This abandonment causes Irene to question her 'punishment', and finally to reject God (*Mother of Pearl,* pp. 22, 13). Yet, in spite of her own experiences, female dependence on male, whether God, father, or husband, is so deeply laid, so unmarked, that Dr August Clemens, the name of 'the first man to rescue her', becomes her prayer (p. 14). This psychic dependence re-creates the female dependency depicted in cultural texts which shaped perception from the earliest days and instances the collapse of the tension between fantasy and reality that Benjamin discusses. Need for parental approval and desire for an ideal mother govern Irene's responses. Cured of tuberculosis, Irene remains at Granitefield as kitchen help, and when one of the male patients accosts her and then appeals to be allowed simply to look at her body, she consents. Her consent is circulated to the other male patients, and Irene begins a career of catering to the patients whom she sees as deprived of human touch and tenderness. *She* may touch them, but they are not allowed to touch her, for she wishes to 'preserve' her virginity. Attempting to rewrite the old scripts, she reads these encounters as 'her small equivalent' of Clemens's sacrifice – his care of the sick – and will later recall the men 'with the helpless fondness of a mother for her absent, roving sons' (pp. 26, 24). In the Jesuitical preservation of her virginity, however, she relives the same scripts. When one of the patients threatens to expose her activities to Clemens, to retell the old fiction of female sin, Irene decides that she must leave Granitefield for she cannot risk Clemens's disapproval (p. 25). More than, or other than, a god, Clemens has become the fantasy mother: not only did he 'save' her life, by providing a job, he also rescued her from returning, 'orphaned and adrift,' to the 'hostile world' (p. 15). On leaving Granitefield, she reflects: her 'childhood had become a murky dream, a sort of pre-existence: it was *this* place that had borne her [the mother's role]. And made her [God's]' (p. 35). Godmother, god and mother, are conflated in Clemens, as is their/her awe-ful power of banishment.

The familial rejection of the tuberculosis victims is seen from the perspective of their loss; the division of the city is initially seen from the perspective of the south. When Stanley and Irene marry, they move to his north-side house on Jericho Street, where she sees the light as 'thin and nordic, the winds from the river hostile. And there was no joy on the sabbath' (p. 36). She perceives the streets as cramped, forbidding, unfriendly, and collapses identity of place and person, imagining a prying neighbor as 'the epitome of Jericho Street – neat, tight-lipped, righteous' (p. 43). Rita's antipathy is more extreme: she dreads any contact with the territory or people of the north, almost as if she fears an infection, a fear she will not examine. When Pearl is discovered with a northern family, Rita imagines that 'she was being given back a stranger who had been suckled by wolves, who had lived among and been loved by the enemy'. She comes 'with *their* blood not hers' (p. 160). Her views are well know to Pearl, who, in adulthood, remembers Rita saying, 'They eat their young over there' (p. 167).

Rita's perspective does not derive from experience, for she does not cross the political divide. Her antipathy seems to emerge from urban legends, those tall tales that do the rounds, harmlessly for the most part. In this instance, the tales provide a negative example of stories shaping reality, but their real danger lies in their unmarked nature: the stories have been so completely internalized that Rita, unaware of their fictitiousness, acts and sees them as facts.

Pearl's north implies different, or additional, possibilities. She constructs her perspective from experience, memories and sensations which Rita has deliberately exiled, shades forced to dwell in the recesses of her mind. One of the shades, of course, is the child Pearl, whom Pearl/Mary reconstructs as Jewel, her lost twin. Searching for a safe place to house her twin, Pearl selects the north side of the city, comparing it to Egypt in her grandfather's story of the finding of Moses. The story of Moses would have been known to children both sides of the border, but devotion to Hebrew, as well as Christian, scriptures is and was common in the largely Protestant north of Ireland, but not in the Catholic Republic, where Christian scriptures dominate. Other instances of Catholic and Presbyterian practices, such as the biblical names of northern streets and the play with Catholic concepts in the south, emphasize these differences and point to the divisions in the Christian as well as the national family. The grandfather's telling of the story may also imply that his attitude is more tolerant than Rita's, just as his desire to live by the dividing river contrasts with Rita's fear of it, as contaminated by contact with the 'other side' (p. 148).

While Catholic jokes dominate the southern section, the story of Solomon's judgement shadows Irene and Stanley's northern story. Although the scriptural story implies that the 'true mother' who wishes to save the child's life is in that case the biological mother, it also suggests that mothering has more to do with nurturing than birthing a child: the mother shows her authenticity by her willingness to save the child's life; similarly, Irene shows herself to be the true mother in the novel, in that she, unlike Rita, would nurture and thus save the child's life.[13] I have conflated Mother Ireland here with the Irish Republic, though of course the image stood for the whole island in the early twentieth century. However, in the recent past, the image has been more current in the Republic than in Northern Ireland. Aptly hovering over the northern section of the text, the story is also an alternative, albeit still patriarchal, perspective to the expectations and legalities of Catholicism and Protestantism. Unmarked by the characters, underscored by the author, the 'cadences' of both the Moses and Solomon stories can be seen as the 'murmurings of . . . mothers' (or fathers in this case – Stanley rather than Irene the likely source), embodying for Pearl the security and love once experienced.[14] Thus her positive response to the Moses story may not be to content, or not solely to content, but also to the distinctive cadences which stirred the exiled sensations.

Pearl's positive response continues into adulthood, as she reads the north through the lens of home. When Jeff, the man she will marry, brings her to meet his northside family, Pearl feels 'a dizzying sense of familiarity'; driving through the burnt-out streets is like being 'in the territory of dreams'; the street names read 'like a ruined and cryptic version of home' (pp. 209, 210). Significantly, Jeff's is the only positive nuclear family presented. Welcomed by his mother as the daughter she never had, Pearl feels at home, and for the first time in her life, 'entirely blameless' (p. 211). Significantly, in the place where she was mothered, nurtured, by Irene and Stanley, Pearl no longer feels the pervasive sense of guilt which usually engulfs herself and her 'mothers'. Conversely, guilt is connected to lack of nurturing, mothering and valuing of female children. Pearl sees the city as 'twins divided at birth', feels 'proprietorial' about this northern home and resents the southern attitude. 'We should cut them off and set them adrift,' she remembers Rita saying. Pearl adds mentally: 'As if we were not adrift already' (p. 205). Pearl is either suggesting that the south, 'we', rather than the north is unstable, or else identifying herself, 'we', with the north. Parodying southern attitudes, she notes, 'We don't consider it *our* war, indeed, for us, it is hardly a war at all' (p. 168; my italics). This dismissal and rejection of the separated twin is a common southern attitude, one which parallels the dismissal and rejection of the tuberculosis patients: as Irene is ignored by Mother Rivers, so the north is ignored by Mother Ireland, the vulnerable offspring abandoned by mothers who bear little resemblance to the oft-cited mythic models.[15]

The same metaphors of loss and rejection shape the lifescapes of the three principal characters, the ubiquity of the textual references to religion underscoring it as a major, unmarked influence in the women's lives. Irene's marriage to Stanley is built on a double loss: Granitefield and Stanley's impotence. Passively if not positively happy, Irene, being certain that she, a southerner, will never be accepted until she 'bear[s] a child, whom they could claim as one of their own', and to quiet a prying neighbour, insinuates that she is pregnant (pp. 40, 43), a woman's value in the north as in the south being determined by her ability to bear children. The gullible Stanley embraces the impossible, delightedly naming the phantom child Pearl, a 'pearl of great price' (p. 47). When the fantasy dissolves in that emblem of Catholic/Protestant, nationalist/unionist division, the Belfast shipyards, Irene begins to desire a child, not for northern acceptance but for her own, Irene's, sake. Revisioning myth, attempting to write her own script, she imagines that doctors have fashioned a child from the ribs they removed from her body and determines to find this child, her 'first loss', 'rightfully hers, the fruit of Eve's ribs' (p. 55). Searching for her own literal and figurative creation, Irene simultaneously rejects the Judeo-Christian myth of origin and recognizes traditional patriarchal appropriation of children, identified by Rich as a tentacle of male power. Again, Stanley has no problem believing that the baby Irene presents is her own, begotten she tells him with a Granitefield ex-patient. 'Whore,' Stanley rages, falling back on the binaries of the old texts, beating and raping the still-'virgin' Irene. Her reaction reveals an acceptance of sexual guilt, so deeply buried as to seem innate. Irene 'smiles' in relief: 'She had finally been punished. Punished for all the things Stanley did not know about her. Everything would be alright now' (p. 78). Despite her intellectual rejection and revision of punitive myth, Irene's psyche has been so trained that this daughter of Eve welcomes the blows, believing like Rita in a male God whom women must placate and hoping that punishment means her debt is paid.

Inserted between Irene's and Pearl's, Rita's story, although also burdened with the ethos of punishment, is the leitmotif, the typicality and humour of which serve to underscore the pervasiveness of the women's plight. Rita's superstitious ignorance foregrounds the linguistic play with religious concepts of sin, guilt and punishment on the one hand, and the ubiquitous inherited traditions on the other. Although the women may be irreligious, traces of religion everywhere present in language signify the unmarked texts that deform their lives. Stanley's name is Godwin; the woman with whom Irene lodges on her journey to motherhood is May Blessed, a landlady who exacts the last penny from her boarders but who threads her language with Christian scriptures, welcoming Irene with: 'Plenty of room at the inn' (p. 56). Rita's friend calls the pregnancy that follows the unmarried Rita's first sexual experience a 'virgin birth', reminding readers of the impossible model Irish mothers are measured against. Her underweight baby retained in intensive care, Rita, rejuvenated by her three-week holiday from responsibilities, reimagines the baby as plump and pretty, and sees herself, Mel, her husband, and her father as a 'blessed tableau. A Holy Trinity' (p. 124). Conflating here Holy Family and Trinity, Rita excludes the baby, her slip underscoring both the absence of maternal desire and the immature drive to be reinstated again in patriarchal favor. When the baby disappears, Rita bargains with a stained-glass representation of the deity and remembers her optimistic fantasy that the eye of God had regarded her with forgiveness on her wedding day, forgiveness necessary, of course, for the sin of pre-marital sex. But, miserable at her baby's loss, she sees the eye closed in a 'malicious wink' (p. 133). Not so, the narrator notes, there is only one eye: years before, a boy equipped with a catapult had climbed the tree behind the church, 'aimed for the bull's eye' and 'taken out the eye of God' (p. 133). That boy was Mel Spain. When Mel himself is fatally 'shot through the eye' (a case of mistaken identity), the narrator, also imbued with 'natural' religious metaphor, remarks on 'God's peashooting revenge' (p. 150). The tone in Rita's section is almost always humorous, the humour distancing readers from the characters as it continues to highlight unmarked texts that focus on women's chastity and patriarchal families. The ubiquity of images and responses reveals the layering of language, and thus of perception, with fragments and distorted scraps of the old stories.

Initially pleased that her childish infatuation with Mel Spain results in pregnancy and thus, in the conventional mores, marriage, Rita feels trapped and resents the baby as the limitations of pregnancy become apparent. Frightened by vague apprehensions, she, like so many young women, hears no actual accounts of maternal experience, of many women's lack of desire for children. Denied real-life alternatives to myth, Rita cannot see, say or comprehend her fears. Only when her baby is taken does she allow herself to realize 'that someone had wanted her baby more than she had', a 'truth' she deems 'terrible' (p. 126). Absence of maternal desire seems so unnatural that she cannot confide to husband, father or even to a friend with whom she jokes about pre-marital sex. The reality of her experience must be suppressed, for Rita herself and her society accept the unmarked text, the myth of motherhood's incorporating maternal desire. Guilt rules Rita until another 'accident', another pregnancy, opens her eyes to the possibility of writing her own story, or as she calls it, making a 'new start'. The ease with which she can re-create gives her a sense of power 'over the official version of their lives' (p. 150). This story, however, is doomed to failure, for Rita does as Irene attempts: ignores history, deliberately excising Pearl's first four years instead of incorporating and revising the story.

Revealing the power of the invisible, repressed history comes back to haunt the present, with Pearl's body as site of the struggling, rejected story. During the years of Pearl's absence, Rita becomes adept at creating new fictions, which, like the romances and fairy tales that underlie her expectations, serve to bolster her self-image. Despite her bargain and what she fears may be its consequences, she invents a story of the death of her first baby, a story she repeats to the recovered Pearl, unable to re-create a fiction with the actual materials of Pearl's loving upbringing in the north. Ironically, from this fiction Pearl fashions her own broken history. Disturbed by the lack of evidence of a first baby, no grave or photographs, Pearl is haunted by an image of the phantom child as orphaned and lost, an image of her lost self, of course, her memories and history, which, thanks to Rita's fiction, she pictures as a lost child. She wakes at night, her cries mingling with those of the phantom sister. Fearful lest this sister displace her, Pearl conjures for her a life similar to that she led with the protective Irene and the fond Stanley. Imaging a desired and loving mother, a contrast to the giddy Rita, Pearl is yet another woman in the series drenched with guilt for her 'unnatural' desire (pp. 170, 192, 200).

As Pearl matures, this 'sister' recedes, only to resurface during her pregnancy. This 'fully formed' child, incorporating the history of the mother who desired her and the one who did not, the 'true mother' and 'evil mother' of biblical and fairy story, stalks Pearl's dreams. It's not the child who is lost, but the mother, she realizes, coming to intuitive terms with her own desperate search for mother. Assenting to what she sees as Jewel's prior claims, Pearl induces an abortion. Loss of history, of 'herstory', thus leads to schizophrenia and violence, a religious and political as well as familial lesson in the divided Ireland of Morrissy's novel. The guilt that Pearl experiences, the belief that her 'savage reversal of natural instinct' makes her unfit to be with her husband, Jeff (p. 216), points to the continuing and corrosive influence of Irish-Catholic-interpreted myth. The reality of her experience is repressed, as Pearl responds to the unmarked fiction, believing herself a 'vessel of guilt, carrier of original sin, a child of Eve' (p. 218). In her divided body, as in Rita's psyche, the myth of maternal desire struggles with and vanquishes the reality of maternal disinclination.

The terms employed by Rich and Benjamin allow us to read Morrissy's family fable, despite its specifically Irish context, as instances of an ancient, almost universal, gendered myth. The problems with myth are multiple: the loss of actual women's history;[16] the distortion of relationships to favour the powerful; and the embedding over time of these distortions in both culture and individual psyche as natural, as unmarked. Rita may ignore history but cannot render it impotent, as we see with Mel's death and Pearl's breakdown, a dangerous signal to those who would see feminist battles as over. The desolate Pearl wonders whether all humans feel as she does, 'an exquisite loneliness, an absence unaccounted for' (p. 218). This absence is not only that of first mother, first home, it is also the absence of women's history. The theory of maternal desire *is* a denial of human history, and a substitution, similar to Rita's, of myth. The bodily and mental rupture replays the loss of history; the guilt the women feel, which keeps them silent, usually tractable, always resentful, points to the psychic hidden success of myth. Morrissy's awe-ful story, like those of other feminists,[17] can be read as a presentation of the reality of mothering rather than the fiction of maternal desire, thus as empowering. In creating this new fiction from the detritus of myth, Morrissy begins to reconstruct the absence Pearl grieves.

*   *   *   *   *

For 'Mary Morrissy: biographical and critical contexts', see Chapter 10.

Works cited

Benjamin, Jessica, 'The Omnipotent Mother: A Psychoanalytic Study of Fantasy and Reality', in Donna Bassin et al. (eds.), *Representation of Motherhood* (New Haven: Yale University Press, 1994), pp. 127–46.

Boland, Eavan, *Object Lessons* (New York: Norton, 1995).

Browne, Noel, *Against the Tide* (Dublin: Gill & Macmillan, 1986).

Burstein, Janet, 'Restorying Jewish Mothers', in Andrea O'Reilly and Sharon Abbey (eds.), *Mothers and Daughters* (New Haven: Yale University Press, 1994), pp. 37–45.

Condron, Mary, *The Serpent and the Goddess: Women, Religion, and Power in Celtic Ireland* (New York: Harper & Row, 1989).

Gamez-Fuentes, Maria-Jose, 'Never One without the Other: Empowering Readings of the Mother–Daughter Relationship in Contemporary Spain', in Andrea O'Reilly and Sharon Abbey (eds.), *Mothers and Daughters* (New Haven: Yale University Press, 1994), pp. 47–59.

Hayes, Trudy, *The Politics of Seduction*, LIP pamphlet (Dublin: Attic Press, 1989).

Heilbrun, Carolyn G., *Writing a Woman's Life* (New York: Ballantine Books, 1988).

Hywel, Elin ap, 'Elise and the "Great Queens of Ireland": "Femininity" as Constructed by Sinn Fein and the Abbey Theatre, 1901–1907', in Toni O'Brien Johnston and David Cairns (eds.), *Gender in Irish Writing* (Philadelphia: Open University Press, 1991), pp. 23–39.

Innes, C.L., *Woman and Nation in Irish Literature and Society, 1880–1935* (Athens: University of Georgia Press, 1993).

McWilliams, Monica. 'The Church, the State and the Women's Movement in Northern Ireland', in Ailbhe Smyth (ed.), *Irish Women's Studies Reader* (Dublin: Attic Press, 1993), pp. 79–99.

Meaney, Gerardine, *Sex and Nation: Women in Irish Culture and Politics*, LIP pamphlet (Dublin: Attic Press, 1991).

Moloney, Caitriona and Helen Thompson, *Irish Women Writers Speak Out: Voices from the Field* (New York: Syracuse University Press, 2003).

Morrison, Toni, *Beloved* (New York: Knopf, 1987).

Morrissy, Mary, *Mother of Pearl* (1996; London: Vintage, 1997).

Nice, Vivien E., *Mothers and Daughters: The Distortion of a Relationship* (London: Macmillan, 1992).

O'Brien, Edna, *House of Splendid Isolation* (London: Weidenfeld & Nicolson, 1994).

Orbach, Susie and Luise Eichenbaum, 'Feminine Subjectivity, Countertransference and the Mother–Daughter Relationship', in Janneke van Mens-Verhulst, Karlein Schreurs and Liesbeth Woertman (eds.), *Daughtering and Mothering: Female Subjectivity Re-analyzed* (London/New York: Routledge, 1993), pp. 70–82.

Phelan, Peggy, *Unmarked: The Politics of Performance* (New York: Routledge, 1993).

Rich, Adrienne, 'Compulsory Heterosexuality and Lesbian Existence', *Signs: Journal of Women in Culture and Society* 5 (1980), pp. 631–60.

——, *Blood, Bread, and Poetry: Selected Prose, 1979–1985* (New York: Norton, 1986).

Robinson, Mary, 'Women and the New Irish State', in Margaret Mac Curtain and Donncha O Corrain (eds.), *Women in Irish Society: The Historical Dimension* (Westport, CT: Greenwood Press, 1979), pp. 38–70.

Snitow, Ann, Christine Stansell and Sharon Tompson (eds.), *Powers of Desire* (New York: Monthly Review Press, 1983).

Viney, Ethna, *Ancient Wars: Sex and Sexuality*, LIP pamphlet (Dublin: Attic Press, 1989).

Walker, Alice, *The Color Purple* (New York: Harcourt Brace Jovanovich, 1982).

Warner, Marina, *Alone of All Her Sex* (London: Quartet Books, 1985).

Chapter 10

Feminism and Postmodernism

Representations of Identity in
Mary Morrissy's *The Pretender*

Anne Fogarty

In a well-known but contentious pamphlet, *A Kind of Scar*, published in 1989, Eavan Boland declared that Irish writing would change fundamentally when women shifted from being the object of literary texts to their subject. At the time, such a demand for the valorization of women authors and their distinctive aesthetic and areas of concern seemed at once politically radical and eminently practicable. The method of gynocriticism, as advocated by Elaine Showalter with its accompanying mission of restoring the lost traditions of female creativity, appeared to be an urgently necessary import to the Irish cultural scene, which was constellated solely by the achievements and symbolic value systems of male writers. However, as Boland herself anticipated, while such a change in orientation might refurbish the nature of the Irish literary canon, it would not of itself alleviate the troubled connections between women authors and their subject matter nor resolve the question as to how the female self might adequately be portrayed. In short, the ethical dilemmas and aesthetic choices faced by the individual writer remain obdurate problems, even if the concrete goals of the first wave of feminist criticism could easily be realized.

Bearing such issues in mind, my essay will concentrate on *The Pretender* by Mary Morrissy, a novel which, as I shall contend, precisely meditates on femininity as an intricate cultural and political convolute, the resonances and limits of imagined realities, and the complex positionings of the postmodern heroine. Published in 2000, this work is a multi-layered and subtly realized fictionalization of the life of a woman who claimed to be Grand Duchess Anastasia, the youngest daughter of the Russian Imperial family. In tackling this story, Morrissy broaches one of the enduring historical enigmas of the twentieth century, which has spawned numerous histories, television documentaries and films. The perennial fascination with the tragic deaths of the Romanovs and with the tantalizing legend of an escape by at least one family member seems to stem from nostalgia for a bygone, aristocratic world order and a romantic identification with the power and wealth once wielded by this privileged social class.

Commentators on the figure of Anastasia tend to divide into two camps: historians, such as R.K. Massie, who accept that the entire Russian Imperial family was assassinated in Ipatiev House in Yekaterinburg, Siberia, in the early hours of 17 July 1918 and attest that no one survived the assault, and biographers, such as Peter Kurth, who are at pains to defend the validity of Anastasia's heroic story of survival. Positivist and romantic approaches to the past in this instance seem to hinge on the question of belief, the authority of factual data, and the problematic status of subjective testimony and experience in the establishment of knowledge. In either case, the tale of the woman who might or might not be Anastasia is retold in line with particular ideological values and narrative imperatives. Massie's dispassionate, rationalist history, *The Romanovs*, casts her as a curiosity and anomaly, while Kurth glorifies her as the leading light of his romantic hagiography, *Anastasia*. Morrissy's fictional exploration, by contrast, brings this figure vividly to life by depicting her fractured interiority and capturing the intrapsychic forces that facilitate the donning of an assumed identity. As Morrissy's title indicates, her heroine is at once someone who lays false claim to a ruling position and someone for whom role play is the very basis of her identity. Unlike historical treatments of the woman who claimed to be Anastasia, *The Pretender*, with its receding chronologies and overlapping stories, is concerned less with issues of truth and falsity than with the extent to which female subjectification and the feminine capacity for masquerade might be used as a prism by which to view the troubled course of twentieth-century history.

In a postscript and a list of acknowledgements appended to the text, Morrissy gives a brief account of the Polish woman Franziska Schanzkowska, who in later life, it is held, assumed the alias of the Russian Crown Princess; she also itemizes the multifarious historical sources on which she drew in depicting the sharply delineated but shifting settings of the plot. In so doing, she deliberately raises a curtain on her fiction-making and suggests that her creation is to be seen as porous and open and not as a discrete, self-contained construct. Equally, it can be argued that this revelatory coda emphasizes the power of art to override and supplement history and make good its omissions and lacks. The real Franziska Schanzkowska, who officially went missing in Berlin in 1920, is given a dramatic afterlife in Morrissy's fiction. The pretences on which novel writing depends enable it to achieve an insight which history precludes or is incapable of achieving. The figure of the Pretender, moreover, symbolically conjoins the activities of the writer and her subject and postulates a correspondence between creative acts of imagining and the convincing delusions projected by the main protagonist. The fear of inauthenticity and the warring urges for self-erasure and self-invention are the purview of both the female author and her leading character. The dyad of writer and subject is at once realigned and held up to scrutiny in the altered feminist aesthetic that the novel proposes.

As a consequence, *The Pretender* cannot simply be construed either as a heroic act of feminist recovery or as an attempt to tap into the sentiment of a popular fantasy. Instead, Morrissy renders the tangled story of her multi-faceted heroine as an interplay of presence and absence that never fully explicates or exhausts its subject. My analysis of this subtly modulated fiction will concentrate on two issues: first, I shall explore the ways in which the author exploits the resources of narrative in order both to probe this elusive female biography and to draw out the contradictory facets of her hidden, psychosexual history. The chief concern of the novel is less to set up the main protagonist as a symbol of oppression or of patriarchal abuse than to anatomize the conditions of her being and to invent a form of psycho-narration which can most accurately convey the lived experience of the several entwined female fates that she encapsulates. The quest for a narrativity that can at once disclose and also question the ways in which women's lives are commemorated and shaped is the fundamental driving force of this compelling text. In this light, Morrissy's fiction may be situated, as will be seen, within pressing Irish feminist debates about the responsibility of the woman writer and the possibility of locating a different symbolic order that can dislodge patriarchal presumptions about, and codings of, the feminine.

A second but crucial aspect of this text that I shall consider is its conscious deployment of postmodernist techniques. Strikingly, in contemporary Irish writing, it is female rather that male authors who have been drawn to this latter mode, Anne Enright, Medbh McGuckian and Mary Morrissy being amongst its most prominent exponents. In analysing *The Pretender,* I shall consider the reasons for this affinity between an Irish feminist aesthetic and postmodernism. Above all, I shall consider how the postmodern predilection for what Rosi Braidotti (*Nomadic Subjects*) has termed the 'nomadic subject' facilitates the exploration of themes that preoccupy Irish public debate. As an exilic figure who wanders between Tsarist Russia, Berlin during World War I, a Poland that is a dominion of Imperial Germany and present-day America, Anastasia telescopes discussions about transnationalism, postcolonialism, the social exclusion of women and migrants, and the dangers of a global economy. Furthermore, in acting as a nexus between forms of memory and as a point of contact between histories written from above and those written from below, her story invites reflection on the ways in which the past is invoked in contemporary Ireland and the difficulty of assuaging collective guilt for former abuses of power. Finally, I shall argue that the adoption of postmodern structures and mindframes enables Morrissy not simply to debunk restrictive views of femininity but also to create a compelling new myth of a metamorphic female identity that shows not only how the self is depleted and inscribed by ideological forces and political regimes, but also how it may fight back against obliteration, speechlessness and subjugation.

I Finding a narrative

Two moments of reported speech open and close *The Pretender.* At the outset a voice, later identified as that of Anastasia, calls for 'eggs', while the novel fades out with the following deadpan declaration of the police officer who has just apprehended the befuddled protagonist and her spouse: 'The King? Ain't you heard, pal? The King is dead' (p. 273). The initial scene introduces us to the domestic disarray in the residence of Anastasia and Jack Manahan. The latter is a history professor with a consuming interest in genealogy, who has married the supposed Grand Duchess in a heroic attempt to rescue her from oblivion and public contempt. He treats her with reverent devotion and tries to provide her with prompts that will enable her to salvage her repressed memories. The querulous demand that she issues at the outset is for an illustrated book about Fabergé eggs, an aide-memoire that fails to awaken her blurred recollections of her past. The closing comment by the highway patrolman is an ironic rejoinder to Manahan's insistence that the silent, terrified old woman at the back of his car is of royal descent. The dead king to whom he refers is, of course, Elvis Presley. Royalty in America in the 1980s is dismissed as a phantom or as a fleeting accoutrement of secular fame. Moreover, it is seen as an inherently male-centered system of meaning that disallows any female parts, such as that of the disinherited 'princess' which the heroine claims for herself. Symbolically, in the jagged trajectories that the novel traces, we move thus from a rare instance in which Anastasia's voice is heard – albeit as an off-stage presence – and her unappeasable neediness is registered to an emphatic rejection of the violent history that she encapsulates and of the irrationality of feminine identifications and projections.

These two framing scenes capture the complex dualities of Morrissy's heroine and the conflicting subject positions that she occupies. To the degree that she is at once a lone survivor and a pathetic relict, a token of value and a sign of abjection, her life becomes an enactment of the warring aspects of femininity. On one level, this multi-dimensional heroine is a vehicle for fantasy, an allegory of truth and an essential link to the hidden dimensions of the past, while on another, she is an embodiment of madness, senility, inauthenticity and obsolescence. For Manahan, the amnesiac Anastasia is a romantic enigma that he yearns to possess, but she is also, as he observes with disappointment when he first encounters her, disturbingly reminiscent of a 'bag lady' (p. 10). After their marriage, she slowly destroys the order of his household and fills their home with a menagerie of free-roaming cats and the detritus that she collects. Her distinguishing traits of imperiousness and helplessness and her liking for chaos and dirt associate her with a childlike dependency and an exotic otherness. In addition, her behaviour bridges two opposing aspects of modernity. Her random hoarding of the disposable objects of contemporary American society such as doughnut cartons, seems to betoken a modern ability to adapt to circumstances and to inhabit a world of mass products that refuses any links to the past. However, at the same time, her unease and 'constant fear of ambush' (p. 5) capture not only her sense of alienation, but also the extent to which modernity is posited upon a denial of the traumatic histories that underlie its seemingly untroubled surfaces. Hence, a phone call in the middle of the night incites terror in her because, Manahan speculates, she dreads pursuit by 'a voice from the dead' (p. 15). The initial section of the text ends with a brief vignette of Anastasia on an American talk show in which the interviewer ventures to question the trustworthiness of her story. She retorts by asking him: 'Can you really prove who you are?' (p. 18). Although she plays the role of the madwoman for many of the people with whom she comes in contact, her confusion and inability to produce incontrovertible evidence of her origins serve to pinpoint the fragile nature of modern identity. As the narrator succinctly observes, Anastasia's nettled response shows that she has 'finally come up with an existential argument – a question of her own' (p. 19).

In exploring this problematic female history that is 'as volatile as the century itself' (p. 14), Morrissy devises a narrative structure that satisfies the demands of sequentiality but also mimics the discontinuities in her protagonist's biographies. Indeed, her very instability raises questions about our need to read for the plot and the propensity to think of lives as readily lending themselves to an ordered mode of narrativity. Unlike historical investigations that exhibit a forensic interest in the way in which the Polish woman, Franziska Schanzkowska, assumed the role of Anastasia and duped others into accepting the veracity of her performance, Morrissy presents this tale of multiple selves as a convoluted drama of consciousness. The focus is less on the peculiarity of the phenomenon of the imposter than on the gap between inner and outer realities, the opposition between a view of selfhood as embodiment on the one hand and as sentience on the other, and the divergences as well as hidden links between female lives.

The Pretender splinters into eight sections. The opening and closing episodes are set in the present. They take place in Virginia but are separated by an interval of five years, spanning the period from 1978 to 1983. They thus plot out Anastasia's gradual decline into dementia as well as probing the losses induced by temporal discontinuity, old age and historical change. The intervening sections follow a backward spiral in time. The second chapter shifts the scene to 1922 and introduces us to the amnesiac Fräulein Unbekannt, who has been consigned to Dalldorf Asylum in Berlin following a failed attempt to drown herself. The third section follows her fate in Berlin in subsequent years as she assumes the character of Anastasia and struggles with the expectations that accompany her new role. This progression is broken by the succeeding fourth and fifth instalments of the narrative which provide us with two contrasting flashbacks, one in which Franziska Schanzkowska's anguished suicide attempt in Berlin on 17 February 1920 is delineated, and another in which the confinement and ultimate massacre of the Russian

Imperial family in Yekaterinburg in July 1918 is portrayed from the first-person perspective of Anastasia. The sixth and seventh episodes shift attention once again and concentrate on the figure of the Polish emigrant Franziska Schanzkowska. They pick up her story at a mid-point, on her arrival in Berlin in August 1914. The sixth section describes her experiences as a worker in the AEG armaments plant, her courtship of a young German, Hans Frahlich, who subsequently dies at Verdun, her injuries following an explosion in the Danger Building of the factory, which lead to the termination of her pregnancy, and the several breakdowns that she suffers following her release from hospital. In one of the numerous moments of duplication in the text, this part ends with a reprise of her suicide by drowning. The seventh episode of the novel takes us back to Franziska's childhood and outlines the events that lead to her departure for Berlin, offering them as a possible key to her emotional instability. It depicts her obsessive love of her abusive father and her jealousy when she is ousted in his affections by her younger brother, Walter. The tragic drowning of the latter constitutes the climax of this section of the text. In keeping with many other actions of the plot, this calamity is given a dual causation as it is intimated that it has been brought about by the frustrated desires of two women. The death of the cherished son, who has become the emotional fulcrum of this family, has been jointly effected by the vengeful actions of Franziska Schanzkowska and of Elena Schanzkowska, her father's first wife, who had died in childbirth. Hence, the ghostly figure of a further forgotten woman momentarily comes to light at the end of the embedded narratives that form the core of the novel.

The delicate circuitry of Morrissy's narrative allows her to undertake a complex probing of the nature of femininity and to test the limits of feminist endeavours to locate and reconstruct the female subjects that have been occluded in male-centered histories of the past. Angela Bourke has contended that different kinds of language are needed to permit the 'silenced voices from the past to speak' ('Languages, Stories, Healing', p. 306) and that new horizons of understanding can only be achieved if we are prepared to listen to stories 'where the normal is turned inside out' (p. 313). *The Pretender* similarly suggests that alternative ways of telling and more expansive notions of selfhood are required in order to trace the contours of forgotten lives and to profile a heroine who persistently remains an outcast and refuses to shed her eccentricity and awkward allegiances. The wager of this fragmented narrative is that it considers the problematic nexus between identity, femininity and negation and yet convinces us of the core reality of the aberrational, self-multiplying heroine, who takes on a dizzying array of aliases in the course of the plot, including Mrs Jack Manahan, Fräulein Unbekannt, Frau Tchaikovsky, Franziska Schanzkowska, the Grand Duchess Anastasia, Sissi, Princess, Baby, and Fräulein Wingender. In tracking the numerous permutations of Anastasia's split identities, the novel invites us to reflect on marginality and exclusion, to consider the exploitative nature of political regimes and social institutions, and to take stock of the dissolution of communal bonds and the increasing privatization of experience in modern culture. Furthermore, even though it deftly dismantles femininity as an ontological and political construct, it still suggests that this story of lost, dislocated and adopted female selves has a persuasive force as a postmodern fable.

The experimental use of narrative structure is one of the chief means by which Morrissy paints a composite but fluid portrait of her protean protagonist. The segmented, episodic structure may be read in two different but not mutually exclusive ways: as a series of fragments or as a sequence of counterpointed experiences that are ultimately implicated in each other. Several images, moreover, fuse and cut across the disparate narratives of Anastasia's lives including the egg, the *matryoska* doll and recurrent allusions to drowning, pools, rivers and water. All of these motifs are linked with notions of surface and depth and with the possibility of calling into play a reverse optics that permits us to see things either from the inside out or from a contrary point of view. This apposition of images that invert and mirror each other builds up a troubling sense of the affinities and disparities between a member of the Russian Imperial family and a Polish factory worker. The flashback in which Anastasia recalls the horror of the murder of her family in Ipatiev House in Siberia and recounts her own death scene ends with her resumption of a game of make-believe that she played as a child in which she 'would pick a girl out on the street, a factory worker, peasant girl, it didn't matter and wonder – what if I were her?'. Through this pretence she seems to escape the fact of her own annihilation and to become 'not Grand Duchess Anastasia, but someone other. A nobody, a girl of no importance' (*The Pretender*, p. 97). Thus it is intimated that Franziska is both Anastasia's Other and her re-embodiment.

Details in their stories similarly seem linked through this inverted optics and process of doubling. Anastasia's benign and loving father is countered by Franziska's boorish and violent one; the cherished Tsaervich, Alexei, is mirrored by Walter, the much-loved son and heir of the Polish family; the calamitous execution of the idealized Romanov family is set off against the festering jealousies and incestuous, sexual rivalries of the peasant household and the murder of a favorite son; Alexander Tchaikovsky the Russian soldier who rescues Anastasia and later marries her, is matched by the emigrant soldier with the same name who propositions Franziska in Berlin and claims to have a necklace belonging to the Grand Duchess Anastasia; Anastasia takes refuge in her dying moments in the fantasy of a peasant girl's existence and, in complementary fashion, Franziska transforms herself for a photographic portrait with her fiancé, taken in a Berlin studio, into a Russian princess by donning 'the Tatiana', a Romanov gown.

The ornate Fabergé eggs described in the opening chapter of the novel sum up the decadence and mystery of the Russian Imperial family, while the utopian fantasy that is evoked by the myth of the Romanovs seems in the heroine's ruminations as 'perfect as a decorated egg' (p. 66). By contrast, the eggs produced on the Polish smallholding symbolize the tragic conflicts of this world on the edges of the German Empire and capture its penury and elemental struggles for survival. The dropping of a basket of eggs by her older brother who becomes ostracized as a simpleton, initiates the heroine's gradual loss of innocence as she registers her father's cruelty towards the son whom he regards as different. The heroine's dreams of 'eggs or the pith of oranges' (p. 193) in wartime Berlin concretize her hunger and gnawing sense of unfulfilment in this world to which she has escaped. In addition, the import of the egg as a symbol of rebirth and regeneration is exploited in a strand of images that limns the shadowy, ineluctable contours of female consciousness. On the one hand, the fragile shell of the egg emblematizes the divisions between an outer self and a hidden inner core, while, on the other, it captures the efforts by the protagonist forcibly to create herself as subject and break through the silence to which she is relegated. Fräulein Unbekannt in the second section of the novel is described as 'incubating' (p. 68) a princess as she gradually thinks her way into the persona of Anastasia, and the explosion in the Berlin armaments plant paradoxically saves Franziska from her 'eggshell universe' (p. 173) and her stereotypical fate as the shamefully pregnant fiancée of a dead soldier. The egg, too, with its fragile shell acts as a symbolic correlative for the painful splitting of female identity between the wholeness of the semiotic sphere where desire seems secure and the losses and frustrations of the symbolic order. In the penultimate section, we are told that Franziska realizes that there are 'two worlds – the inside and the outside' (p. 203). Initially, as a child, she is acquainted only with the former. Eventually, the dissolution of the family through her murder of her younger brother pitches her into a guilt-ridden withdrawal into an existence in which she suppresses her former history and hidden desires.

The *matryoska* doll bought by Franziska, which contains all the members of the Imperial family with the tiny figurine of the Tsarevich enshrined at its centre, also functions as a metaphor for the accumulating layers of Morrissy's novel and for the temporality of experience. *The Pretender* presents the varying stories of its heroine as a series of reticulated narratives that both fit snugly inside each other and need to be prized apart as we read through the text. Furthermore, this metaphor of embeddedness indicates the extent to which female selfhood is overwritten in the text by ideological notions of femininity and madness, by political and social forces, and by the psychosexual scripts of the family. The images of water which interweave the pages of the novel constitute an analogous symbolic nexus that articulates notions of surface and of depth, exclusion and belonging. Such motifs are used too to crystallize the existential struggle of the heroine. Franziska Schanzkowska's suicide attempt by drowning in a canal in Berlin is represented as a longing to fight free of the constraints of individual existence and to enter the anonymous structures of history:

> Down, down, she will rush. Headlong. Her intricate store of memories will
> drown as she enters the freezing water in an icy spray. It is what she wants. To
> escape memory. To become innocent. To enter history. (p. 91)

Her troubled condition is depicted both as a consequence of her sense of
anguish and painful female lot and as the result of the inevitable condition of
the human subject who has to come to terms with mortality and the passage
of time. Entry into history is less a guarantee of perpetuity than an index of
loss. The second version of her bid to do away with herself draws together the
redolent, imagistic repertoire deployed by the author to sketch the
consciousness of her heroine:

> Letting go is like breathy flight, an astonishment of air. In her mind's eye she is
> a hollow painted doll, tossed carelessly by an unseen hand, undone with each
> revolution, her outer shell unraveling to reveal a small, then smaller, version of
> herself until she is no more than a tiny wooden egg. (p. 200)

Here, her compulsive masquerades are shown not just to be pathological
deceptions, but also a quest to locate the core of her identity. In this alternative
view, her wish to enter history is evidence of her pursuit of wisdom and self-
understanding and her desire to fathom the role of subjective experience in the
dispassionate records of the past. The image of the 'tiny wooden egg' acts in
this light as a paradoxical metaphor for the devastations wrought by historical
change on the one hand, and for an implicit belief in the irreducible essence
of human existence on the other.

The novel sustains our interest in its elusive protagonist through its adroit
manipulation of narrative technique, particularly *style indirect libre*. This latter
mode of narration endeavors to penetrate the workings of a character's mind
but fuses such insights with authorial or third-person commentary. It thus
typically knits internal and external views of experience together and gives
linguistic expression to the non-speech of mental thought. Moreover, as Martin
Jay has argued ('Experience without a Subject'), even though the middle voice
of *style indirect libre* sets out to articulate the privatized self, it also depicts
experience as socially constituted and intersubjective. In *The Pretender,*
through the alternation of third-person narration, *style indirect libre,* and
occasional inserts of what Dorrit Cohn calls 'quoted monologue' (*Transparent
Minds*, pp. 58–98), that is, first-person narrative that directly reproduces
interior speech, we partake in the dramas of consciousness of the central
persona while being made aware of her self-divisions and the contradictions
on which notions of subjectivity are founded. This oscillation between internal
and external views of Anastasia also permits us to breach her habitual silence
and to attune ourselves to a discrete, feminine language that would not
otherwise be discernible. Thus, in the second section of the novel, Fräulein
Unbekannt's mute resistance to the questions posed by the doctors is
counterpointed by the distracted course of her unvoiced thoughts: 'Guilt is her

only constant. She has done wrong, hasn't she? All her thoughts end up like this. One question begging another' (*The Pretender*, pp. 26–7).

The splicing of the figural and narrating voice here typifies the novel's primary mode of narration and captures the instability of the heroine's personality. Her internal dialogue both bears out her alienation and evidences her struggle to delimit and give expressive shape to her identity. The description of Franziska Schanzkowska's difficulty in adapting to her new job as factory worker in Berlin similarly intermingles personal and impersonal perspectives: 'Franziska was used to labour, but here she felt weak and puny, dwarfed by her surroundings and her own insignificance in this feverish cycle of masculine work with no visible harvest. One of hundreds – her assigned number was 670 – she was just one more body enslaved not to an end but to an effort, the war effort' (p. 116). The individual's story here is engulfed by the violence of history and incorporated into a collective narrative of events that occludes personal biography. Even those rare moments, offset in italics in the text, in which Anastasia soliloquizes on her experience in first-person terms show that sincerity and truth, authenticity and experience do not necessarily overlap. In the longest and most moving of these asides, Anastasia vividly describes the assault on her family in the basement of Ipatiev House:

> *Their excitement, our terror, it was hard to tell the difference in the stench of blood and the high piercing panic. It was a clammy summer's night. The heat had made them sweat. They sweated as we bled, it was an exchange. Their sweat, our blood. Stubble on their chins as they rummaged among us with their boots, mud caked on their toecaps. The sweet smell of warm, oozing blood. The air palpitating. The shudder of exhaled breath, a hoarse groan, the tiny twitching of limbs after death. They gathered at the doorway when it was all over. One of them struck a match, a searing sulphurous sizzle, and lit a cigarette. They passed it around among themselves, inhaling greedily. The smell of Papa. Papa! Save Me!* (p. 95)

The visceral accuracy of this reportage seems to be grounded in the personal and experiential. Equally, however, the testimonial power of the Pretender's recapitulations of historical events is ironically shown to be the result of her own indeterminacy and capacity for role play.

Despite these complex apprehensions of the problematic nature of selfhood, Morrissy nonetheless encourages her readers to connect with the progress of her heroine, because she stages her story as a progressive drama. Indeed, the successive instalments of Anastasia's life accord with the two leading aspects of consciousness that have been isolated by the neuroscientist Antonio Damasio. He holds that human sentience is composed of two vital components, which he dubs core and extended consciousness. The first of these provides the organism with a sense of self in the here and now and is ultimately transient, while the second is the basis of the autobiographical self and depends on systematized memory and a sense of being as emanating from an individual history. In section two of *The Pretender*, Fräulein Unbekannt's lack of memory and her timorous but dogged attempts to accommodate the hostile world around her in Dalldorf Asylum correspond with Damasio's account of the functioning of the core self (*The Feeling of What Happens*, pp. 168–94). This limited and non-verbal level of conscious existence registers the interactions between objects and the human organism in the lived instant. Tasks that presuppose the use of memory stump Morrissy's protagonist. She recoils, for example, from the question as to whether her mother is still alive and reflects that 'even the word itself seemed strange' (*The Pretender*, p. 39). Instead, her perceptual and intellectual field seems initially limited to her immediate environment. On her first night in the asylum, for instance, she is distracted by the 'cacophony, loud and livid as a nocturnal forest' (p. 33) of her fellow inmates asleep nearby. Her gradual annexation of the identity of Anastasia may be seen as a desire for the permanence of extended consciousness which hinges in Damasio's account of things on 'the consistent reactivation and display of selected sets of autobiographical memories' (*The Feeling of What Happens*, p. 196). In adopting the recollections of a Russian Grand Duchess, she creates the illusion of having a coherent personal story. This projected identity is shown to be in competition with a further autobiographical self that revolves around her history as a Polish peasant girl who migrates to Berlin to escape from a turbulent past. Yet, despite the patent disparities between these rival tales, Morrissy's narrative conjoins them in such a way that she convinces us of the fundamental consistency of her heroine. Although the possession of a memoried self may be deemed to be one of the fundamental anchors of personhood, *The Pretender* presents us with the paradox of a central figure whose individualism is discernible even in the absence of a fixed biography. Fiction hence exceeds the probings of contemporary neuroscience in charting the shadowy workings of consciousness and in raising questions about the extent to which experience can wholly be stamped as private and unique.

II Postmodernism and the ethics of memory

Caught up in the chaos of life in a war-torn city, Franziska, on hearing that the body of Rosa Luxemburg has been rescued from the Landwehr canal in Berlin, pointedly asks: 'How could the corpse of a dead woman make any difference to history, which marched on regardless?' (*The Pretender*, p. 193). This is indeed one of the far-reaching questions which Morrissy's novel addresses. Her protagonist's query is all the more pertinent in that the postmodern techniques that this fiction adopts are frequently regarded as precluding the possibility of historical representation or metaphysical reflection. However, as this section of my essay will argue, Morrissy's postmodernism, in keeping with that of several other contemporary Irish women writers such as Medbh McGuckian and Anne Enright, allows for an exploration of the authority and ethics of memory, the ontological status of the female subject and the possibility of constructing alternative versions of the past.[1] Strikingly, the turn to history is precisely what the encounter between Irish feminism and postmodernism appears to facilitate. Thus, tracing the aesthetic and political alignments of *The Pretender* enables one to gauge its oblique but purposeful engagement with current Irish political and sociological concerns and to establish how it mediates feminist theoretical debates in an Irish context.

Fredric Jameson has argued that in postmodernism reification penetrates the sign itself, thus cutting the signifier off from the signified (*Postmodernism*, p. 96). The conflicting and self-cancelling episodes of *The Pretender* may indeed seem in this light to be a postmodern collage in which random moments from the past are overlaid and pasted together. By extension, the bricolage of female biographies that is conjured up appears to relativize women's lives and collapse them into an undeviating pattern of sameness. Franziska reflects at one point that it 'seemed her destiny to be confined' (*The Pretender*, p. 124) and this inevitable fate is borne out by all her alternate selves who end up either in asylums, in psychiatric homes or imprisoned. Recent accounts of the practice and aims of Irish women's history have argued that this field of inquiry must of necessity question the boundaries of traditional historiography and also confront the problem of diversity, disadvantage and silence.[2]

Morrissy's juxtaposition of the varying stories of the Pretender permits her, I would argue, to take up such challenges and to open up the disparities as well as commonalities between parallel lives. Her protagonist allows us to see history from above, through the perspective of Anastasia, and from below, through the perspective of a migrant Polish worker. Their narratives are counterpointed but they do not fuse seamlessly with each other. Morrissy's novel hence encourages us to reflect on the differences that divide women and alerts us to the politics underlying the types of history that we entertain. Rather than reducing history to pastiche, it shows the necessity of discriminating between stories while taking cognizance of how women's lives might be interconnected.

The Pretender also indicates that a woman-centred history must perforce explore subject matter that is usually omitted from public records of noteworthy events. By focusing attention on topics such as the treatment of insanity and employment patterns and domestic life during the First World War, marginalized existences are coaxed out into the open. Through Anastasia, we learn of figures such as Hilda Scharrel, another inmate of the Dalldorf Asylum, who has been forced into prostitution because of being abandoned by her childhood sweetheart, and of Else Jupke, who tries to commit suicide by jumping into the Spree after losing her job as a waitress. Like Virginia Woolf in *Mrs Dalloway*, Morrissy also demonstrates that women's experience of war differs from that of men. Franziska reacts, for example, with bewilderment and anger to the first letter she receives from Hans in Verdun. It seems to her like a text from a 'stranger' (p. 161) and leaves her feeling bereaved even in advance of his inevitable death. In its pointed commentary on the differences between 'War Time' (p. 182) and 'hospital time' (p. 183), *The Pretender* foregrounds the alternative chronometry of women's historical experience.

However, the novel also problematizes the aims of feminist history in showing that the retrieval of the past is always partial and piecemeal. The protagonist's story is characterized as much by what it omits as by what it encompasses. The Communist Revolution, the defeat of socialism in Germany and the events of two world wars are all pushed to the periphery or invoked only indirectly. Anastasia's imperfect recall of her past hence allegorizes on one level the postmodern tendency to reduce history to nostalgia and to limit it to the private and the affective. Morrissy's multi-dimensional text, by contrast, urges us to make connections between the personal and the political in relentlessly uncovering the extent to which female emotional economies are inflected by social and economic contexts. Moreover, even though household arrangements and family relations turn out to be crucial in opening up the varying life worlds depicted, the heroine proves ultimately to be driven by her desire to escape the traditional female lot of becoming a wife and mother. Both Anastasia and Franziska are eager to escape marriage, domesticity and maternity. The pregnancies which they undergo, for example, are seen as calamities that need to be quickly suppressed. One of Franziska's final bouts of madness is induced by the sight of turnips, which devastatingly represent 'the clogged earth of home, sodden and stale and poor' (p. 187). Female autonomy appears only to be feasible through a rejection of bourgeois values and maternal roles and, by the same token, a dissection of femininity as an ideological construct is still deemed a vital necessity in Irish feminist fiction.

Thomas Docherty has posited deterritorialization as one of the distinctive features of postmodern art. In his account of things, this reflex of contemporary aesthetics stems from its urge to counter forms of rootedness. By creating a transnational fiction, Morrissy disconnects herself from the Irish locations of her previous works, *A Lazy Eye* (1993) and *Mother of Pearl* (1996). In so doing, however, she questions rather than fully rejects notions of national heritage. Fredric Jameson has argued that 'a global cognitive mapping' (*Postmodernism*, p. 54) must constitute the vocation of a political form of postmodernism. *The Pretender*, in following the fate of its heroine who is at once a migrant, an exile, a historical relict and an immigrant, aims precisely at such an investigation of the global dimensions of modern identity. The mixed nationality of Anastasia, who is in part Russian, Polish, German and American, is portrayed not only as a liberating openness, but also as the result of different forms of imperialism and patriarchal domination. Her 'eerie sensation of absence' in the bustle of Berlin (*The Pretender*, p. 152) seems to emanate in part from her sense of dispossession as the inhabitant of Poland, 'a place that doesn't exist' (p. 225) because it has been swallowed up by the German Reich. Her removal from Russia to the United States mirrors a shift from one kind of imperial rule to another; she switches from the autocratic regime of the Romanovs to the Americanized global economy of late capitalism.

Morrissy thus deterritorializes the Irish novel in setting aside the inward-looking preoccupations of local nationalism. However, her meditation on the ways in which postcolonial identity must now be rethought on a transnational stage has a direct bearing on recent changes in Ireland, which has been found to have one of the most globalized economies in the world. Furthermore, her concentration on a heroine who is an outsider in all of the communities in which she takes refuge tangentially addresses pressing Irish concerns with the problems of immigration and of racial prejudice. Above all, *The Pretender* retains a commitment to ideals of justice, in the manner advocated by Seyla Benhabib in her scrutiny of the politics of postmodernism ('Epistemologies of Postmodernism', pp. 122–5), despite its questioning of historical meta-narratives and of determinist notions of identity. The intersecting plotlines of the novel reveal that sexual violence, historical atrocity, and institutional abuse all leave ineradicable traces. Anastasia, as the 'eccentric European' (*The Pretender*, p. 271), acts both as an index of the harmful effects of suppression and an accusatory reminder of horrors perpetrated in the past. In this capacity, she also functions as a cipher for the accumulating scandals about sexual abuse and violence in state institutions such as Magdalene laundries and industrial schools that have beset Irish society in recent times. Despite its postmodern indeterminacy, Morrissy's story alerts us to the need for an ethics of communal memory and the negotiation of a shared morality with which to view the past. Furthermore, the unsettling instability of her protagonist, who is at once a victim of mass murder and herself a murderer, raises complex questions about female autonomy and culpability.

The feminist force of *The Pretender* cannot be attributed solely to its political and sociological subtexts, however urgent and compelling they may be. Morrissy's postmodern fable also fulfils the difficult brief outlined by Eavan Boland of finding literary forms that are capable of representing the problematic dimensions of female subjectivity. Wendy Doniger has argued that the shadow of gender is evident in most fantasies of doubling. Men usually split themselves in reaction to their own evil; women are either split by men to contain the nefarious forces that they represent or else they cleave themselves in reaction to abuse by others (*Splitting the Difference*, pp. 306–9). Greater autonomy hence traditionally accrues to the male rather the female doppelgänger. *The Pretender*, with its multiple stories of duplicated selves, constructs a rich mythography of disempowerment and social exclusion and unflinchingly explores the painful psychoses resulting from female dependency. While its survey of the atrocities and injustices of recent history and the amnesiac tendencies of postmodern culture is necessarily bleak, it suggests that what Marina Warner terms the 'fantastic metamorphoses' (*Fantastic Metamorphoses: Other Worlds*) of its shape-shifting female subject provide the most cogent and engaging means of taking soundings of the deficiencies of our purchase on the past and the exploitative global communities that we inhabit. Morrissy's story of displacement and mutation propounds a resonant myth of female survival and adaptation and of cross-cultural and transhistoric interchange that counteracts the devastating upheavals and losses of the twentieth century. Above all, it reveals the continuing need of Irish feminism to question notions of paternal power and to come to terms with a history and cultural tradition that displace women and consistently silence their presence.

*   *   *   *   *

Mary Morrissy: biographical and critical contexts

Mary Morrissy was born in Dublin. She has worked as a journalist, copy-editor and fiction-reviewer for the *Irish Times*. She has published one collection of short stories, *A Lazy Eye* (1993), and two novels, *Mother of Pearl* (1996) and *The Pretender* (2000). She won a Hennessy Award for short fiction in 1984 and a Lannan Award for Literature in 1995. *Mother of Pearl* was shortlisted for the Whitbread Prize in 1996 and *The Pretender* was nominated for the IMPAC Award in 2002. Morrissy was writer in residence at University College Cork 2000–1. She has also taught in creative writing programmes at the Universities of Arkansas and Iowa. In 2005–6, she was awarded a fellowship to the Cullman Center for Scholars and Writers at The New York Public Library to pursue work on a new novel focusing on the life of Sean O'Casey's sister, Bella.

While relatively few critical studies of Morrissy's work have been published to date, her fiction has been marked as noteworthy in monographs by Gerry Smyth, *The Novel and the Nation* (1997), and Christine St Peter, *Changing Ireland* (2000), while Linden Peach's 2004 study of contemporary fiction, *The Contemporary Irish Novel*, devotes considerable attention to *Mother of Pearl*, which he includes in a chapter about 'abject mothers' and representations of the maternal and femininity in Irish fiction. Essays by Patricia Coughlan ('Irish Literature and Feminism in Postmodernity'), Anne Fogarty ('Uncanny Families') and Sinéad McDermott ('Maternal Belongings and the Question of Home in Mary Morrissy's *Mother of Pearl*') praise her work as both experimentally inventive and usefully illustrative of social change in ideologies of maternity and the family in contemporary Ireland.

Works cited

Benhabib, Seyla, 'Epistemologies of Postmodernism: A Rejoinder to Jean-François Lyotard', in Linda J. Nicholson (ed.), *Feminism/Postmodernism* (London: Routledge, 1990), pp. 107–30.

Boland, Eavan, *A Kind of Scar: The Woman Poet in a National Tradition* (Dublin: Attic Press, 1989).

Bourke, Angela, 'Language, Stories, Healing', in Anthony Bradley and Mary Ann Valiulis (eds.), *Gender and Sexuality in Modern Ireland* (Amherst: University of Massachusetts Press, 1997), pp. 298–314.

Braidotti, Rosi, *Nomadic Subjects: Embodiment and Sexual Difference in Contemporary Feminist Theory.* (New York: Columbia University Press, 1994).

Cohn, Dorrit, *Transparent Minds: Narrative Modes for Presenting Consciousness in Fiction* (New Jersey: Princeton University Press, 1978).

Coughlan, Patricia, 'Irish Literature and Feminism in Postmodernity', *Hungarian Journal of English and American Studies* 10 (Spring/Fall 2004), pp. 175–202.

Damasio, Antonio, *The Feeling of What Happens: Body, Emotion and the Making of Consciousness* (London: Vintage, 2000).

Docherty, Thomas, *After Theory: Postmodernism/Postmarxism* (London: Routledge, 1990).

Doniger, Wendy, *Splitting the Difference: Gender and Myth in Ancient Greece and India* (University of Chicago Press, 1999).

Enright, Anne, *The Pleasure of Eliza Lynch* (London: Jonathan Cape, 2002).

Fogarty, Anne, 'Uncanny Families: Neo-Gothic Motifs and the Theme of Social Change in Contemporary Irish Women's Fiction', *Irish University Review* 30, special issue on contemporary Irish fiction (Spring/Summer 2000), pp. 59–81.

Hayes, Alan and Diane Urquhart, *The Irish Women's History Reader* (London: Routledge, 2001).

Hill, Myrtle, *Women in Ireland: A Century of Change* (Belfast: The Blackstaff Press, 2003).

Jameson, Fredric, *Postmodernism, or, The Cultural Logic of Late Capitalism* (London: Verso, 1991).

Jay, Martin, 'Experience without a Subject: Walter Benjamin and the Novel', in Laura Marcus and Lynda Nead (eds.), *The Actuality of Walter Benjamin* (London: Lawrence and Wishart, 1998), pp. 194–211.

Kurth, Peter, *Anastasia: The Riddle of Anna Anderson* (New York: Little Brown & Co., 1986).

Massie, R.K., *The Romanovs: The Final Chapter* (London: Random House, 1995).

McDermott, Sinéad, 'Maternal Belongings and the Question of Home in Mary Morrissy's *Mother of Pearl*', *Feminist Theory* 3 (2003), pp. 263–82.

McGuckian, Medbh, *Shelmalier* (Loughcrew: Gallery Press, 1998).

Morrissy, Mary, *A Lazy Eye* [1993] (London: Vintage, 1996).

——, *Mother of Pearl* (London: Jonathan Cape, 1996).

——, *The Pretender* (London: Jonathan Cape, 2000).

Peach, Linden, *The Contemporary Irish Novel: Critical Readings* (Basingstoke: Palgrave Macmillan, 2004).

Showalter, Elaine, 'Toward a Feminist Poetics', in Elaine Showalter (ed.), *The New Feminist Criticism: Essays on Women, Literature and Theory* (London: Virago, 1986), pp. 125–43.

Smyth, Gerry, *The Novel and the Nation: Studies in the New Irish Fiction* (London: Pluto Press, 1997).

St Peter, Christine, *Changing Ireland: Strategies in Contemporary Women's Fiction* (London: Macmillan, 2000).

Warner, Marina, *Fantastic Metamorphoses: Other Worlds* (Oxford University Press, 2002).

List of Contributors

Patricia Coughlan is Professor of English at National University of Ireland (Cork). She has edited *Spenser and Ireland* (1990), co-edited *Modernism and Ireland: The Poetry of the 1930s* (1995), and written many essays and articles on Irish writing, including on Irish Gothic, Beckett, Bowen, Kate and Edna O'Brien, Heaney, Montague, Banville, and other contemporary poetry and fiction. Her interests focus on sixteenth- and seventeenth-century colonial discourse and on gender representations in Irish writing. She jointly devised and led the research for the bilingual *Dictionary of Munster Women Writers 1800–2000* (2005).

Anne Fogarty is Senior Lecturer in the School of English and Drama, University College Dublin, Ireland. She was Director of the James Joyce Summer School (1997–2005) and is currently editor of the *Irish University Review*. She has published numerous essays on aspects of Spenser and early modern Ireland, on the historical dimensions of the fiction of James Joyce, and on Irish women writers, including Kate O'Brien, Lady Gregory, and Maria Edgeworth. Her study of Eavan Boland is forthcoming.

Luz Mar González Arias is a full-time lecturer and researcher in the English Department, University of Oviedo, Spain. She has published two books and several articles on female corporeality in the work of Irish women, revisions of Celtic and Christian mythology from a feminist perspective, and Irish women poets and their relationships with nationalism and postcolonialism. She is currently researching the youngest generation of Irish women poets.

Patricia Boyle Haberstroh is Professor of English and Chair of Fine Arts at La Salle University in Philadelphia, USA. She has published *Women Creating Women, Contemporary Irish Women Poets* (1996), and *My Self, My Muse, Irish Women Poets Reflect on Life and Art* (2001). She serves on the editorial boards of the *New Hibernia Review* and the *Irish Feminist Review* and was awarded a Fulbright Fellowship to Ireland in 2002 to research and teach at University College Dublin.

Heidi Hansson is Senior Lecturer in English at Umeå University, Sweden. She is currently finishing a book on the Irish writer Emily Lawless and editing a collection of essays on nineteenth-century Irish women's prose writing. She is also the leader of an interdisciplinary project about foreign travellers to northern Scandinavia in the nineteenth century, and is working on a study of writings by Irish visitors to the region.

Cathy Leeney teaches at the Drama Studies Centre at University College Dublin, Ireland. She is currently completing a book on Irish women playwrights from 1900 to 1939. Her research interests include contemporary Irish theatre, directing, performance theory and Irish women playwrights.

Gerardine Meaney is Director of Irish Studies at University College Dublin, Ireland. She is the author of *(Un)Like Subjects: Women, Theory, Fiction* (1993) and of a short study of Pat Murphy's film *Nora,* for the series 'Ireland into Film' (2004). Her articles on gender and Irish culture have appeared in *Colby Quarterly, Textual Practice* and *Women: A Cultural Review.* She is a co-editor of the *Field Day Anthology of Irish Writing: Women's Writing and Traditions,* Volumes IV and V (2002).

Eiléan Ní Chuilleanáin, educated at University College Cork, has since 1966 taught at Trinity College Dublin, Ireland, where she is now Associate Professor of English. She has published a number of academic books and articles, including articles on Maria Edgeworth, as well as poetry and translated poetry. She edited Edgeworth's *Belinda* for the Everyman Paperback series (1993).

Katherine O'Donnell is currently Head of Women's Studies at the School of Social Justice, University College Dublin, Ireland. She has published widely on eighteenth-century Irish literature and the history of sexuality.

Rebecca Pelan is Lecturer in the School of English and Drama, University College Dublin, Ireland and is the general editor of *Irish Feminist Review.* She lived in Australia for many years, where she lectured in English at the University of Queensland; she returned to Ireland in 2001 to take a position in the Department of English at the University of Ulster. She has published extensively on the subject of Irish women's writing, Edna O'Brien's fiction, feminist/literary theory, and women and the Troubles. She is a member of the editorial board of *Hecate* (Australia), and of the editorial advisory board of the *Australian Journal of Irish Studies.* Her book *Two Irelands: Literary Feminisms North and South* was published in 2005.

Christine St Peter is Professor of Women's Studies at the University of Victoria, Canada. She has published widely in the fields of Irish and Canadian women's writing. Her editing projects have been in the areas of Canadian oral history, Irish drama, Irish women's studies and reproductive technologies in Canada, and she presently serves on the editorial boards of *Canadian Journal of Irish Studies* and *Irish Feminist Review.* Her book on contemporary Irish women's writing, *Changing Ireland* was published in 2000. She is currently working on Irish women's *Bildungsromane.*

Ann Owens Weekes is an Associate Professor at the University of Arizona, USA, where she teaches Irish literature. Her 1990 work, *Irish Women Writers: An Uncharted Tradition,* a discussion of writers from Maria Edgeworth to Julia O'Faolain, was the first work exclusively devoted to Irish women writers to be published. This was followed in 1993 by *Unveiling Treasures: The Attic Guide to the Published Work of Irish Women Writers,* an introduction to the works and lives of over 250 writers of fiction, poetry and drama. She has written many articles on individual writers and is currently working on the fictional representations of women as mothers in twentieth-century Ireland.

Notes

Notes to Chapter 1

1. My Ph.D. thesis and first book were an integrated study of feminist theory and women's fiction: *(Un)Like Subjects: Women, Theory, Fiction*.
2. Particularly 'Stabat Mater' and 'Women's Time'; see *The Kristeva Reader*.
3. *The Ante-Room* was published by Arlen House with an introduction by Eavan Boland in 1980. *Mary Lavelle, Farewell Spain* and *The Land of Spices were published* by Virago in 1984, 1985 and 1988 respectively.
4. For a critical account of the relationship between national, gender and poetic identities in this period, see Eavan Boland. *A Kind of Scar*; Edna Longley, *From Cathleen to Anorexia*; Patricia Coughlan, '"Bog Queens": The Representation of Women in the Poetry of John Montague and Seamus Heaney'; Elizabeth Cullingford, *Gender and History in Yeats's Love Poetry*. In poetry, see Eiléan Ní Chuilleanáin, *The Magdalene Sermon*; Medbh McGuckian, *On Ballycastle Beach*; Nuala Ní Dhomhnaill, *Selected Poems/Rogha Danta*; Paula Meehan, *The Man Who Was Marked by Winter*.
5. See Moynagh Sullivan, *The Woman Poet and the Matter of Representation in Modern and Postmodern Poetics*, for an analysis of this process.
6. Reprinted in *Field Day*, vol. V, p. 1025.

Notes to Chapter 2

1. See Kelly, and for anecdotes of Irish duelling including a reference to the D'Esterre-O'Connell duel, and a description of a duel which took place in 1838, see Lefanu Chapter 10, at *http://indigo.ie/~kfinlay/lefanu70/lefanuX.htm*

Notes to Chapter 4

1. See my longer essay in Irish, which gives detailed references to Peig's writings and related material. I thank the Irish Research Council for the Humanities and Social Sciences for their award of a Government of Ireland Senior Research Fellowship in 2002–3, which assisted me to complete this essay. My view of Peig is developed from my lecture at the annual Blasket commemoration in 1998, and from the ensuing discussions of the topic in Irish national newspapers and on radio, April-May 1998 and 1999 (*Irish Times, Pat Kenny Show, Morning Ireland*). For biographical information on Peig, see Diarmuid Breatnach and Máire Ní Mhurchú, *Beathaisnéis 5*.
2. The best account in English of the history and culture of the Blaskets as a whole is by Muiris MacConghail (*The Blaskets*), who also gives

information about the other classic autobiographies. Feirtéar's television documentaries (1997 and 1998) are an excellent introduction; the latter includes an interview with Peig's youngest child, her beloved Neilí. George Thomson's *The Blasket That Was* and Robin Flower's *The Western Island* are classics of English-language writing about Blasket life and culture; Moreton gives a striking view of the island community's last days in the 1940s and early 1950s.

3.   These are *Peig: A Scéal Féin* [*Peig: Her Own Story*], translated by Bryan (1974), and *Machtnamh Sheana-Mhná* [*Thoughts of an Old Woman*], translated by Séamus Ennis (1962). Ó Gaoithín also published a volume of his own, *Beatha Pheig Sayers* ['The Life of Peig Sayers'] (1970), which is of lesser interest. Bo Almqvist gives a revealing account of Ó Gaoithín's own literary pretensions and readiness to perpetrate an authorial hoax ('The Mysterious Micheál Ó Gaoithín').

4.   Miller's account seems to say that the cost of the passage to America was offered to Peig, but that she refused because she preferred to stay by her mother, who was then an invalid (p. 475). However, it is clear to the reader of all three volumes that in any case she and her family could not, from sheer poverty, raise the passage money, and her friend Cáit Jim did not – perhaps could not – fulfill her promise to send it. In her reference to the matter ('Fulness of Life'), MacCurtain stresses the spiritual bond between Peig and her mother, an emphasis with which I agree (quoted in Maureen Murphy, 'The Fionnuala Factor', n. 21). Maureen Murphy shows a much more positive outlook on the institution of rural family life in Ireland, stressing the altruism of the remittance system whereby emigrant sisters sent financial 'help' home to their siblings; she sees this as a mark of specifically feminine strengths.

5.   These notably included Carl Marstrander, Carl von Sydow, Kenneth Jackson and Marie-Louise Sjoestedt (both frequent island visitors in Peig's time), as well as Flower and Thomson. For von Sydow's striking photographs, see Mac Conghail, *The Blaskets*.

6.   I am grateful to Seán Ó Coileáin for this point.

7.   I thank folklorist and ethnographer Diarmuid Ó Giolláin for discussion of these and some related points with me, though I take responsibility for their formulation here.

8.   Maryann Valiulis ('Neither Feminist Nor Flapper') explores constructions of femininity in the newly independent state; Yvonne Scannell ('The Constitution and the Role of Women') shows that even as the Constitution was being drafted, a vigorous opposition was mounted by women towards its exclusive emphasis on women's role in the home.

9.   As shown by investigation of the archives of Talbot Press (now Educational Company of Ireland) which published the first volume both in its full and school editions, and at the National Publications Office (Oifig an tSoláthair) which brought out the second.

10. I thank Aindrias Ó Gallchoir for this information.

11. This passage from the hero's speech in Bolger's play *In High Germany* makes clear the association of Peig with a nationalism perceived as atavistic and experienced as coercive: 'I thought of my father's battered travel bag, of Molloy drilling us behind the 1798 pike, the wasters who came after him hammering *Peig* into us, the masked men blowing limbs off passers-by in my name. You know, all my life, it seems, somebody somewhere has always been trying to tell me which Ireland I belonged in . . .' (p. 107).

    The publisher's biographical note on Julian Gough's campus novel *Juno and Juliet* credits Gough, raised in Tipperary, with co-authorship of a work called *Peig: The Musical*.

12. The controversy followed a report on my Dunquin lecture by Dick Hogan (*Irish Times*, 'Southern Report', 31 March 1998). Rev. Pat Moore, with an address in Gneeveguilla, Co. Kerry, conducted a prolonged dispute with me in 'Letters to the Editor', vehemently expressing his disagreement with my position, especially in regard to women and their social roles (*Irish Times*, 6, 14, 21, 24 April and 13 May 1998).

13. Máirín Ní Dhuinnshléibhe does, however, give a vivid account of women's shared lore and habits of intercommunication on the island, especially of their daily conversations when they met at the well ('Saol na mBan').

14. Sisters, as well as younger brothers, in such families were forced to leave households and earn their living elsewhere, often in Britain or America, by the prevailing social system, whereby the eldest son inherited the farm, and in circumstances where poverty precluded the financial support of other siblings. I have borrowed the term 'surplus woman' from Leonore Davidoff and Catherine Hall's discussion specifically of middle-class 'redundant' women in the mid and later nineteenth century (*Family Fortunes*, p. 453); see also Tom Inglis for a somewhat controversial argument about the long-lasting effects of the Irish rural system on late marriage rates and on emotional life (*The Moral Monopoly*, ch. 7, 'The Transformation of Irish Society' and ch. 8, 'The Irish Mother', pp. 159–200). I thank Piaras Mac Éinrí for helpful discussion of this topic.

15. Joanna Bourke gives a general account of the conditions of employment of farm and domestic workers in the late nineteenth century (*Husbandry to Housewifery*, 'Paid Workers' and 'Subsistence Entrepreneurs', pp. 25–198, and references therein).

16. See Jessica Benjamin's excellent discussion (*The Bonds of Love*) of intersubjectivity and mutual recognition *versus* the dominant Western tradition of an atomized selfhood predicated on separation and Freudian instinctual drives towards mastery.

17.   For a late twentieth-century emphasis on women's mischievous delight in transgressive play, see the poem '*Táimid damanta, a dheirféaracha*' ['We are damned, my sisters'] by Nuala Ní Dhomhnaill, who herself has a West Kerry background.

18.   Nic Eoin's comment is made in Feirtéar (*Slán an Scéalaí*). The rather literal-minded approach which saw autobiography as a pure record of facts also characterized the reception until recently of the slave narratives of American literature, by both female and male authors. I thank Lee Jenkins for this observation and for the reference to John McWilliams's essay, 'The Rationale for "The American Romance"'.

19.   It seems that in reality Peig was aided in this dreadful task by her neighbour Méiní, a *mulier fortis* who acted as unofficial island midwife and nurse, as described in Leslie Matson's luminous memoir, *Méiní: The Blasket Nurse*. The text's representation of this as a solitary task is itself evidence of conscious narrative design.

20.   This custom is vividly recorded in a more minor, but also under-valued, Blasket classic in English, Eibhlís Ní Shúilleabháin's *Letters from the Great Blasket*. Transport to and from the mainland, across the notoriously dangerous stretch of the Blasket Sound, was by *naomhóg,* the frail but buoyant boat locally constructed of tarred canvas over a light wooden frame, called a *currach* in Connemara (Mac Conghail, *The Blaskets*; Thomson, *The Blasket That Was*). The requirement that a woman travel in the *naomhóg* is a striking instance of the liminality of women and the feminine: a woman was needed for this rite of transition, where the literal passage across the dividing water symbolically prefigured the dead person's passage beyond this life.

Notes to Chapter 5

1.   For a discussion of 'counterpoint' as an alternative to dialectics, see also Wendy Brown, 'At the Edge', pp. 586–9.

2.   I am grateful to Aintzane Legarreta-Mentxaka (Maken) for showing me this connection. Kate O'Brien had a liking for Castilian heroines: her gaunt, androgynous, one-eyed closeted beauty Ana de Mendoza in *That Lady* (1946) was from Castile, as was the brilliant Carmelite, so tempted by lesbian passions, whom O'Brien wrote about in that most unconventional hagiography, *Teresa of Avila* (1951, pp. 22–5, 40–4).

3.   B.A. from New Mexico, United States: 'I watched this movie because I am becoming a fan of the strikingly handsome Vincent Perez . . . The chemistry between Vincent Perez and Polly Walker had a little to be desired though. I am sure this could have been improved if the characters had been able to explore each other a little more instead of trying to cram their story into 1 dance and one afternoon.'
Donald 333 from Fresno, CA, USA: 'The two have little chemistry. The

result: a stilted and perfunctory outing. The only saving grace is the always wonderful Frances McDormand, whose hard-bitten, love-struck fellow governess offers a sad little bit of zest.'

A viewer from Philly: 'I absolutely adore Vincent Perez . . . However, this movie was a drag . . . I felt no emotional attachment to the characters or the passion they SHOULD have had for each other.'

A viewer from Ohio: 'Beautiful as Polly and Vincent both are as actors, I never felt the much needed bond between them that makes a movie a joy to watch.' (http://www.Amzon.com)

4. O'Brien is to use a child's performance of sixteenth-century English poetry to spark a reverie on love to a greater and more complex effect in *The Land of Spices* (1941).

5. Coughlan reads Conlan's appreciation of the beauty of the bullfight as 'of a piece with her admiration of Mary, openly denominated as sexual'. She argues that: 'For the reader, this would seem to entail a division of female sexuality within itself into the binary pattern of dominant and submissive roles, viewer and viewed, familiar from the masculine-feminine stereotype. Juanito and Agatha can be lined up as active agents, desiring *subjects,* each opposite Mary, projected as *object* of desire' ('Kate O'Brien', p. 76). This argument does not hold, as we see Mary becoming a connoisseur of the *corrida.* She even tells Don Pablo that in going back to Ireland she hated to leave the bullfights (*Mary Lavelle*, p. 319), and our final image of Mary is her folding a matador's cape into her suitcase (p. 345).

6. O'Brien is buried in the Carmelite convent in Faversham, Kent; her headstone has the inscription 'Pray for the Wanderer'.

7. In other words, the triangle formed by Mary, Don Pablo and Juanito is better analysed by Rubin's 1984 'Thinking Sex' article than by the 1975 article 'Traffic in Women'. Rubin's later article modified her earlier thesis, which identified the traffic in women as the basis for exchange through the production of sex/gender systems that rely upon compulsory heterosexuality. The later article suggests that the gender identities thus established need not determine sexuality. Eve Kosofsky Sedgwick in *Between Men* gives a brilliant analysis of how the exchange of women between men anxiously maintains a homosociality in the sublimation of a (homo)sexuality.

Notes to Chapter 6

1. States uses Heidegger's distinction, as he has applied it to painting, figuring art as 'a place of disclosure, not a place of reference' (p. 4).

2. See Alisa Solomon, *Re-Dressing the Canon*, and Elin Diamond, *Unmaking Mimesis*, for fascinating commentaries on the relationship between Hedda and the dramatic form of the play.

3.   *Portia Coughlan* was first published in *The Dazzling Dark: New Irish Plays* (1996).

Notes to Chapter 7

1.   Similar figures have been found in France, England, Scotland and Wales but they are much more numerous in the Irish landscape. For an illustrated guide of the Sheela-na-gigs of England and Ireland, see Joanne McMahon and Jack Roberts, *The Sheela-Na-Gigs of Ireland and Great Britain.*

2.   My description of these two figures is based on the catalogue included at the end of McMahon and Roberts, *op. cit.* Among other common features of the Sheela-na-gigs are huge heads (much in the Celtic style of representing the head as the most important part of the human body), wide-open mouths and protruding tongues, as is the case of the Sheela from Cavan Town. As for the female genitalia, sometimes the inside of the vagina is clearly shown and the clitoris represented–the Sheela found in Clonbulloge, Co. Offaly, is a good example. Some figures present a masturbatory gesture, as occurs with the one found in Kiltinane, while others just point to the vulva.

3.   Sheela-na-gigs have not only intrigued women artists. The controversy that surrounds their origins and the impact these icons may have on contemporary Ireland have also attracted the attention of Seamus Heaney, who refers to them in his *Station Island*, and of Michael Longley, who included a poem entitled 'Sheela-Na-Gig' in his volume *The Ghost Orchid.*

4.   In the sculptures of Eilís O'Connell, elliptical shapes are connected with body references and Sheela-na-gigs. Pauline Cummins and Louise Walsh have also used the iconography of the Sheela in *Sounding the Depths,* an installation that abounds in images of the womb and the vagina.

5.   Louise Hermana is the name Louise C. Callaghan adopted at the time *Brigid's Place* was published.

6.   The composition of the poem 'Female Figure' preceded that of the other texts in *Brigid's Place*, as it was written in January 1991 and published in England soon afterwards. The text was used as a starting point for the workshop in which the other Sheela poems were written, in 1992, and re-published alongside them.

7.   The chapbook is not paginated, hence the absence of page numbers here.

8.   My interest in Simone de Beauvoir's existentialist body and my readings of her work under this philosophical perspective were developed after my participation in the seminar 'Sex, Gender and the Body: Phenomenological and Psychoanalytical Perspectives', coordinated by Toril Moi in 1997 as part of the courses offered by the School of

Criticism and Theory at Cornell University. *The Second Sex* has been the subject of some controversy, as Beauvoir's much quoted statement that 'one is not born, but rather becomes a woman' has been read under the light of the sex/gender distinction, which would imply that 'woman' is a gendered category gradually acquired and 'sex' an empty, and again, non-signifying and prediscursive container. This reading of Beauvoir's work involves a misunderstanding of her existentialist philosophy. For an interpretation of *The Second Sex* in terms of sex and gender, see Judith Butler 'Sex and Gender'.

9. For an interesting study of the consequences derived from the sex/gender distinction, see Moira Gatens, *Imaginary Bodies*.

10. The theories mentioned above are just a brief illustration of the wide range of theoretical approaches to this topic, but they are by no means meant to form a comprehensive list. Another useful theoretical source might, for example, be found in Luce Irigaray's well-known theories on the female sex challenging the primacy of the Lacanian phallus as a super-symbol of culture in a move that would reclaim the signifying value of the vagina.

11. This lithograph can be regarded as a contemporary version of the Sheela-na-gig found in Cavan Town.

12. This poem is dedicated to Monica Bates, a professional weaver who uses Sheela iconography in her tapestries. 'Sheela-Na-Gig' had already been published in a *Poetry Ireland* volume titled *How High the Moon* (1991), which included poems by Susan Connolly and Catherine Phil MacCarthy, the two winners of the 1991 poetry competition 'A Sense of Place'.

13. Nuala Ní Dhomhnaill, for instance, has written wonderful revisions of Queen Medbh in which the stories from *The Táin* are significantly altered.

Notes to Chapter 8

1. See Begoña Aretxaga's *Shattering Silence* (pp. 24–53) for an interesting discussion of this kind of 'implicit knowledge', especially from the 'outsider's' viewpoint.

Notes to Chapter 9

1. I take my title from Adrienne Rich's poem 'Diving into the Wreck', in which she discusses the need for women poets to dive into the wreck of gendered western myths.

2. Morrissy may also be pointing to the lack of fundamental change in the political situation of Northern Ireland from the 1950s to the 1990s, despite ceasefires and social/economic changes; the decidedly unfamilial response of south to north has also remained unchanged.

3.   The relevant article, 41, of the Constitution is widely quoted: see Mary Robinson, 'Women and the New Irish State', 41.2.1: 'In particular, the State recognizes that by her life within the home, woman gives to the State a support without which the common good cannot be achieved.' And 41.2.2: 'The State shall, therefore, endeavour to ensure that mothers shall not be obliged by economic necessity to engage in labor to the neglect of their duties in the home' (p. 60). Also, see C.L. Innes, *Woman and Nation*, on the conflation of woman and Ireland.

4.   Vivien E. Nice, *Mothers and Daughters*, p. 229.

5.   Motherhood indicates the whole institutional apparatus which defined/confined women as mothers, not the fact of giving birth.

6.   Rich's essay, like the work of other critics, is simply a small but important part of the continuing conversations among feminist scholars from all disciplines. Rich responds to the occlusion of lesbian existence from feminist scholarship, as subsequent scholars will respond to and qualify her essay. Rich's essay first appeared in *Signs* in 1980; thereafter, it has been included, discussed and qualified, appearing in 1983 in Ann Snitow, Christine Stansell and Sharon Tompson's *Powers of Desire*, and again in 1986, in Rich's own collection *Blood, Bread, and Poetry,* which includes the correspondence between the editors of the 1983 volume and Rich.

7.   Peggy Phelan, *Unmarked*, p. 7. While questioning the binary that implies power resides in the visible rather than the invisible, Phelan's work exposes the ways in which the undervalued, women and/or homosexuals, are marked while the valued are unmarked in 'discursive paradigms and visual fields' (p. 5).

8.   Nice, *op. cit.*, p. 12.

9.   Susie Orbach and Luise Eichenbaum, 'Feminine Subjectivity, Countertransferences and the Mother–Daughter Relationship', p. 73.

10.   I do not mean to imply that Ireland is unique in its deployment of religion as a tool of oppression: contemporary battles about abortion and Foreign Aid funds for family planning testify to the health of this practice in the United States in 2007. Also, the Presbyterian Church in Northern Ireland is as vigilant as the Roman Catholic Church in its care/control of women. Numerous texts treat the western world's, and particularly Ireland's, revision and continued misuse of Genesis, and of myth. See, for example, Marina Warner, *Alone of All Her Sex;* Mary Condren, *The Serpent and the Goddess;* Ethna Viney, *Ancient Wars;* Trudy Hayes, *The Politics of Seduction;* Gerardine Meaney, *Sex and Nation;* Elin ap Hywel, 'Elise and the "Great Queens of Ireland"; and Monica McWilliams, 'The Church, the State and the Women's Movement in Northern Ireland'.

11.   It is important that Irene *daydreams* of a mother, while Pearl *dreams* of a sister; the material of daydreams is derived from the cultural texts,

however imbibed, while the material of the dream is derived from actual experience.

12. Carolyn G. Heilbrun writes of the need for stories on which to model our lives, lives being modelled on stories rather than on other lives. Stories, she says, shape reality, stories incorporating songs, tales, movies, novels, and more. In this context, the images Irene imagines are probably modelled on romances, movies or even the remnants of fairy tales, still so much part of popular fiction. Heilbrun speaks of the images we create as responding to the demands of convention, to the demands we imbibe, then, from society or from story (*Writing a Woman's Life*, p. 37).

13. The first verses of the italicized story of Solomon are introduced in *Mother of Pearl* as Irene and Stanley become aware of each other. In this section, the 'two harlots come to Solomon', each claiming the living baby, insisting the dead baby belongs to the other woman. The second set of verses, the king's plan, follow Stanley's realization that Irene is not pregnant, her fall 'from Grace' (p. 49). The final verses, the 'true mother's' refusal to allow the king to cut the child in two so that each mother may share, appear as the police take Pearl from Irene. The biblical verses not only highlight the ironies of motherhood Morrissy ponders and distinguish northern from southern sensibilities, they also point to the mutual source of Catholicism and Protestantism and thus to the religious difference as familial also.

14. Heilbrun, *op. cit.*, p. 37.

15. The dismissal of the north, particularly apparent among the thriving middle class in the Republic of Ireland, has been the subject of many recent editorials and columns in Irish papers. Several writers engage this issue provocatively in a collection of interviews by Caitriona Moloney and Helen Thompson, *Irish Women Writers Speak Out*. For a fictional account, see Edna O'Brien's *House of Splendid Isolation*.

16. Eavan Boland's *Object Lessons* illustrates this loss in Ireland particularly well.

17. Empowering, independent and awe-ful mothers are most frequently seen in the fiction of minority women. See, for examples, Toni Morrison, *Beloved,* and Alice Walker, *The Color Purple.* See also Janet Burstein, 'Restorying Jewish Mothers', and Maria-Jose Gamez-Fuentes, 'Never One without the Other.

Notes to Chapter 10

1. Medbh McGuckian's *Shelmalier*, which treats the 1798 rebellion, and Anne Enright's *The Pleasure of Eliza Lynch,* which recovers the story of the Irish courtesan who became the consort of Francisco Solano López, the dictator of Paraguay, also marshal the resources of postmodernism to create complex poetic reckonings with the past.

2.　See Alan Hayes and Diane Urquhart, *The Irish Women's History Reader*, and Myrtle Hill, *Women in Ireland*, for a discussion of the varying methodologies and parameters of Irish women's history.

Index